2—

The Last Undiscovered Place

The *Last* Undiscovered Place

David K. Leff

University of Virginia Press
Charlottesville and London

University of Virginia Press

© 2004 by the Rector and Visitors of the University of Virginia

All rights reserved

Printed in the United States of America on acid-free paper

First published 2004

9 8 7 6 5 4 3 2 1

Library of Congress Cataloging-in-Publication Data

Leff, David K.

  The last undiscovered place / David K. Leff.

    p. cm.

  ISBN 0-8139-2264-X (Cloth : alk. paper)

  1. Collinsville (Conn.)—History. 2. Collinsville (Conn.)—

Social conditions. 3. Collinsville (Conn.)—Biography. 4. Leff, David K. I. Title.

F104.C63L44 2004

974.6'2—dc22

                                                2003018257

*For Bekah and Josh, because your
inheritance is as much the future
as it is the past*

The interior landscape responds to the character
and subtlety of an exterior landscape; the shape of the
individual mind is affected by land as it is by genes.
—Barry Lopez, *Crossing Open Ground*

We shall not cease from exploration
And the end of all our exploring
Will be to arrive where we started
And know the place for the first time.
—T. S. Eliot, *Little Gidding (Four Quartets)*

Contents

Illustrations

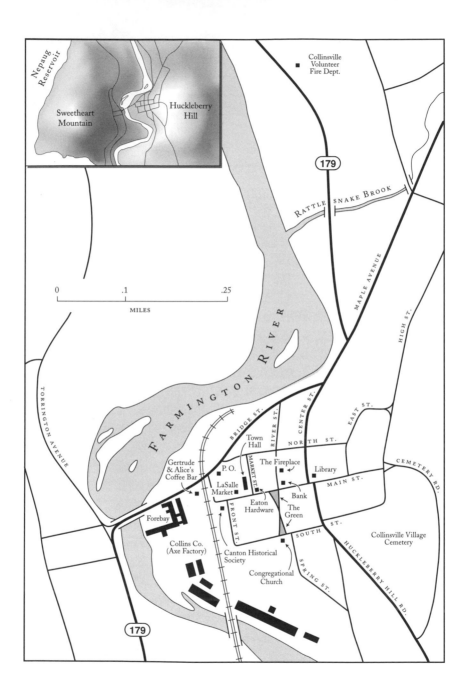

Nepaug
Reservoir

Sweetheart
Mountain

Huckleberry
Hill

Collinsville
Volunteer
Fire Dept.

179

RATTLESNAKE BROOK

MAPLE AVENUE

HIGH ST.

EAST ST.

0   .1   .25
MILES

FARMINGTON RIVER

TORRINGTON AVENUE

BRIDGE ST.

RIVER ST.

CENTER ST.

NORTH ST.

CEMETERY RD.

Town
Hall

Gertrude
& Alice's
Coffee Bar

P. O.

The Fireplace

Library

MARKET ST.

MAIN ST.

LaSalle
Market

Bank

Eaton
Hardware

The
Green

FRONT ST.

SOUTH ST.

Forebay

Collinsville Village
Cemetery

Collins Co.
(Axe Factory)

Canton Historical
Society

SPRING ST.

HUCKLEBERRY HILL RD.

Congregational
Church

179

Foreword

You can't visit the Collinsville depicted in these pages. It's not that the village is a mythical Brigadoon appearing periodically from the mist. To the contrary, you can't find this Collinsville precisely because it is a real place, beset by the give and take of time. With the passage of months and years, residents have died and others have moved away. New folks have settled here. Businesses have opened, and once-familiar haunts have shut their doors. Fires, divorces, births, bankruptcies, marriages, elections, construction and reconstruction, and myriad other occurrences have altered the way things look and the way in which we look at them. But the traveler consulting any road map will still find a Collinsville where Connecticut Route 179 crosses the Farmington River. And although the place may look much like the one described in the following chapters, the people, art, shops and restaurants, and music, as well as the issues confronting the village, will have changed. Yet because this is Collinsville, the creative ferment, the community passion, reciprocity of nature and architecture, and near presence of the past will remain for visitors to discover and rediscover anew. Hone your senses in this village, develop your fervor for exploration, and then go home to kindred experiences. They are waiting. Perhaps you've peeked at Collinsville first, but you live in the last undiscovered place.

Surveying

*Outside lies utterly ordinary space
open to any casual explorer willing
to find the extraordinary. Outside lies
unprogrammed awareness that at times
becomes directed serendipity.
Outside lies magic.*
—*John Stilgoe*, Outside Lies Magic

Becoming Indigenous

Place is forever changed by story. No—by the storyteller. There is no such thing as an ordinary suburb. Our houses, our yards lie on ancient layers of passion and drama.
—*Marjorie Sandor*, The Night Gardener

The sound of rustling leaves penetrated my sleepy half consciousness. Sitting up in bed, I peered out at the muscular limbs of a huge sugar maple framed by a second-story window a few feet away, the leaves painted in shades of green and in golden light. The grand tree's quirky geometry of gnarled branches seemed to embrace me. Though in my early forties as the twentieth century drew to a close, I felt like a child awakening in a tree house. Years have passed, yet often I still feel that way.

A low rumbling became a rising whine, grew louder and faded: a passing car on the macadam road a few yards from my door. It is a quiet local street, but a twenty-second drive leads to a state highway that in turn joins an interstate funneling traffic to New York and Boston. In half an hour I can be at an international airport, flying to any place on the planet. The world, it seems, has made a path to my door. Beneath the pavement stretch copper wires and fiber-optic cable, gas lines, sewer pipes, and water mains, joining me to switching stations, power plants, waste-treatment facilities, reservoirs, and the Internet. I am well connected.

Readying for morning errands, I squinted through the branches while buttoning a shirt, slipping into chinos, and pulling on socks and sneakers. Sidewalks, tidy lawns, and clapboard houses were close on all sides. Down the next cross street were parked cars, utility poles, a hardware store, a flat-roofed old house remodeled as offices, and a small grocery, and beyond them the arching, forested back of a hillside forming the horizon—a typical prospect repeated on thousands of streets in small towns, suburbs, and city neighborhoods. Nothing should draw more than a casual second glance. Yet I found myself in an extraordinary place. It was so, despite seeming so ordinary on the surface—plain and mundane, extra in its ordinariness. It was, quite literally, run-of-the-mill: one among hundreds of tired New England mill towns that pock the region like rust splotches.

The scene appeared familiar and tired. Cavernous, decrepit factory buildings clustered along a swift river squeezed between hills. A white church huddled with a few civic buildings and a small core of struggling shops, some reborn as antique boutiques and galleries, near the mill dam. Simple look-alike homes climb the hillsides, with an occasional group of once-grand managerial residences. Towns like this one are industrial relics where men and women once labored long hours at repetitive tasks, making practical products like knives, springs, and buttons. Run by paternalistic businessmen, these towns gained an air of Roman permanence with their impressive factory buildings and company-ordained routines. But the reason for such places has expired. The trip-hammers, turbines, grinding wheels, and stamping machines are not just rusted and quiet; they are gone, sold for scrap.

My window looked out from house number 4, on a street called The Green for its wide, grassy margins and central location. It's a minute's walk from Canton Town Hall in the village of Collinsville on the banks of the Farmington River. About sixteen miles from Connecticut's capital of Hartford, the village lies on the suburban fringe of that city. Like many places, it is named for something that no longer exists.

Main Street looking toward Huckleberry Hill. LaSalle Market is on the immediate left, Town Hall third on the left. The Collins Company office building is on the immediate right. In a hundred years not much has changed save the vehicles. (Photograph by Walter Kendra)

The Collins Company began manufacturing axes here in 1826, becoming the world's largest maker of edge tools. The company produced machetes, adzes, hoes, bush hooks, hammers, plows, knives, picks, and shovels before closing one hundred and forty years later. The Collins trademark, a muscular arm rising from a crown and grasping a hammer, is probably unfamiliar to you. Yet this company's tools may have had a role in clearing your lot, crafting your house or furniture, cultivating your garden, or assisting in a myriad of your fix-it and repair jobs.

Unless you live nearby or know something about axes or machetes, coming into Collinsville is a revelation. In fact, many who think they have been here before are surprised by their first visit up Main Street and around The Green. Most people pass through on the state highway along the river, skirting the village that remains undetected a block away. There is no reason it should be otherwise. No seminal historical event occurred here; no great ideas were given birth; no celebrities vacation nearby. There is no snow-capped peak, picturesque harbor, deep-cut gorge, or other natural wonder. There is, simply, no special reason to come here. The hilly landscape of Collinsville is pretty, but nothing exceptional.

I came here with my ex-wife, Sarah, largely by happenstance. I went to school nearby, then landed a job in Hartford. When we were searching for a home, a couple of friends I'd met through a schoolmate suggested we give their town a look. Collinsville met our middle-class needs. It was close enough to work, safe, moderately attractive, and affordable—a nice place to raise a family. Collinsville passed the test, but so did many other places. What drew me was the classic New England architectural style I'd admired elsewhere, and the close neighbors and easy walk to small shops such as those I had enjoyed in the town where I grew up. Its gently rundown aspect had enough rough edges to intrigue the lingering college bohemian in me. I had no idea how intriguing it would become.

With the security of conventional surroundings, I easily fell into a sleepy routine. Weeks piled into months and years of driving back and forth to work, mowing the lawn, raking leaves and shoveling snow, picking up milk and eggs at the grocery, and making deposits and withdrawals at the bank. I enjoyed backyard barbecues, Memorial Day parades, and street-corner conversation. And somewhere in that blurred passage of time, amid comfortable monotony and traditional surroundings, I discovered a remarkable world. Collinsville was neither dull nor prosaic, though it was indeed ordinary. As Walden was merely a pond at the edge of a town, or Henry Beston's "outermost house" another shack at the shore, so was Collinsville just a mill village. Like Thoreau and Beston, I gradually discovered in simple workaday territory a realm both curious and singular.

The first hints of Collinsville's magical dimension came to me on returning from vacations. After weeks paddling through Labrador or tramping along the Appalachian Trail, or a few days walking Boston's busy streets, I found that the ease and the desire to explore remained. Refreshed by a change in routine and scenery, I brought back with my occasional souvenir stones and used-bookstore finds a habit of seeing and listening that made home seem more engaging.

We may get away to lie on the beach or speed down a mountain on skis, but on vacation we also find that buildings more readily draw the eye, trees and flowers more easily provoke our curiosity, and people on the whole seem more interesting. There is a vibrancy that home lacks, as if we see in living color while away but only in black and white when we return to our usual haunts. This is not to say that Levittown can be Aspen when glimpsed through a traveler's eyes, any more than Collinsville can become Quebec. But we can sharpen perception and make the most mundane surroundings interesting by learning to read our own everyday landscapes as we would places thousands of miles away. Why not cultivate the traveler's way of taking in the world in the forty-nine weeks we remain home? "The most dully monotonous environment is full of wonders," observed the naturalist educator Elliot R. Downing in 1922. We just need to know how to look.

Returning from a trip to Oregon years ago, I confronted a world grown seemingly puny and impoverished to me after endless stretches of Pacific beach, expanses of emerald farmland, and trees so large our tallest oaks appeared mere shrubs. Weighted with melancholy, I sought out the soothing flow of the Farmington River and gazed into the current as it threaded among partially submerged rocks. As I walked along the shore, I soon found myself wandering through the old axe factory, a hodgepodge of weather-beaten brick, stone, wood, and corrugated metal buildings situated among piles of rubble and rusting machinery. The broken windows, cracking brick, and peeling paint reinforced my depression. A once-vibrant factory that had created jobs and practical products and served as a vehicle for community life was quiet and moldering in neglect—a ruin. It might as well be the broken remains of an ancient civilization, I thought.

Suddenly I was seized with the comical notion of the axe factory as an acropolis. The bizarre thought took a twist and became an epiphany of sorts as I imagined the mill like a dilapidated medieval castle, or an industrial Machu Picchu. Weren't ruined sites essential to the identity of Greece, Scotland, and Peru? Could the decrepit mill serve the same purpose here? After all, the Collins Company epitomized the American manufacturing revolution, as significant to civilization's advance as Greek architecture, the Scottish feudal system, and Inca technology.

I saw questions posed in unusual building shapes and sizes, in their odd angles in relation to each other and the river, in power canals coursing around and through them. Why this out-of-the-way location for a major industry? Why axes rather than buttons or pots? How did the shapes of the buildings relate to the processes within, and how did production move from raw material to finished product? Where did the massive iron railroad bridge lead? Walking just below the dam beside the three-story brick polishing shop, I felt the power of the water crashing on the ledges vibrate in my chest. How did this flow drive machines that made tools shipped around the world? Who were the men who poured molten steel, operated forges and stamping machines, and ground blades to a fine edge?

Hungry for answers, I began talking to old-timers who conjured for me the gritty whine of edge grinding; the sweet odor of machine-shop cutting oil; the acrid smell of hot metal, sweat, and soil; hands callused and creased with grease; the trip-hammer echoing like a village heartbeat. The routines of packing, stacking, and loading came alive in their voices, in memories of a time at once hard and heroic. Resentment was there too, in pensions unfulfilled and the slow, agonizing death of friends from grinders' consumption. Yet always evident and insistent were the deafening clatter and hum of machinery, pounding, stamping, and clinking, and the connections to bustling Main Street, where anything could be purchased within walking distance of the shop—medicines, clothing, groceries, hardware, furniture, appliances, automobiles, sporting goods, and books.

I decided to trace these stories deeper, beyond memories and into stacks of photos and files of documents tucked into library alcoves and historical museum cabinets. In a faded typescript, Samuel Collins's diary revealed his dream of affordable, quality axes and a wholesome village, a dream he saw threatened by poor materials, labor strife, floods, drought, faulty technology, unreliable managers, and greedy banks. I uncovered photos of Costa Rican firemen sporting Collins axes, and accounts of Cuban revolutionaries wielding deadly machetes made in Collinsville. A letter from Admiral Robert Peary praised the Collins ice lances, hatchets, and shovels used in his assault on the North Pole. Each file demanded the opening of another; one story found the next. Collins blades were used in the building of the Trans-Siberian Railroad, and by marines hitting Pacific beaches during World War II.

The past refused to be confined to print and photos as it beckoned in the buildings and streets around me. The abolitionist John Brown, Central Park's designer Frederick Law Olmsted, and Elisha Root, the model for Mark Twain's mechanical wizard in *A Connecticut Yankee in King Arthur's Court*, had walked my streets. A congressman lay buried in the cemetery up the hill, among Civil War soldiers, company presidents, bankers, doctors, an embezzler, a murder victim, and a female novelist. Immigrant German, Scandinavian, Irish, French Canadian, and Italian workers were buried nearby, their presence suggesting an explanation for the village's varied array of churches. I began to see not only what was here and now but what had been. Collinsville gradually became for me a place in time as well as space, and I found myself occasionally and unexpectedly breaking through to the past as if through a fragile layer of ice.

As I began discovering the village, it intruded even on the vacations that had once made home seem so dull. Collins swords were behind museum glass at Gettysburg; a tool-kit axe aboard the first nuclear submarine, Nautilus, bore the familiar trademark. I found Collins axes still in use beside a pile of firewood in Olympic National Park, on fire pumpers in Saint Louis. Sporting my Collinsville Fire Department tee shirt as I waded through the crowd at a New York folk festival, I was stopped by a man who spent ten minutes describing his family's use of machetes for planting and harvesting in his native Honduras.

I began taking long walks through the maze of steep village streets, all bearing functional names befitting practical places. Spring Street is still the location of bubbling water, Main Street is the primary commercial district, Cemetery Road leads to the graveyard, and New Road was once the new way to nearby Avon. I walked East, North, High, Front, South, River, Center, and Bridge Streets. I measured the village's growth by the age and location of houses, and its prosperity in the transition from simple workers' cottages to substantial managerial residences with columns, broad porches, and big windows. Every street was at a quirky angle, every turn provided more to see—differing clapboard widths, doors, railings, and light fixtures; stone arches, slate roofs, and gingerbread trim. My growing awareness was born of a mixture of old-timers' tales, library articles, and an appreciation of architecture and landscape. Collinsville began to grow larger, more vivid and resonant to me. At my doorstep, I found what travelers seek in distant regions—originality and authenticity.

Wandering led me to the edge of the village—up hillsides near hawk roosts, on gray schist ledges beside sunbathing garter snakes, and through mountain laurel whose June blooms are a thousand soft pink eyes. From this vantage point I saw hills narrowing and hastening the river, revealing the geographic inevitability of the water-powered factory and the logic of building shapes and street angles.

Peeking into the aged mill buildings through grimy windows, I discovered machine shops, car repairers, sign makers, and antique restorers. Among them were artists and artisans drawn by cheap space and picturesque surroundings—glassmakers, potters, leather crafters, sculptors, woodworkers, and painters. Occasionally the rhythmic vibrations of rock music issued from bands practicing in the old packing shop in the predawn hours.

Such activity at the factory enlivened the village as it had in the days of tool production, and Collinsville now erupted with artistic inspiration where once it had boomed with mechanical creativity and the growth of businesses. Galleries emerged around Main Street in buildings that had once housed clothing and bookshops, or lawyers' offices, or auto parts stores. Gertrude and Alice's Coffee Bar opened in the long-vacant freight station, featuring music and showcasing local painters and sculptors. The Acts Factory Players, born over coffee shared among friends, soon performed works by Shakespeare, Neil Simon, and A. R. Gurney in the Town Hall. The example of local amateurs who dared to perform encouraged others with conventional jobs to lose their stage fright and talk about their passion for guitar playing or poetry, flower arranging, soap making, woodworking, watercolors, and pottery.

In a place meant for foot travel, with houses and shops nearby, I found myself bumping into neighbors at odd moments, not just when we were prepared for a visit. We swapped stories, laughed, and voiced concerns about the kindergarten or a newly erected stop sign. The clustered village of stores and public places where residents mingled encouraged neighborliness. It attracted people committed to the traditional art of being neighbors. I joined the volunteer fire department, was appointed to the historic commission, and moderated town meetings. A bouillabaisse of people and happenings infused me with a sense of belonging, of ownership beyond a freehold interest in property. Collinsville seemed to yield a special atmosphere the way mountains are said to create their own weather.

It seemed too good to be true, and it was. Interesting people moved away, a couple of galleries and that petri dish of creativity, Gertrude and Alice's Coffee Bar, closed. There were fewer plays on the Town Hall stage, and the fate of the factory buildings was left uncertain by a soured real-estate deal. But new people moved into town, businesses quickly filled vacated space, and LaSalle Market initiated Friday night folk music. At times I lamented the loss of old town life, while at others I was drawn to the new. I discovered that the change itself intrigued and generated excitement. Eventually neither the past nor the present fascinated me as much as the adaptability of this place over time.

If such magic could be found in an everyday place like Collinsville, I wondered, why not elsewhere? "Outside lies utterly ordinary space open to any casual explorer willing to find the extraordinary," observes the Harvard professor John Stilgoe. Exploration, he argues, "begins in casual indirection, in the juiciest sort of indecision, in deliberate, then routine fits of absence of mind." Perhaps my discoveries make Collinsville seem special, but this is principally because I have taken the time to look. The discovery of interesting places depends on neither great events nor the detection of rare minerals or unusual animal species, but only on an intrepid explorer. My casual investigation of the surficially dull, well-to-do suburb of Avon, for example, reveals an intriguing past tied to explosives manufacture, commercial canal traffic, and political power. Rare Jefferson salamanders lurk on the traprock ridges at its eastern boundary. Impoverished urban areas like the north end of Hartford have a power to hold the imagination, too, with cemeteries home to black Civil War soldiers and Frederick Law Olmsted, and a past that includes shade tobacco growing and visits by

Martin Luther King Jr. Recently a moose wandered through an urban park along the Connecticut River.

Collinsville is my home, the place I know. I offer my explorations not to demonstrate that this village is any better than anyplace else but to foster discovery of other places. There is no particular formula for doing so. The nature of each place will dictate its own research methodology. I merely suggest that there is an unknown world of endless fascination at our doorsteps, and that we underestimate the depth of our belonging, the extent to which we are shaped by our surroundings. If we grow to know our communities, they will enrich our lives, and we will learn to care for them and work to make them better.

It is easy to sleepwalk through familiar surroundings. We might drive many miles to climb a mountain or fish a river without ever venturing onto trails in our neighborhood or casting a line in a nearby stream. I have friends familiar with the bird migrations of Cape May and Mount Desert Island who seldom bother with binoculars at home. I was long more familiar with the museums of Manhattan and Boston than the treasures of art and history a few miles distant. Our communities often remain mysteries to us until out-of-town vacationers begin posing questions, discovering beauty and intrigue we overlook. The places we inhabit might not seem vacation destinations, but the disposition of travel—the habit of seeing and listening, and a willingness to wonder—can serve us no less at home than in some exotic locale. There is nothing special about Collinsville in this regard. No place is commonplace.

Outlaw Village

My house could not be built today. It is not that the skills of nine-teenth-century craftsmen have been totally lost. There are tradesmen adept at mortise-and-tenon construction who would also welcome the challenge of horsehair plaster and a fieldstone foundation. Perhaps the cost would be high, but money is not the problem. Though generations of families have been sheltered under its roof, building this house today would be illegal—deemed by zoning ordinance detrimental to the community's health, safe-ty, and welfare. The same is true for the house next door and those down the street, the businesses around the corner, and apartments up the hill.

My street is anchored at one end by a traditional white New England church, and at the other by a four-story red-brick building, the old Valley House Hotel, now converted to condominiums. Known as "The Green," this short X-shaped road terminates in grassy triangles, with three houses on each side. Stately Greek Revivals vaguely recall the Parthenon, slate mansard roofs hearken back to nineteenth-century France, and wide overhanging eaves with decorative brackets echo Italian farmhouses of a century and a half back. Around the corner, Main Street features small shops in two- and three-story buildings of masonry and clapboard. It is an attractive scene, elegant, almost beautiful. People stroll slowly along the sidewalks, and drivers sometimes pull over to snap photographs. Occasionally a painter will set up an easel on the corner. Yet the law no longer tolerates places like this.

Over seventy-five pages of zoning regulations now make construction of such a village impossible even if every safety provision in the building and fire codes is satisfied. Though many find this cluster of homes and shops along narrow, tree-lined streets charming, they are anathema to the rigid geometry of zoning. On a bright blue-sky day with the hillsides and every structure perfectly outlined, I wondered how laws with the noble intent of ensuring safety from fire and flood and preventing overcrowding could prohibit the building of such a fortunate place.

An overthrown pass bounced on the sidewalk in front of me, and I tossed the football back to my neighbor's kids. It would be only a slightly longer throw to the bank, where my first errand was withdrawing weekend cash. The Collinsville Savings Society is a strongbox of brick, granite, and brownstone with broad stone arches. It was built around the turn of the twentieth century, and its heavy materials and squat design evoke the purpose of a bank: a place where money is secure. Although friends who once lived next door found it a good neighbor, the zoning ordinance now forbids such close proximity between businesses and residences, especially without a single yew bush, arbor vitae, or Lombardy poplar screening one from the other. Nevertheless, the two buildings have sat nakedly beside each other for a century with barely a shrub or sapling. New banks, as well as new stores, are typically required to be separated from houses, not just by a few feet or yards, but in wholly different zones in what amounts to a commercial ghetto. The restrictions make shopping inconvenient and require considerable driving.

Like many people with homes over a century old, I often play amateur carpenter, electrician, and plumber. After cashing my check and chatting briefly about a recent house fire with Deb, the assistant bank treasurer, who was minding the teller's counter, I headed to Eaton Hardware for cabinet hinges. The walk usually takes less than a minute, but on a Saturday it's longer because of streetside conversations with friends and neighbors. I paused to catch up on garden plans with Rosemary; David wanted to know if the state was buying a piece of land along the river; Colleen asked about the next scout meeting and had an anecdote about the pinewood derby.

The street had more than the weekday complement of cars, and parking spaces on Main Street were scarce. As I climbed the worn bluestone steps it occurred to me that absence of a parking lot would prevent this shop, which has been selling hardware since 1867, from opening today. Zoning demands an adjacent no-man's-land of striped asphalt: there is none here. Were I to drive to Wal-Mart I could find the legally requisite spread of pavement, and undoubtedly pay less for a broader selection of screws and nails. But it would take at least forty-five minutes, and I would leave without the one thing Eaton offered free that Wal-Mart does not carry: a taste of neighborhood life.

As I scanned the battered wooden drawers for the correct hinges, I caught myself admiring the ancient tin ceiling of pressed squares. Above are second- and third-floor apartments which mark the building with the ominous-sounding zoning designation of "mixed-use occupancy." Simply put, residences and businesses are in the same structure, a throwback to a time when shopkeepers lived above their stores. Zoning laws do not generally countenance these living schemes, yet such arrangements have been common for centuries, providing both security for the businesses and reasonable rents for householders.

Hinges in my pocket, I climbed Main Street's steep slope away from the village's tiny commercial hub. It was too nice a day to be indoors fixing a cabinet without a quick stroll first. The higher ground is dominated by two-, three-, and four-family dwellings. Most are long, low, clapboarded structures with center chimneys and large ells behind. Changes to porches, windows, and siding over the years have made each distinctive despite their common origins, like siblings. But these multifamily houses disregard one of the most sacred principles of modern zoning: they are mixed with single-family residences. Zoning typically separates such houses in a de facto caste system. Apparently, something about apartment dwellers demands they be set apart. Could it be their neighborliness, generosity, or civic devotion? Surely economic status cannot be the sole reason for this segregation: one need not live on New York's Central Park West to know apartments can be pricey.

I savored the comforting, domestic jumble of this hodgepodge of houses. Such a village cluster, observed planner and Appalachian Trail founder Benton MacKaye, "is the natural home of homes." Perhaps this variety of buildings also nurtures a paradoxical appreciation for the rigidity of zoning. We cherish the strict rules that help keep Collinsville distinctive. Zoning prevents any flattering imitations. There is an energizing, almost adolescent rebellious pleasure to be taken in the discrepancy between what exists and what is allowed. We who live here revel in our singular and idiosyncratic place.

If the mix of single- and multifamily dwellings were the only zoning violation among these houses, it might be ignored, and their duplicate doors and porches disregarded as fussy design features. But these houses, often terraced into the hillside, fail to adhere to the cardinal rule of residential zoning: the lots are too small—some less than a quarter acre in a zone that demands at least twice as much. Despite surviving fires, wind storms, and floods while nurturing a succession of families, these structures are considered unfit by today's standards. They hug the street, some as close as five feet from the road when forty is required. They have too little space between them, and too large a percentage of their tiny lots is covered with buildings and paving. Side-yard regulations demand at least ten feet between structures, but some are only a foot apart. Many houses, built with a nineteenth-century economy of space, do not meet today's minimum square footage requirements. Streets are too narrow, too steep, and too irregular, and the houses lack sufficient frontage.

Regardless of the fact that this place defies the fundamentals of zoning, there are no citations pending, no arrests. There is no imminent threat to public health, safety, or welfare requiring the immediate attention of the sanitarian, police, or fire company. The village is legally "grandfathered," its inadequacies accepted as a consequence of development in what was presumably a less-enlightened era. And like a grandfather, it is respectfully ignored as an interesting relic with little current relevance.

Many of my neighbors wear this nonconformity as a badge of honor. They take pride in the irregularity of their homes in these days of formula subdivisions, when houses are placed with tiresome precision like cookies on a baking sheet, and developments fill with homogeneous people of a certain income, age, and number of children. Authenticity is our competitive edge.

Being different exacts consequences, of course. Property owners must often obtain variances from the zoning regulations for fences, tiny outbuildings, and some of the minute home improvements people routinely make in other parts of town. Our businesses require "special exceptions" for small changes in the way they carry on trade. This continual need for variances and exceptions reinforces the notion that we are rogues, constantly bending rules.

Reaching the road's crest above the graveyard, I stopped and caught my breath. The wind was gusty, and leaves scuttled along the pavement. Across the valley mica-flecked ledges sparkled on Sweetheart Mountain, and far below the river there was an irregular band of silver light. Descending into the cemetery, I walked on uneven grass among granite, marble, and brownstone monuments terraced into the slope like the village houses. Soon I stood at the simple obelisk for Samuel Collins, father of this place. From all accounts a hawkish-looking man with piercing eyes and a beard, Collins must have spent time enjoying this view of the river and hills. These were the raw materials from which he created a world.

Unlike today's entrepreneurs, Samuel Collins, his brother David, and cousin William Wells, all younger than twenty-three, were not enticed by tax credits, convenient highways, water and sewer infrastructure, or low-interest industrial-development bond financing. What caught their atten-

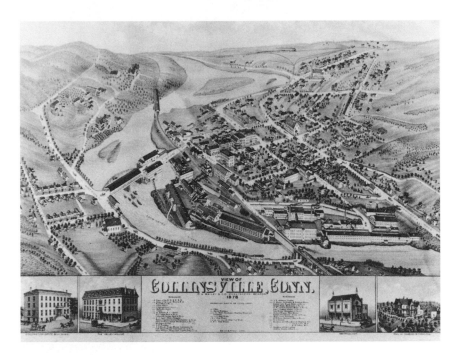

A bird's eye view of Collinsville, 1878. (Courtesy Canton Historical Society)

tion were foaming white rapids descending a rugged staircase of bedrock with sufficient force to spin machinery. This geography of hills and river gave birth to their dream of mass-produced, presharpened axes. Fulfillment of that dream, they knew, would take a village.

Business started slowly in 1826, but even the few workers that Samuel hired required homes in this sparsely settled area. Within a year the company had built three simple clapboard houses overlooking the factory. One of them still stands one hundred and seventy-five years later, sheltering the family of a man who once ground blades against massive grindstones. Eventually, the Collins Company owned nearly two hundred single-family homes, duplexes, and boarding houses, employing a small army of paper hangers, painters, plumbers, and carpenters to maintain them. It sold land for stores, operated the fire department, created a recreation hall, and built a church. The bank, school, library, and other enterprises were born in Collins's offices. The village, no less than the production lines which forged and polished steel blades, was an engine of industry, without which business would have been impossible. When logging from Maine to Michigan demanded axes; when coconut, rubber, and banana harvesting in the tropics called for machetes; when the gold rush required shovels and picks and sod busters on the plains needed plows, the factory provided them. The Collins Company grew, and with it the community.

The village developed with all the confidence of an enterprise destined for the ages. It was the Collins Company that first induced the stagecoach and then the railroad to come to town, that built a bridge over the river and lured a post office. Samuel Collins promoted stores, churches, and schools because he believed they encouraged loyalty, sobriety, and hard work among his employees. He envisioned a place where factory and family could flourish, a place built for both business and the business of living. "I would rather," he wrote, "not make one cent than to have men go away from here worse than they came." By the time he died in 1871, his notions had become institutionalized into company culture. Thus, while the village took shape without land-use regulations or formal planning, it appears carefully laid out, developed by a single mind, albeit a corporate one. The details of lot size and street width were not an issue. Business necessity, community welfare, and the rigors of the landscape dictated the details of construction. The Collins Company's dominance in the area allowed it to act without the compromises and rules necessary for efficiency and fairness in today's zoning process. For the Collins Company, owning was zoning.

Contemporary zoning regulations treat Collinsville as if it were some ancient experiment gone awry—a mistake, a dead-end of civic evolution. Yet our zoning commission is not solely at fault. There is little public support for replicating the cluster of mixed uses that naturally evolved to make Collinsville so engaging and livable. Few people today want anything built near them except carbon copies of their own homes. They demand that only houses take up residential areas, and they seek to keep businesses confined to commercial ghettos. The result is tiresome suburbs where woods and fields have been gobbled up for broad lawns and illusory privacy. In such a world as this, Collinsville remains a unique island, not as Disneyesque fantasy or Williamsburg anachronism, but as a place that works.

The view from Samuel Collins's grave is handsome and orderly. Below is a cluster of homes, shops, churches, and offices descending toward the hulking structures of the old axe factory along the river. It is a prospect that might defy the usual notions of planner's map, engineer's scale, or surveyor's transit, but the village of Collinsville is a good place to live.

Roadcut

Geology is the epic of this place,
of any place. The challenge is to see
something so big, to focus on a reality
so enveloping.—John Elder,
Reading the Mountains of Home

Strange as it may seem to neighbors who regard me as a staunch conservationist, if not a tree hugger, I enjoy wandering across the river to a place once blown to pieces by dynamite and hacked apart by bulldozers. One day when my son, Joshua, was five years old, I described to him how the echoing sounds of exploding rock and debris, roaring diesel engines, and clattering machinery once reached our front porch a quarter-mile from the site. His enthusiasm for heavy equipment and explosions was enough to overcome the usual dread of a walk with Dad. Of course, I didn't tell him that today this road cut through solid rock is quiet except for passing cars. People drive through without an inkling of the upheaval that took place little more than a generation ago. Yet every time I pass the rock face, its contorted shapes and subtle bands of color fire my imagination. When I told Josh we could read the rock like Egyptian hieroglyphics and learn the hidden reasons for Collinsville's existence, his soft brown eyes brightened. "Are there pyramids?" he asked hopefully.

"No," I admitted," but the rocks are much older."

Josh and I briskly walked down Main Street, the long green ridge of Sweetheart Mountain rising beyond the brick factory buildings ahead of us. We passed the sacks of neatly arranged fertilizer, shiny wheelbarrows, and garden tools cluttered at the entrance to Eaton Hardware. Skirting the well-worn stone steps at Town Hall, we peered into the windows of LaSalle Market, the village's kitchen and pantry, and briefly watched the regulars making sure work of doughnuts and coffee, the morning cup calling them as dependably as the sunrise. His interest flagging, Josh asked for a blow-pop; I lured him on with the promise of one on our return.

Turning onto Bridge Street, toward the Farmington River, we soon reached the bridge and passed the Forebay, a square pond framed on two sides by mill buildings mirrored in its dark surface. A kind of industrial reflecting pool, it collects river water to feed the factory canals.

The Farmington River Bridge is a broad and sterile concrete span more suitable to an interstate highway than a small-town road. Tempted by wide shoulders and clear sight lines, traffic speeds across more quickly than safely, and I held Josh's hand tightly for fear he might be blown away in a tractor-trailer's gust. Below us the river plunged over a granite dam and was churned to a froth in a pool of boiling hydraulics. It crashed out of the Forebay on one bank and poured from a defunct hydroelectric powerhouse on the other before cascading down rugged and irregular ledges beside the factory.

"This place was special to the Indians," I told Josh. He looked up, eyes suddenly wide. "They came from miles around to fish for salmon, herring, shad, and alewives swimming upstream. Fish had trouble making it through the fast water, so they were easier to catch."

A long series of little-boy questions ensued. Were the Indians still here? Where did they live? Did they wear feathers in their hair? Did they make fires and eat the fish? Who were their chiefs?

Pointing to the dam and powerhouse, I explained how the water once turned machinery to make axes at the factory and later to produce electricity.

"Water can do that?" Josh asked skeptically.

"Water even demolished the old metal bridge in a humongous flood," I told him. "That's why this huge concrete thing is here. The place I'm taking you tells the secret of why the Indians fished this spot, why the factory located here, and how come the bridge is so big."

"Neat! Let's go."

We passed a couple of men in baseball caps fishing from the bridge. A thin, sallow fellow with a wisp of mustache had a twelve-inch rainbow trout in a plastic-joint-compound bucket. (Josh was more interested in the Styrofoam cup of worms, and asked if he could take one home as a pet.)

Once across the Farmington we walked a minute downstream past the stone arches and tower of St. Patrick's Church. Opposite the church, a narrow side road dips toward the river and meets an iron truss railroad bridge now part of a bike trail. Before the 1955 flood, this side street was the principal road to Unionville, the next mill village to the east. Today the main route goes straight ahead on higher ground, toward a low shoulder of Sweetheart Mountain. To make way for it, a three-story-deep trench hundreds of feet long was blasted through solid rock, exposing that which, though typically invisible, shapes what is most familiar around us.

From the trench, Josh and I looked up as if out of a cellar hole. "This rock is underneath everything—our house, our garden, the street, even the river," I told him. "That's why they call it 'bedrock,' because everything rests on top of it." I pointed to the twisted oaks and tangled laurel thicket growing in the veneer of clay, stones, sand, and humus at the edge of the precipice above us. "Dirt is like the skin on your face," I added, "and the rock is like the hard bony skull underneath."

We typically consider rock homogeneous, or at least as having a regular pattern. But the road cut is neither uniform nor smooth. Nothing within these greenish-gray walls of schist and gneiss is regular, simple, polished, or symmetrical. Instead, layers lie one on top of the next in varied thicknesses. Sections tilt in opposing directions—folded, fractured, bulging, and twisted. Veins of lighter rock, where mineral-rich gases and liquids seeped into cracks and slowly hardened, meander through the dark background. These sinuous seams, known as pegmatites, often hold large crystals of mica and feldspar that rock hounds treasure. Occasionally I see someone with a hammer chipping away at the rock face, eager for gemlike pieces of bedrock.

The schist and gneiss that serve as the muscle of Collinsville's landscape are metamorphic rocks, formed under tremendous pressure and heat from ancient ocean sediments. Schist is a flaky mix of minerals such as mica, quartz, garnet, aluminum-containing kyanite, and graphite. The gneiss is more coarse-grained, unevenly layered with alternating light and dark bands, typically with less mica and more feldspar. The light bands contain quartz, a feldspar called plagioclase, and almost colorless muscovite mica. The dark bands include hornblende, garnet, and the black mica biotite.

I felt Josh tug at my sleeve, hard. "Is this it?" he shouted with stern disappointment, straining to be heard over the whoosh and whine of passing cars resonating within the rock walls. I nodded.

"Where are the pyramids?"

"I told you there *weren't* any pyramids." He stamped his foot, scrunching up his face. "Where are the pictures of Egyptian guys on the wall?" he demanded. "I thought there were bulldozers."

"I didn't mean real hieroglyphics, it's just . . ." I paused and drew a breath. With a dramatic flourish I pointed to the wall nearby. "Look at that!" I commanded, as if warning of an avalanche. "These rocks were formed over five miles below the earth's surface when continents crashed together 500 to 250 million years ago!"

"Were there explosions and volcanoes? Earthquakes?" he asked. I nodded in response, describing with tall-tale vividness the cataclysm that forced a thousand-mile-wide ocean basin and volcanic island arc into Connecticut's hundred-mile width, creating mountains rivaling the Himalayas.

"There were mountains here so high the snow never melted and trees couldn't grow. No person or machine could do this," I said, pointing to the wrinkled, crimped, and twisted rock around us which had been turned at difficult angles and in impossible shapes by forces so powerful they seem unreal, though the result is set in stone.

"Awesome!" he exclaimed. "But where did the mountains go?"

"At least a couple times the earth cooled, massive glaciers moved like slow rivers of ice covering everything and grinding down the mountains. The last time was twenty thousand years ago and the ice was a thousand feet thick."

"Wow!" said Josh impressed. "Just like the South Pole."

"Sort of. But the ice was so heavy that it chewed away the weaker parts of the bedrock. Eventually it got warmer. The glacier became soft and water trickled underneath. As the ice melted it dropped the stuff it had scraped up, leaving a mishmash of clay, gravel, sand, and rock that later mixed with decaying leaves and other living things to make soil."

"Is the glacier coming back?"

"Not for thousands of years. Something more important, though, is wearing down the mountains all around us every day: water."

Josh eyed me suspiciously. "How could water tear down a mountain?"

Indeed, how *could* rocks be worn away by something so smooth it slides down your throat? But with unrelenting persistence over eons, water is the solvent of stones and mountains.

Worn down for millennia by water, the rugged hills around Collinsville are merely the roots of once lofty peaks, like teeth ground to the gums. Though our land has been wracked with earthquakes and volcanoes, the gradual, peaceful, and unrelenting process of erosion at a rate of about four-hundredths of an inch annually has dominated the last billion years and continues today. It seems no less fanciful than a collision of continents, but clearly does not inspire a five-year-old.

"Erosion," said Josh, "is boring."

I showed him where water had washed rock fragments from the road-cut wall and small trees had broken the stone face by wedging their way into cracks. I reminded him of the great tusks of winter ice that cause pieces of the once-buried ledge to weaken and fall away. Though the rock wall seems unassailably solid and permanent, broken pieces of it lie scattered everywhere. He picked up a fragment and put it in his pocket. "I have some-thing millions of years old," he said proudly.

"Much of the rock in Collinsville is very hard," I explained. "Because this rock is so hard it wasn't worn away as easily as rocks elsewhere. The Farmington gets squeezed between hills and runs faster here than in other places where softer rock gets eroded away and allows the river to spread out. The fast water which could power machines is why Sam Collins built his factory here. Because of the factory, we have Collinsville."

"Did the hard rock have gold?" Josh asked hopefully. Cartoon Network and the Disney Channel have embedded the notion that prospecting precious metals is the only reason for an adult's interest in rocks. "Did he dig through the mountain to get here?"

"No, but he explored the whole river valley."

"Did he have ships like Columbus?"

"Not exactly."

There were no roadcuts in the rugged topography Samuel Collins encountered during the two years he spent searching for a mill site in the mid-1820s. The underlying substance of the earth was hidden by soil and trees, with only weathered gray outcrops hinting at what was underneath. Nevertheless, though Collins probably thought little of geology, it determined the location of his factory and was as important to the business as was his ability to raise capital and develop the technology to manufacture axes.

Collins spent time exploring upstream in Barkhamsted. Perhaps when returning to Hartford, where his impatient brother was already beginning to make axes, he took the rough road along the river. He would have noticed how the broad valley and generous floodplain a few miles upstream at the confluence of Cherry Brook grew smaller as he approached South Canton. Among steep slopes thick with pine and hemlock, the valley sharply narrowed, sluicing the river between Sweetheart Mountain's gray schists and the darker, coarse-grained gneiss of Huckleberry Hill. Pinched by the bedrock into a tight channel, the river surged with the energy he needed. Resisting the water's erosive force, the valley remained narrow enough for a dam. And though the area had been settled a hundred years earlier, there were few houses to interfere with the mill pond because the steep, shadowed hillsides left little arable acreage, and thus discouraged farmers.

On May 22, 1826, the Collins brothers and William Wells paid $2,800 for about five acres of land, a small grist and saw mill at the site of a defunct iron forge, and the right to erect a dam. Their ability to use a river valley that had frustrated farmers brought an entirely new way of life to a sleepy area. Within twenty-five years the noisy factory was making its own steel and producing hundreds of tools each day. In the bustling village it spawned, clothes and groceries were sold, children walked to school, and trains arrived and departed carrying people and goods across the continent. As business grew over the next hundred years, factory buildings, homes, and shops were built along the riverbanks. The population and locus of civic activity shifted from the area's agricultural communities to the mill village. New immigrants came not to farm but to take jobs at the axe works.

Josh, tiring, broke my reverie. "Dad, can we go now?"

"I'm not done with the story about Sam Collins."

"You told me it already. Besides, it's boring."

From the roadcut, we walked back to the side street and down by the large rusting railroad bridge spanning the river. Reminded of the smoke-belching locomotives he had seen during antique-train excursions and on videos, Josh stopped abruptly, seeing the technological past as I was the geological. "Why is this a good place for the railroad to cross?" I asked. Josh shrugged his shoulders. "Because the river is narrow since the hard rocks prevent it from getting wide."

Across the water, decrepit factory buildings crowded a narrow floodplain. The massive concrete-and-steel highway bridge stood upstream with the dam just behind it, the small two-story brick hydroelectric powerhouse to the side. Just as geology had discouraged early farmers and seduced the Collins boys into setting up business, so too had it hastened the company's decline. By the 1920s internal combustion engines fired by coal and oil and electricity from distant power plants made water power obsolete. Factories in the cramped river valleys whose location had once been a boon found themselves at a disadvantage. Economies of scale and competition demanded larger plants, and newer technologies favored sprawling single-story operations. The advent of truck transportation, and the increasingly common use of cars by employees, required space for parking. A factory sandwiched between steep hills had difficulty expanding and modernizing. Many companies left such areas for the flat, well-drained soils of old cropland, places that offered broad, easily developed expanses that could accommodate massive buildings and hundreds or even thousands of vehicles. The electric grid and fossil-fuel boilers liberated manufacturers from the need for falling water to drive machinery. Factories could be anywhere.

When fourteen inches of rain fell in the Farmington River Valley in about twenty-four hours during August of 1955, the river's geological restriction resulted in a crippling blow to the factory. From its modest origins in the Berkshires, the Farmington gathered water from the myriad swollen streams and creeks that had supplied factory power for over a century. Brown with silt, the river rose quickly, overflowed its banks, and became a roaring torrent, carrying off trees, lumber, cars, parts of houses, and other flotsam.

A great clot of debris caught in the river's constricted throat at Collinsville. The flood rumbled and roared in the narrows. The ground vibrated. The relentless force gnawed away at the iron-truss predecessor of today's highway bridge until at last the sound of wrenching, scraping metal briefly rose above the noise of the river as the water ripped the structure from its footings and tore it apart. The road where we now stood was deep beneath the flood, and the powerhouse was midstream, the river lapping at second-story windows. "We would have drowned!" Josh exclaimed.

Demolished buildings, broken pavement, mangled trees, and unrecognizable rubble were left by receding water. A layer of gooey mud coated everything. After the '55 flood the Collins Company limped along for a little over a decade, but never fully recovered.

The current road bridge, out of all scale to the river it spans and the village it is part of, was engineered against the ultimate deluge. The road along the river was rebuilt for local vehicles, but a new one, on higher

The 1955 flood at the site of the Farmington River Bridge. The raging torrent destroyed roads, homes, and businesses. (Courtesy Canton Historical Society)

ground, was constructed for through traffic. A straight shot without regard to topography, the new road required a cut.

"A road that could never drown," Josh observed.

"Exactly. See how the river, the bridge, the roadcut, the factory, and Collinsville are related to the rocks underneath everything?"

"I guess," he shrugged. I smiled and tousled his hair.

"How about that blowpop?"

"Yeah! Let's go!"

After the factory closed in 1966, Collinsville was transformed. Without the busy axe company providing work and setting life's routines with its paychecks and steam whistle, the village declined. Though the mill eventually housed small machine shops, auto repairers, furniture strippers, woodworkers, and start-up businesses looking for cheap rent, the buildings were too small and antiquated for a large single employer like Collins.

Without the factory, retailers saw fewer customers, and many stores moved to busier locations. Collinsville lost its pharmacy, newspaper, bakery, and other neighborhood institutions. Property values dropped and buildings fell into disrepair. Collinsville assumed the aspect of a run-down low-rent district, its small lots and multiple family dwellings an anachronism in days of sprawling single-family subdivisions. It became a place people moved to until they could afford something else.

New stores ignored Collinsville for flatter locations with spacious parking and wider streets unconstrained by our geology. As in the days before the Collins Company, the area became a backwater, bypassed for more suitable locations. Only small businesses with a niche market survived. The rugged topography of Collinsville left no room for the vast selections of Stop-n-Shop, though LaSalle Market provided many necessities we easily run out of—milk, bread, eggs, bananas. Fleet Bank's main office would be cramped, though tiny Collinsville Savings Society, whose president is greeted by first name, continued after almost one hundred and fifty years. Center Spirit lacked the vast selections of the strip-mall discount houses, but it was an easy walk for a bottle of wine at dinner or a beer after mowing the lawn. There's no extra charge for the premium conversation over the register with George, a large man with a soft voice and easy manner who was once in the tree-care business.

Lacking more lucrative economic opportunities, Collinsville grew quaint in its decline as the factory's smoke and noise faded in memory. Craving the authenticity new subdivisions lacked, newcomers eventually discovered the tired, forgotten houses and began making repairs. The fast river and steep green slopes that had caught Samuel Collins's eye more than a century and a half earlier drew painters, sculptors, glassmakers, woodworkers, and other artists and artisans. Attracted by natural beauty and a quirky village, they found cheap studio space in the old factory with its tall, light-filled windows and high ceilings. Photographers focused their lenses on the picturesque mill, and painters set up easels to capture the stately Green. Canoeists plied the mill pond and rapids, while fishermen spent hours by the dam and in the pools nearby.

As Josh and I made our way toward LaSalle, we passed antique shops and galleries that had found a bygone setting compatible with their goods. Taking advantage of the river much as Samuel Collins once had, a canoe store and a fly-fishing shop sprouted in locations where lumber and dry goods were once sold. People now came to pursue their passions for art, fishing, boating, antiques, history, and the outdoors.

Collinsville's bedrock, glaciation, and soils not only connect us to the earth's distant past—they are essential to the location of our homes, businesses, and gardens. They will determine our future in the layout of roads, sites for commercial and industrial expansion, and location of open space. To experience earth's processes it isn't necessary to travel to the Grand Canyon or survive a California earthquake. A walk down the street is sufficient.

A Landscape of Mind
that Matters

The places where we spend our time
affect the people we are and can become.
—*Tony Hiss,* The Experience of Place

Occasionally, after agonizing over nine innings of the Red Sox, I unwind with a stroll along the placid waters of Boston's Backbay Fens— dark, plump, pondlike river impoundments teeming with tadpoles and ducks, the shore a mix of lawn and reedy marsh. Perhaps it is merely the fantasy of a distraught fan looking for a comforting image after a blown save, but the nearby buildings, traffic sounds, and ragged mix of tended and unkempt shoreline occasionally remind me of the Collins Company mill pond. A similar sensation hits me when, after seeing *Rigoletto* or *Tosca* at the Met, I walk into Central Park, where the broad, path-crossed lawns vaguely suggest a magnified version of the Collinsville Green. Perhaps I am drunk on Italian poetry and music, or just homesick, but the large overhanging trees and dappled sunlight, inviting walkways, and manicured lawns at the edge of a bustling area seem strangely familiar. For years I kept these parallels to myself, but one day I came across the fine print of a foot-note that joined the words "Olmsted" and "Collinsville."

Frederick Law Olmsted, father and foremost genius of American land-scape architecture, lived for only about a year and a half in Collinsville. But as a student in his late teens receiving the only formal education necessary to his future profession, he was likely forming the basic impressions and attitudes that were to define and sustain the remainder of his life. Had he designed a little bit of Collinsville into the Fens, Central Park, and many of the nation's other classic urban green spaces? Walking through these places, it seemed to me that a part of Collinsville never left him.

A poison-sumac thicket and the needs of the new Congregational church conspired to bring sixteen-year-old Olmsted to Collinsville around Christmas of 1838. When he was an adolescent, a tangle with sumac left his face inflamed beyond recognition, forcing his eyes closed and rendering him almost blind, and so dashed all hopes of attending Yale. Months after-ward, his condition improved, Olmsted was sent by his father to study with Frederick Augustus Barton, a surveyor, civil engineer, and mathematics teacher at Phillips Academy in Andover, Massachusetts, who was himself studying for the ministry. On completing his studies, Barton was called to the Collinsville church. Young Fred, a serious-looking fellow with dark hair, penetrating eyes, and a prominent nose, came with him.

Axe manufacturing had started only about a dozen years earlier, but Collinsville was already a busy village of about five hundred souls, most of whom were Collins employees. A new dam had been built the year before, and houses and other buildings were going up along the dirt streets. Trees were being chopped down to clear lots, and burning brush scented the air. Masons were busy fitting stone blocks into foundations and bricking chimneys, while the steady percussion of carpenter's hammers echoed among the buildings. Collinsville was not a settled community with historic associations but a rough and raw place under construction.

Whether it's a peephole cut into plywood on a city block or a new house in a suburban cul-de-sac, construction draws an audience. In the 1830s Collinsville must have been pure adrenaline to a young man studying civil

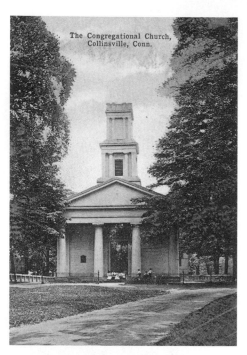
The Congregational Church, Collinsville, Conn.

Young Olmsted likely daydreamed from the church's stone steps. (Author's collection)

engineering; Olmsted could see roads terraced into hillsides and drainage systems laid out, and watch around him, the lessons far more compelling than those offered in dry lectures and dusty books. He witnessed an entire landscape being tranformed. How could he not have been impressed with the land's plasticity, the possibility of a place yielding to a person's vision?

The Congregational church where Fred spent much of his time was only a couple of years old when Barton and Olmsted arrived. Built by the Collins Company to guide residents' spiritual life much as the factory shaped their daily routines, the church was planned as the focal point of the village. From its steps Olmsted could look across The Green, then a meadow without houses, crisscrossed with paths. Only a year before there had been a frog pond in its center surrounded by brush, but now changes were under way. Mr. Collins had big plans for this site, which would remain a broad, open expanse in the midst of densely packed street of houses and shops. It would be the centerpiece of his wholesome workingman's village. From the church door Fred may have admired the elm saplings Collins had begun planting along the streets. Paths and roads lined with the graceful, vase-shaped trees would be a signature element in Olmsted's future designs.

In front of this same church my children waited for the school bus. They listened impatiently for the sound of the rumbling diesel down the street, and dared each other to jump from the broad stone steps on which Olmsted

Rebekah and Joshua Leff in front of their home at 4 The Green. (Photograph by the author)

once stood. They played tag among the tall fluted columns, their voices shattering the morning calm. Entranced by the inexact symmetry of the view, I was often almost insensible to the noise. The substantial Valley House is opposite, but just off-center from the white church. The six stately houses that face each other across the X-shaped street—one of which was built by Reverend Barton—vary greatly in design and orientation. The grassy triangular islands at each end of the road are shaped slightly differently. The tall maples along the street that replaced Collins's elms following the onset of Dutch elm disease do not precisely mirror each other.

Olmsted was gone before either the first houses on The Green or the hotel were built, but he is said to have amused himself by drawing hypothetical town plans as all around him Samuel Collins was laying out a village with bricks, mortar, clapboards, and nails. With Collins's plans taking shape as Fred watched, perhaps the young man formed and recast his own church-door view. The scene has changed greatly since Olmsted's time, but why shouldn't the off-kilter balance and quirky regularity of today's view also intrigue and inspire?

As the bus roared away, I waved to my daughter and then to my mischievous son, who was coveting the bumpy backseat. I wondered what my children saw as they looked down The Green. Surely they had no idea of the elegance of their church-portico bus stop. As do many children, they spent hours with wood, foam, and plastic blocks constructing houses, stores, and forts. Will growing up in Collinsville kindle some unexpected creative impulse later in life, as perhaps it did for Olmsted? Would they see the world differently if raised in a fancy subdivision dubbed Foxcroft Estates or Blackshire Farms, a place with a stone entryway and three-car garages? Often I have scrutinized their crayon and pencil drawings for clues, and looked at their Lego creations from odd angles. What will be the residual power of this place?

The morning quiet returned as grinding bus gears and diesel fumes faded. Maybe The Green's neatly enclosed space inspired Olmsted's concept of outdoor rooms, those reflective places he created with shrubs, walls, and bridges. No one will ever know for sure, but certainly I, in the optimistic hours of morning at least, find this Collinsville view inspiring. Surely, even as a young man, a genius like Olmsted was not insensible to what was around him.

While for Samuel Collins the topography of Collinsville met the practical necessity of providing factory power, Olmsted would discover in it a power for otherwise shaping people's lives. With his eye for scenery, the future park designer must have been struck by how perfectly the mill village was ensconced among the hills along the winding river. Today this prospect makes visitors reach for their cameras. It captivated me on my first drive through Collinsville, and prompted me to explore this place when I later looked for somewhere to settle down.

Olmsted was restless and bored under Barton's tutelage, though he learned the rudiments of surveying and civil engineering. The landscape, bustling with industrial activity, beckoned to him. "I was nominally the pupil of a topographical engineer," he later wrote in his autobiography, "but really for the most part given over to a decently restrained vagabond life, generally pursued under the guise of an angler, fowler or a dabbler on the shallowest shores of the deep sea of the natural sciences." Like many Collinsville children today, he whiled away his time wading in the Farmington River, climbing the ledges of Sweetheart Mountain, and day-dreaming under trees. A short walk quickly took him beyond the factory, houses, and noise. Perhaps here he felt his love for simple, rural scenery deepen and first sensed that remoteness could be found close to urban activity if buildings were screened by hills and green spaces.

Like every boy before and since, Fred probably peered into the factory windows. In the grinding shop he would have glimpsed men sitting on wooden levers in front of massive spinning stone wheels, sharpening axe-heads in a dusty atmosphere where water dripped continuously to keep the metal cool and particles out of the air. If he ducked into the forge shop he would have experienced what the local historian Paul Wittmer called "an infernal din from the pounding of great trip-hammers and other tools, with the glaring fires intermittently lighting up an otherwise primeval gloom, and sweat drenched, half-naked workers straining at their jobs." Seeing men so hard at work in difficult conditions may have inspired Olmsted's belief in the power of rural scenery to preserve the physical health and mental tranquility of urban dwellers. Country surroundings, he would later maintain, had a restorative effect by occupying workers' imaginations "with objects and reflections of quite a different character from those which are associated with their bent condition." Young Olmsted must surely have been impressed by such difficult "bull" work being done so close to the natural world he later came to view as its antidote.

Wandering among the decrepit factory buildings remains a voyage of discovery. "This is like an Indiana Jones adventure place," Josh said one day as we stepped over broken pavement winding among a hodgepodge of neglected buildings and dotted with piles of rubble. In a corrugated metal addition to the cavernous old rolling mill, a ponytailed man banged away at a Chevy that had skidded into a phone pole. Captivated by the work, Josh asked if he could practice on my car. Walking on, we glanced into an open door at piles of used motorcycle parts, and through grimy windows at sawdust drifted up beneath a band saw in a shop where musical instruments were fashioned from exotic tropical woods.

Hard labor at nature's edge might have remained nothing more than a romantic notion to Olmsted had he not been in a place where woods and fields were being purposefully transformed, changed into a community that would sustain not just the workman's effort but his free hours and family as well. Here was a landscape re-formed with a social purpose, for Collinsville was not just a place to mass workmen as if they were so many mounds of coal or bars of iron. According to a company history published almost a hundred years later, the village also provided a "clean, sane intelligent life with streets shaded with beautiful trees, with ample spaces, neat and orderly . . . fine water, excellent drainage, churches, schools, library and stores." Collins himself observed that "it has been said that our manufacturing villages have a demoralizing tendency. I wish to show there can be an exception." The notion of creating such an exception, of infusing sanity in a place of bustle, was essential to Olmsted's faith in his ability to transform marginal urban lands and integrate them into a city's fabric as calming green space. That balance between bustle and calm, between nature and culture, is still part of life in Collinsville.

Olmsted left Collinsville as dogwoods and lilacs were blooming in 1840. It was a place the burgeoning genius did not quickly forget. On March 20, 1841, he wrote to his stepmother, "How I long to be where I was a year ago: midst two lofty mountains, pursuing the uneven course of the purling brook, gliding among the fair granite rocks, & lisping over pebbles; meandering through the lowly valley, under the sweeping willows, & the waving elms, where nought is heard save the indistinct clink of anvils & the distant roaring of water as it passes gracefully over the half natural dam of the beautiful Farmington . . . then & there to be—up to knees in mud & sand chasing mush-quash." More than a century and a half later the hills and flowing water still beckon.

My daughter Rebekah and I climbed Sweetheart Mountain's steep slope through thick stands of young trees and under a midday twilight of dense hemlocks. We made our way up a rocky staircase plush with moss, and over gray schist ledges stippled with garnets. Though less a mountain than a long, forested hillside, Sweetheart rises abruptly from the river's west side and forms a backdrop to the village. It was a cool mid-May day, with the trees recently leafed out, and the air smelled of damp soil. I imagined young Olmsted wandering here just below the ridge generations ago. What caught his eye?

Since Olmsted's time, the hillside had been stripped for charcoal, pastured, had houses built on its lower slopes, and boasted a series of ski trails with a rope tow powered by a car engine. Bekah couldn't care less about such things, and was clearly not interested in chunks of milky quartz or a fallen blue jay's nest. She was annoyed when I stopped to point out a trillium growing in moist soil beneath a ledge. Stubbornly determined not to like anything that Dad called to her attention, she had her thoughts focused on Gertrude and Alice's Coffee Bar in the old freight station, where I'd promised a game of crazy eights over a Snickers bar and hot chocolate if she walked with me.

"How much longer?" was the refrain whenever we paused to rest. The sound of our breathing mixed with that of the leaves rustling in the breeze around us. When the wind quieted, the soft whoosh of tires on pavement reached us, filtered through the faint sound of falling water from the river below.

Gaining the trail's high point at a ledge surrounded by laurel thickets, we began a steep descent, but the path soon flattened as it looped around several large trees. Suddenly Bekah stopped. "Wow!" she said, "Look at this." Though we had passed this clearing overlooking the village a dozen times before, this was the first time she had seen anything. "It looks like a model train set." She gestured with her arm at the regularity of streets and houses rising up the slope of Huckleberry Hill toward the cemetery on the opposite side of the valley. As if counting, she recited the names of neighbors whose homes were visible . . . the various stores . . . Town Hall. "You can't see anything in the woods," she said, "and it's like everything feels so far away, and then suddenly it's right in front of us which makes it seem close, but it still looks so small—like toys. I mean I can't believe we're going to be back in a few minutes and everything will be real size again." I nodded and smiled. Perhaps this is what Olmsted saw. Will this perspective some-how make its way into her view of the world?

On an evening not long after, Josh and I carried our canoe down to the river. The day had been hot and humid and the cool dank air was deli-cious wafting off the water. We paddled among flotillas of waterfowl, Josh quacking all the while, calling them his "war navy" and urging them to launch an attack on the seagull forces occupying the nearby sandbar. At Rattlesnake Brook, a small stream partially flooded by the mill dam, we squeezed below the bare beams of a bridge damaged in the 1955 flood and paddled between the Department of Transportation's sand pile and the sewage treatment plant.

Just beyond, we heard rustling in the bamboo-like Japanese knotweed that grew thickly on the steep bank. Suddenly, a large beaver, brown and glossy, plopped into the water. Josh giggled, and we stealthily gave chase just as Olmsted did with his "mush-quash." Silently, gracefully, the beaver glid-ed through the water, with only its broad, dark head visible above the sur-face. Then, without warning, it gave a loud tail slap and disappeared into the dark stream. We waited a couple of long minutes for it to surface, but it was gone: all we saw were reflections. Suddenly there was a shadow in front of us and a bump on the bottom of the boat as the beaver swam beneath us. Josh and I turned toward each other and laughed.

If, as Olmsted believed, landscape can subtly shape our character, dispo-sition, and outlook, how are my family and neighbors affected by Collinsville? Does the visual isolation of this village squeezed between hills reinforce a unique character or viewpoint? Does it matter that we can walk downtown for groceries and dart into the woods a few moments later, even though just over those hills are cookie-cutter subdivisions and miles of strip malls?

Olmsted strolled on streets we walk today and spent time along the same river and on slopes we here and now traverse. Great cities have spent mil-lions of dollars creating his style of rural scenery in the midst of urban activity, while a step outside my home is a great man's inspiration. It could belong to anyone.

Membership

Tell me the landscape in which you live,
and I will tell you who you are.
—*José Ortega y Gasset*

Neighborhood Genealogy

Every neighborhood has a genealogy of engaging people, often eccentric and sometimes seemingly ordinary. The buildings that are a neighborhood's most prominent feature are merely representative of the people who occupy them. They are erected, demolished, rebuilt, sold, and passed down according to the successes, failures, and whims of their inhabitants. Even the plainest postwar subdivision likely has a cast of characters in its past: a farmer and his crops, an enterprising developer, soldiers returning from war, perhaps women who worked in defense plants. Like Collinsville, such places may appear ordinary, but fascination pulses just below the surface of the houses and streets we see every day.

Neighborhoods are going concerns and, like people, grow and change, passing through readily identifiable cycles of life. Since before the Civil War, three houses have faced three others across our short street with its broad, grassy margins. But when Sarah and I moved here in 1984, the neighborhood had grown old more than architecturally in manner. We purchased our house from a frail, gentle old widow who was moving to a nursing home. Her husband had once been the Collins Company's purchasing manager. Across the street Guy Whitney, the last plant engineer, then in his mid-90s, spent balmy days on his porch. Next door to him a former Collins vice president and his wife were also enjoying their ninth decade. A third house, at the corner of Main Street, was carved into apartments. The young couples on either side of us had been resident less than two years, having bought from people very much their seniors. A toddler in a house to our south was the only child for a block around. The cumulative ages of the seven people on the street's east side did not come close to that of the three on the west.

Within a half dozen years the elderly residents were gone and children outnumbered adults. A neighborhood once as staid as its classic Yankee homes was again enlivened with shouts of children chasing each other and the racket of dribbling basketballs, touch football, and home-run derbies. Trees became jungle gyms, bicycles lined the sidewalks, and skateboarders played chicken with traffic. Plastic toys in colors never contemplated by nature were often scattered as if in a tornado's aftermath. Yet according to some old-timers, it was no more noisy or chaotic than when the Meconkey, Whitney, and Hough children, the youngsters of our predecessors, filled the same streets and yards with joy and monkey business a generation earlier.

People tend to consider their neighborhoods as an equilibrium of couples and singles, children and elderly. Names may change, but otherwise the collective composition of people seems as stable as the buildings. Change is judged by structures, in their state of repair or use. We watch in amazement as children grow and achieve mastery of life's first pursuits, mark time as they climb the ladder of school and career, and often fail to see the transformations that their growth creates in a neighborhood. Likewise, we are often blind to the contributions of older residents, whose long lives have been filled too with raising children, earning a living, and adding to a community's civic energy. Understanding generational shifts—the stages of life

The Green around 1900, looking from the church toward the Valley House. (Author's collection)

in our communities—gives places a depth and texture that otherwise escapes us.

Guy Whitney used to sit on his porch soaking up sun like a turtle on a rock. A couple of years passed before I realized that as plant engineer he had been responsible for a busy factory, two hydroelectric stations, and about two hundred houses. In dark glasses he sat shrunken and sphinxlike, an enigma in headphones, wearing a box on his chest into which I shouted to be heard. Had he lost his hearing to pounding trip-hammers, roaring generators, and clanking machinery? Our conversation was an effort rewarded by his tales of climbing into turbine pits, repairing leviathan steam boilers, and navigating tidal waves of mud and debris carried by the '55 flood. He painted a picture of a heroic age, of muscular men laboring hard and proudly making something practical that was recognized around the world. Through his words I saw glowing molten metal poured into molds and the sparks flying from grindstones, and heard the din of axes and machetes being hammered and stamped. Occasionally, with a wry smile, he would tell a ribald story of youthful exploits. Once he allowed as how he would enjoy dating an old girl-friend—if he had the strength to dig her out of the cemetery first. His words were labored and his inflection flat, yet he held me in thrall with stories of a place that seemed far away, even though it was only down the street.

Despite our conversations, only on reading his obituary did I have the vaguest notion of what a dynamo Whitney had been: volunteer firefighter, town moderator, secretary of the Board of Education, library board member, vice president of the historical society, justice of the peace, member of the regional water commission, chairman of the Farmington Valley Flood Control Commission, civil defense director, and life member of the Republican Town Committee. Humbled by his accomplishment, I was shamefaced at the fact that I failed to see more than an interesting old man.

Leonard and Marion Hough, contemporaries of Guy Whitney, lived next door to him but were never glimpsed on their porch. They were somewhat reclusive, their entire house hidden behind a palisade of bushy hemlocks. Sarah and I met them walking the brick paths of our garden one weekday afternoon when we were normally at work. Thin and wrinkled, slightly bent, they were a dapper couple, neatly dressed and with a formal, old-fashioned manner of speech. Embarrassed at having been discovered on their semiweekly stroll to admire our flowers and vegetables, they brimmed with apologies we assured them were unnecessary. Despite our professions of a standing invitation to visit and an offer of tea, they were extremely shy and in a hurry to leave. Afterward, we saw them occasionally walking around the block, always quiet and self-effacing, radiating a polite formality.

Shortly after Leonard Hough died, I discovered that he had been vice president in charge of sales for Collins. In the mid-1940s *Fortune* described him as "a fast operator." Fluent in Spanish in deference to the dominant Latin American machete trade, he traveled widely. A photograph from the time reveals a lean and handsome man with a confident air. It was the essential demeanor for representing the company at trade shows and for dealing with rough competitors, government bureaucrats, demanding customers, and the public. Over several years we had had occasional conversations about flowers, the weather, his health, and once, oddly enough, the quality of beer. Why had we never talked about the dynamics of foreign trade, or how he arranged government contracts during the war, or why the company closed despite a flurry of orders? I felt foolish, as if I'd squandered something of great value. He had been one of the essential people of Collinsville and once again all I had seen was a pleasant elderly gentleman.

A village is more a manifest set of relationships among people than it is a mere collection of houses. After all, houses are dwellings, and the genuine act of dwelling is to spend time, to share surroundings and events. Guy Whitney and the Houghs taught me how day-to-day connections and personality build a place as much as lumber and brick. The houses they lived in were put up long before their time, but their jobs at the company and their volunteer commitments had created a community that flourished even as the factory closed and the surrounding buildings deteriorated. Though we were often too busy with our own lives to notice, they were living examples of how the weight of time would cast the rest of us in new roles and relations.

Experiences with Guy Whitney and Leonard Hough left me wondering how I related to my house and the people who had previously lived in it. In hours both at the museum, a building where the company had once finished and stored plows, and in the air-conditioned vault at Town Hall, I gathered bits of information and supposition about my house as if I were organizing pieces of a large jigsaw puzzle. Though it was among the last of the facts I uncovered, the story of my home commences with the Collins Company annual meeting of October 7, 1846.

In the tiny wooden office building that once stood at the corner of Front and Main Streets, the directors adopted a policy to sell private building lots. The first went to Charles Blair at what would become 6 The Green, immediately to the south of my house. It was a challenging time for the company and the decision could not have been easy. Perhaps they needed the additional revenue that property sales would generate, or wanted to encourage investment by others. It was one of many issues Samuel Collins and his fellow directors faced. Demand for axes was high, labor was tight and restless, difficult factory additions were under way, and a September drought that lowered flows in the Farmington River hindered production.

The land for my house was carved out of the landscape and became a parcel of real estate on October 19, 1847, when the company sold it for $225 to Nathan L. Polk, who later ran the local pharmacy. In a looping script of fine and shadowed ink, the plot was described as being bounded by the "open common by the meeting house on the south." The noted dimensions are to within one-thousandth of a foot: 126 and 187/1000 north, 96 and 666/1000 east, 126 and 318/1000 south, and 97 and 930/1000 west. Signed by Samuel W. Collins himself, this document is the Collinsville equivalent of a grant from the sovereign. Thus was 4 The Green created, and with it the boundaries of my proprietorship, the limits of my kingdom. Use of the lot is limited to a "dwelling house with outbuildings for family and domestic use," and erection of "any shop or store or manufacturing building or business" is forbidden. (Could conversion of the garage to a maple sugarhouse and the sale of syrup run afoul of these words from a century and a half ago?) Collins was creating a village, and The Green was a tranquil oasis fixed by his private zoning.

Polk took two mortgages, one for $800 and another for $500. By year's end a house stood on the property, and a couple of years later a barn was built. He sold the property in 1850 and within fifteen years 4 The Green was conveyed a fourth time. The third owner was also the fifth: Samuel Woodbridge, a justice of the peace, deputy sheriff, and livery stable owner. The property remained in the Woodbridge family until 1892, when dentist J. B. Flint, living next door at 6 The Green in the house his wife's father had purchased from Collins, bought it for $2,500. Flint flipped the property to the company the following month. It then housed a series of Collins employees until it was sold to John Meconkey and his wife Dorothy in 1962. Meconkey was the company man charged with implementing Collins's divestiture of residential properties. In 1984, Dorothy Meconkey sold the property to Sarah and me, the first people to live here in over ninety years who were not associated with the company.

Somewhat fancifully, I sometimes wonder whether characteristics of those who have long owned a home are passed along to successors in a kind of genetics of tenancy. Could my obsession with this place's past have been seeded by John Meconkey, who in the twilight of his career was given the unenviable task of selling the factory's assets? Vern Eads, a self-described "mortician to industry" who brokered the deal, said Meconkey, a courtly gentleman not given to displays of emotion, handled the divestiture with professional efficiency, but admitted that it left him in tears. He could not bear tearing down one hundred and forty years of history.

Known as "Mr. Canton," Meconkey was said to have given two hundred and twenty-nine years of public service to the town when he died in 1978 at age seventy-seven. He served for many years on the school and library boards, as registrar of voters, and on the Republican Town Committee. He was also town auditor and wrote award-winning annual reports. Sarah and I have been on the town plan update committee, and she has chaired the conservation commission, sat on the land-trust board, spearheaded development of a wading pool for children, and been involved in other efforts. I have chaired the historic commission, answered the bell as a firefighter, moderated town meetings, and served on the museum board of directors. Has Meconkey's civic spirit infected us both?

Regardless of who has lived in them, the village's buildings have relationships to each other, have their own history and connections reflecting economic, natural, and social conditions. Their ages, style, number, and state of repair tell stories about the ebb and flow of community success and decline, of optimism and depression.

Although a few houses appeared earlier, twenty-one two-family homes were built by the company on the river's east side in 1831 and twenty-four more on the west the following year as demand for axes led to intensive worker recruitment. Each a story and a half, with apartments built side-by-each around a center chimney, they cost $500 and rented for $25 per year at a time when wages were $12 to $16 per month. Still, accommodations remained so scarce that renters were required to furnish lodging, board, and washing to two men in addition to their own family. These houses are plain, cottagelike structures whose simplicity and uniformity reflect the economic exigencies of a young and expanding business. A Harvard professor of landscape, John Stilgoe, an adventurer in ordinary places, found them "a new sort of community space—the village of identical houses." While visiting Collinsville in 1836, the author John Warner Barber observed that these houses "are built precisely of the same form, are compactly set together on the side of a hill rising with considerable abruptness from the water" and "are painted white and when contrasted with the deep green foliage in the immediate vicinity, present a novel and beautiful appearance." When I walk among them today, they seem not so much clones as cousins with a remarkable family resemblance. Over time, not only have colors differentiated, but so have porches, windows, siding, and doors. They have grown more distinctive as successive generations adapt them to their needs and design sense, and well illustrate the individuality of their inhabitants.

In the 1850s the Collins Company's vibrant exporting business—featuring over one hundred and fifty patterns of axes and machetes along with adzes, hoes, picks, bush hooks, plows, shovels, and other tools—brought wealth and talent to the village. Houses more stylish than the early workers' cottages were built. Greek Revival was the rage, and many homes of the time bear the friezes, pediments, columns, and pilasters reminiscent of the Parthenon. The style was perfect for an industrial village, the simplicity and economy of its lines together with its balance and symmetry reflecting the practicality of manufacturing. With its august allusion to the classical past, Greek Revival architecture lent an instant importance and permanence to the new and still-rough working village.

As the Civil War began, Collins was considered the world's largest edge-tool manufacturer. Production of swords and bayonets cemented its reputation for quality. The company's wealth and that of the village grew rapidly, and by 1870 roughly six hundred and fifty workers were turning out over three thousand tools per day. Annual sales exceeded one million dollars. During and after the war, large and boxy multiple-unit tenements with nicknames like French Block and Swedish Boarding House were built, reflecting the waves of new immigrant workers.

Following the South's surrender, success in the age of Grant and the railroads was marked by the first masonry commercial buildings on Main Street, including an urban-looking company office building with columns and the Collins trademark stamped in metal along the roofline. The Valley House Hotel was erected across The Green from the church to accommodate foreign buyers of the company's products. Built in the elaborate French Second Empire style, the Valley House was considered the height of modernity and fashion. With its prominent chimneys, slate mansard roof, and large wooden entrance canopy, it still has commanding stature. Prosperity also allowed updating of some Greek Revivals with Second Empire additions. The house across the street from mine was totally transformed with a third story, mansard roof, and new porch about 1870. Around the corner, a South Street Greek Revival had a Second Empire tower added, which featured a stained-glass window. The national financial panic of 1873 brought an abrupt end to both the Second Empire style and Collinsville's rapid expansion. New houses were built afterward, but never at the same pace.

Better times greeted the dawn of the twentieth century. An elaborate Queen Anne–style house with a spacious porch and steep roof featuring intersecting gables was built on Main Street. Next door at 2 The Green Dr. Cox added a third story to his flat-topped house, the new Palladian window and pitched roof lending it a fashionable Colonial Revival appearance. Not long after, a Craftsman-style house with exposed rafters under the eaves and tapered square porch columns was squeezed between two Greek Revivals on Maple Avenue. The century's turn also brought a brick Town Hall sporting pointed gothic windows, a hip-roofed post office of brick, and a granite, sandstone, and brick bank with broad Romanesque arches. These buildings reflected the Collins Company's growing need for more office space. No longer could the office building accommodate a public hall, post office, and bank.

Collinsville did not grow much after the early years of the twentieth century. New construction gave way as repairs, renovations, additions, and the demolition of existing buildings became the main engine of physical change in the village. As with the years of rapid expansion, this shift reflected the nature of the company, a somewhat fusty steady state slipping into decline.

Beyond the genealogy of houses or neighborhoods, or the relationship of houses to one another, there is a synergy of buildings and people. A village's design and setting will often attract individuals of a particular economic position and outlook on life. Neighborhood layout can promote mutual civic effort and a sense of belonging through proximity and such common points of interest as a riverside park, or general meeting places like stores.

Built as a working person's town with crowded lots, small houses, and multifamily dwellings, Collinsville today maintains greater economic diversity than do many nearby communities. It is a place where truck drivers, teachers, waitresses, store clerks, and municipal employees can afford to live alongside doctors, lawyers, and business executives. Someone just starting out can find an apartment, and artists can afford the low-paying day jobs that allow them to practice their craft. Reasonable cost and small dwellings ensure a continuous influx of newcomers, who bring fresh personalities and energy to the world of longtime residents.

Being flat, The Green has always been an anomaly in this hilly place, a sort of industrial version of the town common. It was viewed by Samuel Collins as an oasis in a densely packed factory village, a locus for public events that, its church predominant, would be a spiritual and civic focal point. In a blue-collar town, The Green has traditionally been an address for professionals and executives. Nineteenth-century residents included the company president, bankers, leading merchants, a minister, a doctor, and a company vice president who also served as plant superintendent and state representative.

After World War I ended and automobiles and telephones became common in Collinsville, Dr. Cox, who delivered most of the town's babies, resided at number 2 with his wife, Florence. At that time my house was the home of M. Stanley Neal, a Collins foreman, and his wife, Laura, the strict high school English teacher whose sharp features earned her the nickname

"Chisel Chin" among some students. Plant superintendent Charles Smith lived at number 5 with his wife Nellie. Number 6 was the home of a dentist named Flint, and across the street lived the walrus-mustachioed William Hill, Collins Company president.

Today The Green continues, with remarkable consistency, to be populated by professionals. There are two psychologists, a lawyer, a business executive, a symphony violinist, a corporate chief financial officer, and a state-agency commissioner. That this remains a professional enclave might be attributed to the larger, fancier houses, but they are neither fancy nor large by current standards. Indeed, with their tiny lots, short driveways, and limited privacy, they are generally quite different from the standard built for professionals today. Clearly, people who live here do not seek trophy houses. Perhaps they are drawn by the handsome and substantial look of traditional construction. Maybe it is the rough symmetry of the street, or its centrality in the village, or the overall coherence of the buildings in relation to shops and other houses nearby. Whatever the reason, this locale seems to draw people with a similar sense of belonging, regardless of politics, upbringing, or personal habits. The Green, like the rest of Collinsville, is one of those rare places where residents brag about their neighborhood rather than about their houses. Samuel Collins planned well.

Yard Work and the
Theory of Relativity

I've come to relish the meeting on the street,
the serendipitous coffee, the borrowings and
gleanings of my days and what they ask of me.
—*Kathleen Hirsch,*
A Home in the Heart of a City

Digging, gardening, and doing yard work in Collinsville invariably take longer than elsewhere. This is due not to an Einsteinian time warp, but to the pleasures of everyday interruptions and digressions. People walk in Collinsville, and in good weather they actually stroll without the excuse of an errand at the bank, the grocery, or the post office. The sight of a neighbor doing yard work becomes an opportunity to chat about the season's progress, a recent budget referendum, the size of a garden pumpkin, or the baseball standings.

On my first Saturday in town, I cut our lawn, which had grown long and tangled with neglect. As I raked the unsightly clumps left by the mower, Jim, one of our new neighbors, stopped on his way home from the hardware store. A real estate broker, former selectman, and state legislator who lived a couple doors and a street crossing away, he took the time not just to introduce himself, but also to chat about the neighborhood and engage me in local issues. His father's dairy farm two miles distant had become the local golf course, and his wife's father was the last president of the Collins Company.

The conversation began with the mulch value of grass clippings, but soon became a discussion of how grass and leaves clogged catch basins and the regularity with which the road crew tended them. We moved on to the health of street trees and the impact of cars on small villages. Before long, his relaxed, deliberate words and expansive thoughts led to a scheme for diverting traffic from busy Maple Avenue to an old railbed. With a Yankee earnestness, he advised me not to pass on any chances to talk with Mr. Whitney as he sat on his porch, or with Rhett behind the counter at the hardware. "This place has seen some hard times," he told me, running his long fingers through thinning gray hair, "but I think we're on the rebound. This is a surprisingly resilient place."

Shortly after Jim left, my next door neighbor walked over to welcome me. A small woman with chestnut hair and brown eyes, waddling in late pregnancy, Karel was curious about our plans for the house. She and her husband, a Brooklynite like my father, were relatively new to town, and I think she sought some comfort with another outsider among people who had long known each other. It turned out that we were alumni of the same university, and joined somewhat by this happy coincidence and our ethnic backgrounds and careers in the professions, we found that the conversation flowed easily. My thoughts on replacing the gutters on my house and about removing the unkempt, overgrown yew bushes around its foundation seemed to put her mind at ease. After all, in a place where houses are so close to each other, who your neighbors are and what they do with their property assumes great importance.

By turns I asked how her pregnancy was progressing, and we complained about the summer heat, and she told me about the town pool. As we spoke, I raked the grass into piles while her toddler daughter played on the fire hydrant, convinced in a child's fashion that it could deliver scrambled eggs Automat style. Fifteen minutes disappeared as we recounted plans for gardens and walkways, new storm windows, kitchen renovations, and family vacations, until the hydrant was abandoned for stiff tugs on mom's arm.

As I spread grass over the garden, an elderly man with a white crew-cut and a gravelly voice stopped by. Whitey had a hint of bulldog in his face and kindly eyes. Living in one of the first houses built by the company in 1827, he came from French northern Maine to Collinsville in 1946 to work as a grinder. "It was real bull work," he recalled with a slight accent that betrayed his roots, and he went on to describe how he hovered astride a seat called a "pony," pressing blades into the massive grinding wheel in a shower of sparks, grit, and noise. The job required great arm and leg strength, and small men had a hard time. "Starting at about one hundred and forty pounds was tough, but I was at two hundred and five when we closed in '66." Gaunt and bent as we spoke, Whitey took me back to an age when factory lights burned late and sleeping was difficult as the trip-hammers pounded on second shift.

That first weekend set the pace for outdoor projects. I welcomed company, but found that nothing—whether it was planting bulbs, painting, or sealing the driveway—got done in time. Once awash in half-finished projects, I have since learned to adjust for these visits, which make even the most tedious tasks enjoyable. In fact I have learned that a neighborhood's quality is directly proportional to the amount of time it takes one to do yard work.

Belonging to a community is akin to engaging in conversation. In fact, conversation is the very stuff of community. For me, a walk around the block is less about air, exercise, and scenery than it is an opportunity to run into Kate and arrange a play date for our sons, or to see Eric on his porch and inquire about his North Carolina trip, or to chat about the progress of daffodils over the garden fence with Rosemary.

Sometimes I stop in a local shop more to take the village pulse than to make a purchase. I'll find my friend Alan, who lives just up the hill, peering over the paint brushes at Eaton Hardware. He's fixing his fence and I offer to help. I mention the planning commission's review of a subdivision as he rubs his graying mustache. He is equally adamant that the developer is offering useless, inaccessible open space, and that the neighbors are being unreasonable simply because they want nothing built near them. A city planner in a nearby community, he speaks with authority and does not suffer fools gladly. Before I leave the store with a bottle of car wax, we agree to go to a ballgame that evening.

LaSalle Market on Main Street is an extension of many a family kitchen with its tempting aromas and its domestic chatter. I find out how Greg's leg is healing and whether the Department of Transportation has gotten him a new payloader to operate. A burly volunteer fire policeman, he laughs when I tease him about using his injury as an excuse to avoid directing traffic at a midnight motor vehicle accident the day before last. I can tell what Donna is having for dinner by her armload of last-minute groceries. A tall, lithe woman, she moves gracefully, a skill she has learned waiting tables. A couple of neighborhood kids in dirty tee shirts come up the street with a stringer of trout just as I am walking out. They've been casting into what fly-fishers call the "axe factory pool," just below the three-story brick polishing shop. Their worms—especially night crawlers—have been deadly, or so they tell me.

Just like yard work, a walk to the bank, or the fly shop, or even the market can take five minutes or thirty-five. The newspaper I buy at LaSalle is more valuable to me for the encounters I have than for the stories I read. Community is an ecosystem of relationships. We adjust, make room for one another. In Robert Frost's poetic rural New England good fences may make good neighbors, but in Collinsville it is good neighbors who make good fences. Indeed, neighbors are sturdier and more reliable than fences.

Examples of this abound. I have returned from a week away to find my lawn unexpectedly mowed. Sarah came home with newborn Rebekah from the hospital on a snowy day; the next morning the driveway was cleared before I'd awakened, and that night the first of eight dinners was delivered to our door. After my back surgery one autumn, a crew of neighbors raked leaves. On an afternoon when Sarah ran out of rubber cement in the middle of a project and found herself stuck in the house with a napping infant, our grandmotherly hardware store proprietor came around and delivered a tube. Hearing of such neighborly acts, an outsider might think Collinsville had experienced a natural disaster, for we tend to hear of such fellowship solely in the wake of fires, blizzards, floods, and power outages. These considerate gestures emphasize that a community is a going concern of common effort, no less than a business, a club, or a family. When we complain about lack of community we are often not investing the time to build one.

In his 1967 short story "The Wild Birds," Wendell Berry has described this sense of belonging to a place, or a neighborhood, as a "membership." As an elderly man in Berry's fictional town of Port William, Kentucky, puts it: "The way we are, we are members of each other. All of us. Everything. The difference ain't in who is a member and who is not, but in who knows it and who don't." Perhaps Berry's sense of belonging assumes greater importance nowadays, when joining a country club, environmental group, or political party seems to suggest a greater sense of common purpose than sharing in the basic life of a community.

Perhaps "membership" is natural in a place once dedicated to the common purpose of creating a product, something simple and useful not just in a remote market but in the yards and homes of the people making it. Indeed, employment with the company was once a form of membership. Collinsville was a place of corporate purpose extending beyond the factory to homes and stores, and to the layout of streets. It was also a place that suddenly and traumatically lost its reason for being: a way of life disappeared when the company closed. Only after a generation and a half is a sense of purpose reemerging from a common appreciation of natural beauty, village atmosphere, and historic singularity.

Membership recognizes a shared place. Collinsville residents have, perhaps, a stronger sense than most people of why they live where they do. Many come from families that either worked for the company or provided it with goods and services. My friend Bill, an officer in the fire department, works forty-minutes distant, but has stayed in Collinsville because home is where his father packed machetes and his uncles polished blades. Rhett, who runs the hardware store, is here because four generations of his family stood behind the counter before him.

Many who came from elsewhere were attracted by the reasonable rents typical of tightly packed, multifamily houses. Others were drawn by large and inexpensive spaces in the Collins Company buildings, spaces that were ideal for repairing engines, blowing glass, fixing cars, making jewelry, and other small businesses. Like my immediate neighbors, I came for the village atmosphere that easily permits sidewalk conversation, as well as for a topography that offers green hills for wandering and a river to paddle, skate, or fish. Collinsville piqued my interest as a realm to explore, not just as a place to live.

Nevertheless, the village is hardly a showcase of political, religious, or musical harmony. Not everyone is gregarious. At times we clash angrily over taxes, or zoning decisions, or about which kid is a bully in school. Some neighbors are remote, and feuds can extend for generations over matters as serious as property lines or as trivial as whose father peed into the high school furnace seventy years ago. Our town historian tells of the four-foot-wide "spite house" built just to block a neighbor's view. But despite such differences and disagreements, common here as anywhere, there is an attachment to this place that joins us to the village and each other. *Where* we are has become part of *who* we are.

It is almost impossible to be in Collinsville for any period of time without earning that essential badge of membership: recognition. A wave and a "hello" are common whether one is walking to the river with a boat or a fishing pole, cashing a check at the bank, having a pizza, or buying a gallon of milk. There are abundant opportunities for patter about house prices, school teachers, fishing spots, eagle sightings, and relationships. The grace notes are everywhere. On a frosty winter day Bekah's hot chocolate is poured and awaits us as we enter the coffee shop. The woman behind the counter at the post office knows Sarah wants only commemorative stamps. After years of buying Kit Kat candy bars at LaSalle Market I am seriously questioned when I set something else down on the counter. "Sure you want *that*?" asks the surprised proprietor. "Yes," I nod, and as he takes my money he wants to know if anything new has happened. It hadn't occurred to me that I was breaking a habit. Such simple and familiar encounters in all weather and moods are the membership's lifeblood.

Occasionally we transcend membership, momentarily or for a lifetime. Intimacies grow over coffee and late nights talking out a divorce, revealing emotions and details about sex and finance that no mere neighbor should know. Tears bond us at a parent's graveside where long-submerged details of childhood struggles and arguments surface unexpectedly. Friendship grows in attending and witnessing a wedding, and there dancing, joking, eating, and drinking together. Warmth and tenderness are grafted onto common experience over time. Alan, Sarah, and I have shared an apartment while touring Chicago with six-month-old Bekah. We have spent evenings with each other's families, gone to ballgames, hiked in fair weather and in rain, visited historical sights, slept in the same room. We are neighbors, and more than neighbors.

In spring, before the flashboards at the dam deepen the mill pond, the islands at this bulging bend of the river sport broad and sandy banks. Some years we have loaded canoes with grills and coolers, badminton sets and Frisbees, and boom boxes and squirt guns and ventured out to these grassy spits of land. Surprised motorists on the road gape as we lounge in beach chairs, toss baseballs, and sun ourselves on the state's smallest, least-crowded beach.

Summers mean an occasional block party. I call Police Chief Humphrey and The Green is temporarily barricaded to traffic, turning the pavement into a playground. Neighbors assemble. Michael and Pat attend to the logistics of tables, grills, invitations, condiments, and a myriad number of details. Leslie, Jim and Barbara, David and Jean, Karel and Howard, Kate and Rob, Bev and Dave, Colleen and Scott, and many others bring their kitchen creations into bright daylight. A table fills with salads, pasta, cakes, and pies while bluish-gray smoke rises from several grills. Rob, a big man with a booming voice, gathers his band (several members of which live in walking distance) to play blues and rock long into the afternoon, while his young son strums air guitar with them. In dark glasses, shorts, and a day-old stubble, Dave looks like a hip cruise recreation director as he sets up a net and drags out balls, birdies, rackets, and gloves and bats. Volleyball, tag, badminton, and Wiffle-ball games erupt in the languid humidity. One year we hired a magician who scooted around on a unicycle, turned balloons into magical animals, juggled, and swallowed fire. We talk, relax, sway with the music and share the place around us.

The week before Halloween, Sarah and I sometimes host a cider-making party, putting our guests to work squeezing as many as a dozen boxes of apples through an old-fashioned, muscle-powered cider press. The cider draws a harvest of foods that, in turn, sharpen the thirst. Conversation hums through our yard, and the shouts of running children echo among the houses. Our driveway fills with adults and children fashioning faces on pumpkins for our front-stoop carving contest. Cheers go up for ribbon winners: a traditional but elaborately detailed design; a pumpkin carved wholly in stars; a suicidal gourd with a knife to its head; a Picasso-like abstract with eyes and mouth skewed; a small ornamental with a baby's pacifier.

In December's icy darkness several families convene for a pot-luck dinner and Christmas carols. During the long and lazy supper, we catch up on small talk as the children swarm, eventually settling before the television. With full bellies we bundle up and venture out with flashlights, sleigh bells, Santa caps, and reindeer antlers. The children vie for the chance to ring each doorbell, often making enough noise on the porch to render a ring unnecessary. Our neighbors are invariably grateful, or at least polite. We sing at LaSalle Market, the coffee shop, the police station. Walking the streets with flashlights and songbooks, we recall years that were colder and snowier; years before the children came along when we carried flasks; the time a grumpy cop kicked us out of the station because we were making too much noise. One year we sang the dreidel song for a Jewish family during Chanukah.

Of course, nothing is as harmonious or coherently neighborly as it seems in retrospect. Our days are more a ragged quilt of events, errands, and emotions. Not all endings are happy; nothing stays the same. Collinsville is not Mayberry or Lake Wobegon, after all. But neither is it Peyton Place or Spoon River. Oh, we have shoplifters, alcoholics, drug addicts, "unconventional living arrangements," rough divorces, and adulterers. All this is juicy stuff to read and talk about, no doubt, but such trash can be had from any newspaper or street-corner gossip in any town. No membership required.

Learning with Buildings

Improving home facilitates, aids
every other end and pleasure of life.
—Orson Fowler, The Octagon House

       If the citizenry of Collinsville is a membership, then our badges of belonging are our homes. The words "quaint," "charming," and "classic" may come to a visitor's mind, but a villager's thoughts more likely run to roof shingles and flashing, wiring, insulation, and window sashes. We are joined together in constant repair, at once tied to the past and shaping the future.

       Perhaps the age of our houses and their time-wrought imperfections do indeed reflect our lives. In them we see not only our flaws, but our creativity, craftsmanship, persistence, and dedication to something simultaneously useful and beautiful. Like it or not, our lives are often judged by our homes. Their size, style, location, garage space, state of repair, and even color communicate something of the people inside. In Collinsville, where houses are relatively small and simple, it is not so much their size or opulence that typically draws comments. Rather, it is the work we lavish on them.

The malleability of wood and its tolerance of mistakes makes handymen of us all. We live with and even love the unfinished project, the sweat that produces a functional kitchen, a floor that glows with bright woodgrain or a porch whose brackets and spindles become visible with a multichromatic paint job. We are devoted to learning with our homes, to having them teach us about the past, about relations among neighbors, and the practical skills of carpentry, plumbing, and wiring. If, as the Czech writer Karel Čapek has said, "love of one's home is a rite, similar to the veneration of some celestial godhead," then there is much worship in this small village, and veneration with saws, pipe wrenches, wire cutters, and nail punches. In this sense, perhaps it is fitting that many Collinsville houses, mine included, are built in the Greek Revival style, meant to evoke the classic lines of an ancient Greek temple.

"By much slothfulness the building decayeth," according to Ecclesiastes. Actually, it doesn't take as much sloth as one might think. Even as we set about to worship on nights and weekends with our tool boxes, new opportunities for prayer and repair spring up like mushrooms on late-summer lawns. Buying a place neatly finished may save us the effort of construction, but it begets the greater challenge of reconstruction. In our home there is always a floor to refinish, a light fixture to replace, a leaking joint in the water lines, a rotten clapboard, a broken pane of glass, a cracked driveway or a loose shingle. Always we wrestle with wedding today's needs to old forms as we add insulation, plumb a dishwasher, build closets, or wire computers in buildings whose builders never anticipated them. It is a lifelong hobby.

At one time I was hopeful hard work would lead someday to a nominally completed house, but the endless multiplication of projects is a source of remarkable frustration. Even now nothing ever seems finished, and in the early days I felt my home was becoming a quagmire of energy and money. It took years of effort for me to realize a finished product was irrelevant: what counted was the relationship between inhabitants and habitation. A home is not just shelter like a hotel room, and its repair and maintenance are not merely drudgery. It is as essential a marker of our lives as is a snail's shell, a bird's nest, or a bear's den. There is joy in tinkering.

Much of this tinkering is necessitated by one of the planet's most useful and abundant materials. Though sustaining the life around us, water is the root of all evil in building maintenance. Wet wood is food to insects and fungus; wet flashings and gutters corrode; masonry joints erode. I learned this lesson in a vivid manner during a torrential August downpour shortly after we moved to Collinsville. Gazing through the kitchen window, I marveled at the raw force of nature that made it seem as if I were peering from behind a waterfall. But my reverie was interrupted by what sounded like an open faucet gushing in the basement. If only it had been! I could have ended the flood by turning a knob. Instead, water poured from several places in the fieldstone foundation, rapidly filling the cellar despite a floor drain of uncertain destination. This dike had more leaks than I had fingers, so I grabbed whatever was at hand—newspaper, fiberglass insulation, some wadded-up rubber gaskets. The effort was futile against hydraulic pressure that was surely the envy of a medium-sized water company. Fortunately, the storm abated when the flood reached ankle depth, and the drain sluggishly funneled the water away.

Oddly, I felt inspired by this basement disaster. After weeks of debate Sarah and I selected shoring up this sorry site as our first major home improvement project in a house screaming with myriad needs. I threw myself into the job with an enthusiasm usually reserved for some eagerly awaited pleasure, like an exotic vacation. I awoke early with anticipation the next Saturday, and before breakfast I was below ground among the spiders and still packed boxes. The problem was immediately evident: the mortar binding the stone foundation had turned to dust. Repointing—a term I learned from the mason who had rebuilt our collapsing chimney— was in order.

The foundation seemed a logical place to begin renovations since it was built first and was the most essential of the elements supporting a house. Taking the stairs two at a time, I hurried to the bookcase for a couple of home-repair manuals that we had received as house-warming gifts. Forking

E. J. Smith Hardware, predecessor of Eaton Hardware, about 1926. If they didn't have it, you probably didn't need it. (Courtesy Canton Historical Society)

scrambled eggs and spreading jam on a muffin, I read of dressed, semi-dressed, and undressed stone. Sarah sipped tea as she looked for tips on mixing mortar and reviewed the proper use of a trowel and various chisels. Extensive direction was offered on laying and repointing bricks and the building of stone walls and patios, but crumbling fieldstone basements went unmentioned in fifteen hundred pages of do-it-yourself advice.

In less time than it took to read up on Portland cement, I was standing on the worn hardwood floor of Eaton Hardware, where nails, screws, fixtures, tools, and advice had been offered continuously since the presidency of Andrew Johnson. With a couple of customers ahead of me I listened to instruction on replacing copper water line and advice on reseeding a lawn. My eyes wandered over the power tools, especially the Milwaukee Sawsall. Rarely have I been in the store without craving a new tool for an as yet undefined project. Perhaps it's intoxication with the smells of fresh paint, oil-coated pipe, cardboard packaging, and grass seed that inspires. A good hardware store is as much a feast for the nose and eyes as it is for the imagination, and there is something about a tool that makes your hand itch to possess it.

Rhett stood behind the cash register and listened patiently, cracking his trademark wry smile as I described a problem he had heard many times before, nodding all the while like a doctor with a stethoscope to a patient's lungs. In five minutes I walked out with a forty-pound bag of mortar, a small trowel, and some idea of what to do. I also had a new keyhole saw unnecessary to the work at hand, but which I had always wanted and had a notion of using in another project. (I confess that in almost two decades since, that project has never come to fruition, but I have used the saw on several others that I'd not anticipated.)

Repointing was a dirty and tedious job in the dank basement. With a screw driver and paintbrush I cleaned the powdered mortar, dirt, and cobwebs from between uneven stone chunks. Mixing mortar in an old roasting pan, I shoved it as far into the joints as trowel and screwdriver would allow. Slowly, ever so slowly, I mastered the intricacies of the work and made progress. It was not a pretty job, but a basement need not look nice. Basements are an amateur's classroom.

With nothing but time for a task that kept only my hands occupied, I contemplated the wall's geology of uneven stones—some flat, others rounded pieces of schist and gneiss found nearby, perhaps in the cellar hole itself. These broken pieces of the surrounding landscape, rocks hardened in millennia past by heat and pressure far beneath the surface, now supported my home. Beams with bark and knots recalled trees growing nearby one hundred and fifty years ago. The wood bore the marks of the water-powered saws and hand planes that had shaped them into lumber.

This cellar must have been a dim vault of darkness only slightly brightened by candles, whale oil, and kerosene lamps in the years before the advent of the wires and the bare bulbs that now illuminate all but the furthest corner. Electricity is a home's most useful and versatile labor-saving system, and no room in the house has benefited from it more than the cellar, transformed by light from a creepy storehouse for turnips, apples, and canned goods to a useful repair shop, laundry room, or, in many homes, game room. A ganglia of wiring has shifted the basement from the strapping role of Atlas supporting the floors above to something like that of a central nervous system.

Stapled to beams and joists above me was a veritable history of American house wiring, much of it still venerable knob and tube. In this scheme separate positive and negative wires were strung, without a ground, from porcelain knob insulators and carried through beams with porcelain tubes. There were also yards of modern cable wrapped in fabric, metal, and plastic, each easily dated from its technological introduction or its appearance in building codes. Small and rusting fuse boxes were fastened beside a shiny gray circuit-breaker cabinet. Today that cabinet is fed by a service cable as thick as a man's wrist, which provides 200 amps of power for a microwave, computers, stereos, portable heaters, a range, refrigerator, and countless other gadgets. Wires carrying information throughout the house run alongside the streams of electricity, permitting telephone conversations, ferrying music to speakers, and drawing in Internet computer data on a thin coaxial snake.

As I gazed around the room with its maze of pipes and wires I recalled the dictum of Stewart Brand, the Whole Earth Catalog founder, who said that buildings are shaped by money, technology, and fashion. When, I wondered, were sufficient funds available to replace the unfashionable outhouse and kitchen handpump with toilets and water lines? Hidden by clever boxes in the wall or by false bathroom floors, a network of water and sewage pipes now slithered through void spaces. Out of sight, they were out of mind except in the basement, the house's most functionally expressive space.

In a village known for technological innovation, central heat was likely installed in a company manager's home soon after it became generally available around the turn of the twentieth century, though some nearby houses did not have it until the 1990s. In my house, basement ceiling patches indicate that an earlier series of hot-air registers were later replaced with the current low-pressure steam system and accordion cast-iron radiators. Marks on the concrete basement floor show that a larger furnace once stood where a lunking H. B. Smith retrofitted coal boiler now sits. The use of coal explains the cinders I've uncovered outside while digging a garden. Concrete has replaced a dirt floor except in the crawl space below the kitchen, where exposed soil has remained undisturbed for a century and a half. Oil tanks, the remains of kerosene lines that once fueled a small kitchen heater, and bulkhead steps incorporating a factory grindstone all tell stories. My tale of a basement only half remortared is not about giving way to the tedium, dust, or frustration, but giving in to the demands of other tasks.

A whole series of projects grew from a second storm that October. The rainfall rivaled that of any summer thumper, and I panicked as water poured from the walls despite the weeks I'd spent filling cracks with cement. I was desperate to find the source. Without a raincoat, I darted outside and slipped on a clotted mound of leaves. Soaked to the skin and chilled, I ran frantically around the house and discovered rotting gutters and broken downspouts channeling water to the basement. These would have to be replaced before I could finish remortaring.

The rain passed and with a ladder and screwdriver I poked and prodded the rusted gutters and misaligned downspouts. These would be my top priority. But I also noticed that the asphalt shingles were brittle, and some were broken and buckled, where the gutters joined the roof. The house was also peeling badly and some sofits were rotten and needed to be replaced before new gutters could be hung. Of course, new wood requires paint. From the ladder I noticed dried, cracked, and missing window glazing, such that some panes rattled in the wind following the rain. Glazing came before painting and required removal of storm windows.

Descending the ladder into a thicket of overgrown yew bushes, I saw that these were brushing against the house, trapping moisture against the cracking and peeling clapboards. Large roots pried at the foundation stones I had been busily cementing together. Suddenly, I felt overwhelmed with all the collateral repairs involved. The gutters were not a project to be started in autumn. Sarah and I took the only option available to resourceful home-owners. Using the better part of a roll of duct tape we patched the biggest leaks in the gutters, and then wired the downspouts in place and used scrap pipe borrowed from a neighbor to lead water away from the house.

Autumn brought colder weather, and wind-driven drafts and those rattling windows focused our attention on the attic. The scant three inch-es of rodent-chewed rock wool under the floor boards was a bad omen for warmth and fuel bills. But the Indian summer day on which we began insu-lating mocked our efforts to offset winter. The attic was hot, and dust and fiberglass hanging in the air stuck to our sweaty, itchy skin. We ripped up floorboards and pulled out the rock wool, discovering a few 1940s-era news-papers, yellowed and brittle with age. We paused to read headlines of elec-tions and school budgets, as well as ads for ice, patent medicines, and brassieres. We found a photograph of the long-gone railroad bridge over the river, and also a rat skeleton with desiccated skin. Small wasps nests cling-ing to rafters were the only other sign of wildlife, though our neighbors' homes have hosted squirrels and bats.

The dry floor boards we pulled up were fastened with squarish black-smith-forged nails banged into place by nineteenth-century carpenters, with a few modern common nails used in later repairs scattered among them. Nails are the most humble but essential items in a wood-frame house. A 2,000-square-foot modern dwelling contains about 75,000 of them. Made tediously one at a time, nails were a valuable commodity in the colonial era and were mentioned in wills as an important part of an estate. Old nails vary slightly in their thickness and length, whereas today's nails are each precisely the same, millions rapidly produced by clipping off pieces of extruded wire. Though we take them for granted, these humble fasteners that hold our homes together can teach us about metallurgy, manufactur-ing, economics, building construction, and technical innovation.

The widespread availability of inexpensive nails led to invention of balloon-building construction in 1833. This technique replaced the heavy timbers of post-and-beam with studs, sawn lumber in relatively standard small sizes such as two-by-fours, that were uniformly spaced to form a light, rigid wall. The term "balloon" was at first pejoratively applied to emphasize a lack of solidity compared to post-and-beam construction.

Our house is a bridge between the two methods. Studs run from the foundation sills to the attic rafters, but heavy timber with carefully chiseled mortise-and-tenon joints fastened with large pegs form the basic frame. Clearly, the carpenter who labored here in 1847 was not comfortable enough with the new technique to trust the whole house to studs and nails. Balloon construction quickly supplanted those traditional techniques in which skilled carpenters spent a great deal of time chiseling and joining large beams, and reduced by half the quantities of wood necessary for sturdy construction. It is still the mainstay of domestic building, except that studs now run from floor to floor rather than the height of the house.

We arranged cotton candy–like pink fiberglass between joists and replaced the floor boards. There was room for only six inches of insulation when twelve was needed. We could lay an additional six inches on top of the floor, but then the attic would have been useless for storage. We sat there in the still, hot air, muddy sweat running through the dust on arms and legs, contemplating how the space would look when filled with the boxes of keepsakes, old clothes, and camping gear now cluttering the basement and garage. Wasps darted in and out of their papery honeycombs, squeezing through gaps in the window frame. (New sash and glazing needed, I noted.)

In a patch above us Sarah noticed a few light-colored roof boards surrounded by others that were charred and blackened: evidence of an old fire. What had started it—sparks from the chimney, lightning, an early electrical short, a candle? Had the house filled with smoke? Whose family was evacuated? The patch fueled our fascination with the house's history. From our reverie about those new boards grafted to old, it occurred to one of us to lay the insulation on the old floor and to build a new series of plywood pallets for storage. In the subtle joining of the ages above we found an inspired solution. Clearly the old house held new lessons.

Repairing and rebuilding connect us to previous owners, for as we remove some of their stamp we make the place our own. Peeling away layers of kerosene-soaked kitchen linoleum, stripping yards of wallpaper, installing new light fixtures, building a stone wall, patching plaster, replacing windows, rebuilding stairways, installing cabinets, and stripping woodwork—all these projects have fostered an intimate relationship with our house. The process has also bound us to our neighbors, equally busy designing terraces, repairing porches, rebuilding chimneys, and removing asbestos siding to restore clapboards. The work provides us with a common language, understanding, and purpose as we watch and talk about each other's progress. Tools are borrowed, advice given, and, when time from other project allows, hands and backs are lent to new efforts. We have papered eight rooms in our house—two of them twice. Not a single sheet has gone up without our friend Alan's hands at the task. His assistance has helped us build our home and a friendship. With only the mildest Tom Sawyering I have coaxed neighbors to join me with a paintbrush, and building our stone wall would have been difficult without the methodical patience and strong back of Sandy from over on East Street.

While houses are opportunities for learning, they sometimes suffer from too much "amateur-hour" carpentry: moldings not exactly joined, shelves out of plumb, hidden screws visible, doors not planed precisely to fit. Hiring someone can seem like admitting defeat, but it is frequently necessary. Though we are often unhappy with our own work, doing the job offers more satisfaction than it does perfection. As a carpenter in Tracy Kidder's book *House* observes: "Perfection is an insult to the gods." Clearly, we do not want to offend heavenly powers, so it is not always for the want of a few dollars that we do the work ourselves. We do it for the pleasure of the ordeal.

Ultimately, we learn that while our houses are inanimate, they are not passive, and we literally build a relationship in the ongoing repairs and the discovery of their eccentricities. The places that shelter us become something akin to lovers. They welcome and warm us, offering reassurance and comfort. The metaphor is altogether fitting, since they can also be confining, leaning on us for time, effort, and money, and nagging us with temperamental mechanical systems, peeling paint, or cracked windows. We luxuriate in their protective bosoms and chafe at their demands. "Age plus adaptivity is what makes buildings come to be loved," observes Stewart Brand. "The building learns from its occupants, and they learn from it." That is what grows a house into a home.

Home is the innermost house, a quirky, battered refuge of domesticity whose appearance, and especially whose imperfections, become emblematic of its inhabitants as its structure is saturated with memories. Our homes are not merely built of nails, timbers, and fieldstone, but of idiosyncrasies that only time and life can confer. They have proven themselves as shelter for a continuum that embraces all: lovers and lovers' quarrels, children running up and down the stairs shrieking and slamming doors, pets from dogs to snakes, hours of quiet conversation over coffee, Christmas trees and trick-or-treaters, the sounds of piano practice and the smell of Thanksgiving. Their banisters are smooth, their kitchen floors worn, their door hinges tired. They are not merely machines for living, investments, or shelter from the elements. They themselves live.

The projects in Collinsville homes are often works-in-progress, intended for completion but not often finished. Despite a flurry of effort, a certain sustained disrepair lingers, a kind of casual unkempt domesticity of peeling paint, leaning fences, scraggly hedges, and leaking gutters. Unencumbered by the philosophy of "fix up and move on" endorsed by those eager to "trade up," we worry less about wrapping up the work because we envision ourselves here to the finish. Thus we live months— and sometimes years—with unpainted walls, bare bulbs hanging from wires, exposed plumbing, ripped-up floors, and tools scattered around like children's toys. The building waits while we pursue a craft, spend hours as volunteer soccer coaches and firefighters, or play with our children. "Let the floor go uncarpeted, and the wood unpainted," observed that advocate of well-repaired houses, Gustav Stickley, "that we may have time to think, and money with which to educate our children to think also."

But despite all our efforts, a home is built not just out of the work we lavish on it, but from routine daily tasks like cooking, cleaning, and laundry, and of seasonal activities like shoveling snow, watering gardens, raking leaves, and installing window screens. The words "habit" and "habitation" share the common Latin root, *habēre*—to have or keep. Domestic tasks are drudgery only when we make them so. To see them fresh, like our efforts at reconstruction, we must transform them from nuisances to nuanced exploration. "A house," says Wendell Berry, "is not simply a building, it is also an enactment. That is the first law of domesticity, even the most meager. The mere fact must somehow be turned into meaning. Necessity must be made a little ceremonious." Thus, cooking can be an opportunity to explore the flavors of different cultures, the origin of foods, their cultivation and processing. Fall leaf raking offers time to think about the ecological function of trees, the uses of compost, and the childhood joys of jumping in the gathered piles. Snow shoveling is the starting point of snowmen and snow balls, a chance to examine crystals even as the back hurts and the wind blows. Drudgery? Yes, but not only. We are smart enough to invent an arsenal of domestic labor-saving devices; why are we not sufficiently clever to enjoy our labors for what they can teach us?

More than merely a shell of identity or a stage for dreary routines, our homes undertake to shape us with their layout, size, room types, window styles, and assembled conveniences. A contemporary house with huge master bedroom, walk-in closet, and satellite bathroom encourages more private time than does my typical Collinsville home, with its eight-by-ten bedroom and a closet too shallow for a hanger. In a house lacking a substantial den or game room, our living room is wholly devoted to the actual business of living. Unlike those commonly found in houses built today, my kitchen is too small for a table, and thus dining takes place in the dining room, and the sharing of meals is kept distinct from the work of preparing them.

This dining room, by far the largest space in the house, is poised at the crossroads of domestic traffic, the junction of hallway, kitchen, and living room. It is, as nineteenth-century phrenologist and domestic architecture critic Orson Fowler proclaimed it, "the great central living and congregating room of the whole family." Meals make it a center of sociability, the spot where guests are likely to be entertained and where the family most regularly meets and talks. It is also a room for reading newspapers and magazines and a distribution point for materials moving through the house. It is a likely location for Sarah to pay a few bills, for the children to scribble their homework, for a family card game, and for craft projects requiring the table's expanse.

The dining room provides the best link between family and neighbors, whether a couple is formally invited for dinner, or the kids next door join us for tuna fish sandwiches at lunch, or friends sit for an impromptu visit that includes a cup of coffee. Here it becomes clear that although preoccupation with home may seem self-absorbed it is hardly narcissistic. "The impulse to care and to preserve our home," writes urban pioneer Kathleen Hirsch, "gives rise to the patterns and internal order that make it distinctly ours. . . . Structures build upon structures, and before long, if conditions are right, the habits of home reach their arms into the larger tide of any neighborhood worthy of the name." Of our homes, we build our community.

Firelines

*After you are a firefighter for a while,
it becomes instinctive in any situation to
help people, because that is what you
have been trained to do.*
—*Dennis Smith,* Firefighters

"The kid must have been flying," Willie said, shaking his head with a low whistle. The gray Plymouth had blown through a guardrail, snapped pole-sized trees, and bounced like a pinball among massive oaks. It lay on its side in a snow-covered gully, crushed like a roadside beer can. I was half-awake at two AM, peering through the fractured windshield with a flashlight. In the darkness we couldn't see much—an unresponsive victim who had bounced from steering wheel to windshield to ceiling to door, his face obscured by oozing blood.

Down the embankment firefighters came, wired on adrenaline, puffing fog. Hydraulic hoses linked, the jaws-of-life sounded like a wheezing, pulsing lawnmower. Jeff and Bill, two members of the responding company, wielded the bulky spreaders like a massive pair of tweezers, pushing the door away from its frame with the snap and buckling of metal. Halogen lights cast a stark eerie sheen on EMTs, who were busy laying out a stretcher, spider straps, head immobilizers, oxygen, and bandages. The Plymouth's windshield shattered into sparkling glass beads, and the posts supporting the roof were snipped and the top peeled back. A mangled, blood-spattered body was strapped to a backboard. Hand-over-hand we lifted the victim up the steep and icy slope, oxygen mask over his nose and mouth, forehead wrapped in gauze, IV bag held above. His face was contorted, purplish with bruises and drying blood, one eye swollen shut and the other barely hanging from its socket by a gelatinous thread. An arm was folded as if quadruple jointed, like a circus contortionist's trick.

Retrieving tools, I looked into the car past jagged shards of metal. Beer cans, papers, a magazine, a thick black wallet, and french fries and a burger were tossed about randomly. Blood spattered the seat and pooled, black and coagulated. A helicopter whirred overhead. Carrying an IV kit and Halligan tool, I reached the road as the bird landed in a whirlwind of gritty dust.

A fifty-something man in a flannel shirt appeared on the scene as the victim was being secured in the flight stretcher. This new arrival had a tough construction worker's build and an ex-marine's no-nonsense bearing. How did he come to be here? Maybe he was responding to a kitchen-counter scanner and the dispatcher's vehicle description. Perhaps a firefighter, recognizing the boy, had made a cell phone call. Unprofessional, I suppose, but with volunteers, the victims are friends and neighbors, not statistics. The man looked grim and determined, but dazed, like a boxer registering a hard right cross to the jaw.

The flight crew paused as they loaded the stretcher into the chopper's belly. The big man staggered back, struggling with tears. In the harsh white light and rumble of idling machines, he must have seen the uncounted years to come draining away from his son. Maybe he recalled changing diapers, or that first school bus ride to kindergarten, or the struggle with high school algebra, or a piano lesson, or football exploits. He grew old in moments, sullen and pasty and frail, and it seemed he might pass out as his mouth moved inarticulately. A slight, attractive flight nurse led him gently by the elbow aboard the waiting copter.

The chopper streaked across the sky like a shooting star. Billy, Greg,

Willie, and I picked up cribbing, medical supplies, and tools as the sleepy tow-truck driver surveyed the scene and griped about being roused from his deepest sleep in a month. The blood in the car began freezing. A cold wind picked up, sliced through my coat and rocked the frozen, creaking crowns of trees overhead. I knew it wouldn't be long before the contorted, blood-smeared face faded from my dreams: I'd seen worse. But the father's look was indelible.

At the firehouse we restocked the medical kits, gassed up the Hurst motor, and cleaned and folded the tarps. I worked quietly, away from the usual banter that dispels the ghosts of a gruesome accident. Despite a restive wakefulness I didn't stay long. I hurried home, and ran up the stairs and looked into Rebekah and Joshua's bedrooms. Both of my children were deep in sleep, a safe distance from my worries.

During our second year in Collinsville, Sarah and I watched the annual jamboree fireworks with Babe and her family from the well-tended lawn in front of her house, which sits on a rise overlooking the mill pond. A soft-spoken woman with a kind and welcoming face, she was still running Eaton Hardware at the time, and we were honored to be her guests. As the first rockets were launched, the lights dimmed on the midway along the river. The Ferris wheel stopped and the carrousel grew silent. The river shimmered with red, blue, white, and green trails of sparks, explosions of stars that reflected on the still water. Smoky clouds drifted toward us. The night became a bright theater of shifting color and shapes.

"Who sponsors the fireworks?" I asked, as the music resumed and lights once again shone below.

"Fire department," said Babe. "Volunteers. Jamboree raises money for equipment and the like."

Having grown up in a large suburban town I'd never considered that as a citizen I might have a responsibility to protect my community. Whether the emergency was smoking wires, or a car crashing into a utility pole, or a flooded basement, or finding yourself locked out of the house, you simply dialed the phone and "they" came.

Still held in thrall by the spectacular display, and a little embarrassed by my newcomer's question, I surprised myself by asking, "Think they need help?"

"Imagine so."

Of course, in topsy-turvy Collinsville my suburban assumptions were not too far from the mark. Atypically, firefighting was historically not the job of volunteers here. Collins Company workmen, not unpaid citizens, were first charged with responding to calls, though the distinction was probably not readily apparent. In the interest of protecting the factory, Samuel Collins purchased a hand-pumped engine to fill buckets from nearly the moment that axe making began. But the company did not serve only its own property; it covered the entire village and reached into neighboring towns. When the Collins Company closed its doors in 1966, its firefighting apparatus and the tiny, garage-like firehouse were turned over to a newly formed volunteer fire department for one dollar.

Just after dinner on a sunwashed Monday in June, a tall, dark-haired man stood in the firehouse door and shook my hand. "Drill's been canceled for a private meeting," Marq explained in a hushed tone. "We had a member hit by a car and killed during last week's drill." He swallowed hard. "Come back next week. Please come back."

The rejection was oddly exhilarating. Apparently firefighting was more than rushing to car accidents and chimney fires with axes and hoses. I was being invited into something where belonging made a difference. I wasn't turned away because my father and grandfather weren't firefighters, or because my slight frame was too puny, or because I was new in town and didn't know a single member. I was urged to come back another time because the department had family business to attend to at present.

At my first Monday drill I shook a few hands, filled out a form, and was introduced to Jeff, a lanky, red-headed paramedic who lived down the street from me. As he worked on the air packs, Jeff took pains to explain the function and workings of the regulator, low-air alarm, O rings, and the hose and fittings to me. We examined the tank and cleaned the face masks. Although not mechanically minded, I got the hang of it quickly. Within a few months I felt competent with generators and hydraulics. I gained the practical manual knowledge of how to join hoses, cut a car with an air chisel, and operate a pump and trouble-shoot air leaks.

I soon discovered that boyhood fantasies of poles, ladders, dalmatians, and shiny trucks faded as quickly as the testosterone intoxication of macho invincibility. In their place grew a sense of responsibility for others, knowledge of how to take charge, an appreciation of teamwork, and an awareness of surroundings. At day's end, after the wet stuff is poured on the red stuff and the fire is out, volunteer firefighting is about caring for a community.

Flashing lights and sirens ripped through the black first night of the year while somewhere a retired couple listened to a band, danced, and sipped drinks comfortably among friends. Before the evening was over they stood in the street wearing their party finest, shivering in the chill breeze as their house burned. Their grave and tear-stained faces were fleetingly lit by strobe pulses of red and blue. The flames reflected in the grandfatherly man's glistening eyes, while his wife dabbed at her tears with a tissue, worrying quietly to him about her smeared makeup, and wondering aloud in a quavering voice whether more trucks would be coming. There was nothing to do but watch.

Members of the truck company were quickly on the roof, chainsawing a hole to release heat and gases and lift the smoke so that the attack crew could see as they pulled a hose through the front doorway. A piece of flaming gable trim dropped off as the truckies retreated quickly from a volcano of fire erupting from the opening they'd cut. Asphalt shingles bubbled as the bright orange and yellow flames jumped into the air, starved for breath. The fire roared like a tractor trailer passing at sixty-five miles per hour.

The attack crew kept low in the hot air, crawling blind in the dark and smoke, feeling their way through rooms and around furniture and debris until they found bright patches of fire. Wayne, a burly fellow who had studied meteorology and now works in an explosives factory, became entangled in the wiring of the fallen Christmas tree. Disoriented, he paused momentarily, gripping the hose marking his route of escape to the door. He tried to shake himself loose, and seemed to get caught further. Precious air was lost.

Fear crept in closer, but the situation drove him past it, and with a deceptively easy twist he was free.

Outside, nozzles were aimed at the fire as it alternately vanished and erupted. The roaring flames tore into the house over the rumble of pumps and shouting voices. The blaze gnawed through the roof, and flurries of ash rose into the sky on the fire's hot, dry wind, floating to the ground like black snow.

Ultimately the fire was beaten. Despite a partially collapsed roof, broken windows, and blackened siding, the house was structurally intact and could be rebuilt. Inside, the smell of charred wood mixed with the stench of smoldering upholstery and melted wiring. Water dripped from the ceiling and pooled in inky puddles as if in the dim recesses of a cave. Dark stalactite icicles clung to burned wood. The furniture, food, appliances, and knick-knacks remained both strangely familiar in their arrangement and foreign in their blackened, dismal setting. Moldings were charred like half-used fireplace logs. Food cans had exploded, picture frames were cracked, and plastic containers and kitchen tools had melted into surreal shapes. A silver tea service was cast in on itself, as if it were pulled from a haphazard forge. The floor was a marsh of carpeting, plaster, insulation, and half-burned magazines.

As I returned to the truck with a pike pole, I saw the owners' faces in the flashlight beam. Their home had been grossly violated, and no burglar or vandal could have taken more from them. They could replace the living room lounger, the television set, and the refrigerator and microwave, perhaps with better than they had. But no insurance could restore the photographs of children and parents . . . a table given by a deceased aunt . . . the ceramic bowl made by a fifteen-year-old now grown to middle age . . . the venerable wedding dress.

Several of us sat on an engine bumper sipping a jug of Gatorade in the first gray light of day, our faces smeared with ash and our bodies clammy with sweat. The initial burst of energy and excitement was spent. I savored the sweet exhaustion and the small talk of a mission accomplished: a fire-fighter's high. There was quiet laughter, and pats on the back, and low whistles about near misses, and then sudden silence as the elderly couple, accompanied by a tall policeman, walked stiffly past us toward their home. A look inside, we knew, would only quell their hope. What for us was an adventure with the unexpected—an escape from the workaday world, a test of mettle—was their tragedy. I felt like swallowing my heart.

Just as they got to the door one of the men, face smudged and turnout gear filthy, emerged with a large book under his arm. He handed the couple a photo album resplendent with weddings, children playing, pets, and vacations. They turned back toward the police cruiser in smiles and tears.

Pictures, plaques, framed news articles, commendations, and awards line the walls and fill firehouse shelves like family heirlooms. Photos of ancient engines hang beside those of past chiefs and memorable fires. Parade trophies commemorate the most men in line, or the classiest shirts, or the best tanker or rescue truck. Fire departments celebrate corporate anniversaries with parties, parades, and ceremonies; they gather for holiday celebrations, funerals, birthdays, and weddings. You do not join a fire department so much as you give yourself up to it. This too is a family, with all its joys and dysfunctions.

And like the family dinner table or most any other regular gathering place, the fire station is a hothouse of rumor, a place rampant with innuendo. Everyone knows everyone else's business—not just out of natural prurience, but because they often care for each other with genuine, if distant, affection, and must rely on one another in the most demanding circumstances. In a crucial way that most of us seldom experience, here it matters whether one's colleagues are sick, tired, or distracted by personal troubles.

The stress of interrupted meals, worried sleep, and home events canceled at the sound of pager tones sometimes adds to personal problems. Frequent drills and meetings can drive spouses to fits of jealousy. Firefighters become immersed in topics that remain arcane to our partners, and develop tight friendships that are hard for them to penetrate. Guilt often hovers over the firehouse like dense smoke, as we watch a friend's pain growing partly from our mutual dedication.

Several years ago a married couple who had met through the department endured a messy firehouse divorce when a new member married to an outsider had an affair with one of them. The couple were officers, well liked, and among those essential people always involved in organizing events and bringing others together. The sour disintegration of the marriage tainted everything in the firehouse. A free-floating anger met the simplest event.

When the triangle responded to calls, the scene sometimes took on the bizarre quality of a soap opera. Observing one of them bandage a patient or apply traction, we would go about our business, ever watchful lest a crack in the veneer of professionalism reveal ugly, simmering emotions. An affectionate smile or tap between the two lovers, and the frozen longing of the third, was worse to behold than many bloody accident scenes.

The pain was personal, but it was also department business. There was a tear in the fabric of the membership. Conflict and distrust insinuated themselves into the firehouse family, loosening the group's cohesion. Years later, even with all three gone, painful scars have not fully faded.

While life with the fire department can thus drive wedges in personal relationships, it can also bind people together through the shared meals, games, life events, and parades in which spouses, offspring, and siblings participate. Children are drawn to the firehouse at an early age because it offers them a chance to sit behind the wheel of a pumper, aim gleaming nozzles at imaginary flames, and try on respirator masks. The child who once crawled over hoses can become a cadet or junior firefighter at the age of fourteen, and can join the department four years later. Such legacies bind the generations as few experiences can. They can also engender painful conflict.

A few years ago a twenty-three-year-old firefighter, who many remember as a boy playing on the trucks, challenged his father for election to assistant chief. With his wispy smudge of a mustache paling beside his father's robust growth, many of us wondered why he was choosing this way to declare his independence. The assistant chief's mantle was a part of the old man's identity. In the brief nominating speeches each lauded qualification stabbed at the opponent's weaknesses. The father had a knowledge of fires that the younger man could not even remember, was proficient with the most arcane rescue gear, was a professional driver, and had long command experience. The Eagle Scout son was hailed for understanding OSHA requirements, keeping meticulous records as a truck lieutenant, installing a dry hydrant, and appearing at late-night calls.

Many of us shook our heads, glanced knowingly at each other, stared away in discomfort. They were like prizefighters throwing punches at points we could not see. Was this the fallout from a breakfast table argument? Did it have something to do with the father's reaction to his son's girlfriend, or with the younger man's recent move?

Ballots were passed in a room leaden with silence. Had the son plotted this as payback for years of sitting in his old man's shadow? Votes tallied, the former's landslide victory was met with restrained applause, absent the typical handshakes and backslapping. The boy beamed. His father's eyes burned darkly with betrayal. Sickness roiled my stomach as I recalled battling my own strong-willed father.

But in time the wound between father and son healed, as it did among department members. It had to. We are a family.

Carrying the defibrillator, ropes, and medical kits and racing through a field under a blazing sun, several of us plunged into the woods and looked frantically about for the sure-shot path to the river. A woman had flipped an inner tube in the rapids, caught her foot among the rocks, and ended up pushed under by hydraulic force. She had been underwater for ten minutes or more. Our first choice of a route ended in a tangle of brambles; turning, we charged through a maze of trails and finally arrived at the steep river bank. We waded awkwardly upstream over odd sized cobbles, clambering over boulders.

The victim, a fleshy, sallow-faced woman in her thirties, had no pulse as we lifted her limp body from the water. We engaged standard operating procedures: Her swimsuit was scissored away, the defibrillator was placed against her chest, the oxygen mask was pressed to her face, and a towel was thrown over her hips. The regular count of chest compressions betrayed the urgency. CPR continued as we lifted the stretcher. We stopped briefly to apply the defibrillator once more and shock the heart. Her limp body shook with the stretcher's rhythm as we moved her slowly over uneven ground.

Suddenly her husband appeared, eyes bulging and lips atremble. He asked to help, but there was nothing left for him to do. He looked around vacantly as if this were his first view of the world. He gazed up into the sky through the trees and I saw him mouth the word "please." A big man, he seemed at once ready to tear something apart and to cry. We may have been working on a lost cause, but fixed by his gaze we continued CPR. Hand over hand we lifted her over the ledges, all along counting the compressions and breaths. We moved quickly through the woods. I felt queasy. The rushing river echoed in my ears. At the edge of the trees we loaded the victim into a waiting pickup, which took her to the Lifestar helicopter where she was pronounced dead. In shock, the husband wandered through the knee-deep grass in the beautiful sunwashed field, his face a mask of anguish. "We'd just gotten married," he said, to no one in particular.

Puffs of dust rose like mist as people crossed the midway under strings of bright lights. The air was heavy with the scent of grilling burgers, french fries, and fried dough. The crowd shuffled between the game booths on one side of carnival alley and the food stands whose proprietors were hawking cotton candy, popcorn, and soda on the other. Beyond were rides—Ferris wheel, carrousel, roller coaster, Himalaya—their outlines lit in a florid display of neon blooms against the night sky. Squeals, screams, and shouts echoed from this Edisonian aurora borealis as children rocked, twisted, and turned in gravity-defying ways.

At the carnival game I operated, softballs were being tossed into the open mouths of three plywood cats. Nearby, older folks gathered at the money wheel. The splashing, banging, and verbal torment of the dunk tank reached me from just beyond the food shacks. "Come feed the kitties! I've got hungry kitties," I called to coax the timid customers, cajoling the scornful and enticing those who thought themselves above such a simple game. "Four balls for a dollar. Three in is a winner," I called in a singsong, taking money, giving away a few cheesy stuffed animals, and chasing the balls that ricocheted around the booth.

Thousands of dollars raised during the annual Collinsville Volunteer Fire Department Jamboree have paid for air tanks, boots, water rescue equipment, portable pumps, tools, and turnout gear. For weeks this particular year twenty-five firefighters had been busy with all that preparation demanded: They built fences, repaired roofs, raked gravel, set up lights, erected traffic signs, slathered paint, moved refrigerators and food, banged nails, spliced wires, and fixed plumbing. The ladies auxiliary had similarly attended to cleaning, ordered food, organized mountains of paper goods, taken inventory, and collected pots and utensils. All this accomplished, mechanics and salesmen flip hamburgers, doctors direct traffic, and computer wizards call numbers at bingo when at last the awaited day arrives. Lawyers pick up trash. Truck drivers, factory workers, electricians, nurses, and government officials run games. Secretaries, bankers, and college kids serve food.

At my booth, uncoordinated fathers made valiant efforts for their wide-eyed children. Little boys and girls threw the balls awkwardly. The young toughs found they were not so tough. Teenage girls with shaded eyelids and bright lipstick made sure the right people were watching. "Looks like you're about to throw a no hitter," I cried to a sixtyish man who fixed his eye on the cutout cats. "Strike one . . . strike two . . . oh, close on the third," I remarked as he pitched. "You look like a young Bob Feller," I said to him, aware all the while that he may very well have seen Rapid Robert in his prime, my voice betraying an inevitable W. C. Fields archness.

These three days are more than a fund raiser: they're an essential part of the annual life of the town. The jamboree means chatting with people I seldom see, watching grade-schoolers grow up and infants begin to toddle. Youngsters leave exhausted with memories. Parents with lighter wallets remember their own humid evenings in the midway, and that particular heady combination of frying food, sweat, tobacco, perfume, bubble gum, and damp grass.

The final night's fireworks draw thousands with splashes of starry color and echoing martial booms. Under explosions of fleeting green and red arcs, fellow fireman Bill and I, dressed smartly in our white uniform shirts and silver badges, walked around with buckets, begging for donations. As we waded among people craning to look skyward from blankets and lawn chairs, I wondered whether any of them would be inspired to join the fire department as I had been. Maybe the possibility of rescuing a crying child from a crushed car or of dashing through flames with a charged hose draws people to the fire service, but the bravest act of all is volunteering itself.

Volunteer fire companies offer more than the obvious protection to a town. They strengthen a community with shared caring and responsibility in a direct and personal way. Everyone gets more than they put in. We live in a bottom-line society, and volunteer firefighting delivers the goods.

Celebrating

Community is where community happens.
—*Martin Buber,* Between Man and Man

Communities reveal themselves through their celebrations: Independence Day fireworks, St. Patrick's Day parades, Veterans Day ceremonies, hoopla over groundhogs in February and school closures for Lincoln's birthday. A holiday is not just a festive occasion; it is literally, as the word's roots suggest, a holy day. Holidays foster a sense of membership by joining a place and people to time, to shared ideals, stories, and the yearly cycle.

Although we gather together to commemorate each occasion with parades, Collinsville's two principal public holidays stand in stark contrast to one another. Memorial Day is the culmination of spring, when all is green and rainwashed, the air soft. Begun over a hundred years ago as Decoration Day, a time for placing flowers and flags on the graves of Civil War dead, its roots are deep in that central conflict of American history, with its notions of sacrifice, duty, and democratic ideals. And despite the light and easy manner of the family picnics that are now a tradition as well, the day carries a somber, introspective weight. A child may thrill to a parade resplendent with uniforms and fire trucks, but Memorial Day is also a time when the image of heroic deeds meets the heartfelt reality of a widow placing a flag beside a headstone.

Coming at harvest with crisp air and falling leaves, Halloween originates in the haze of Celtic bonfires and offers of sweets to roaming malevolent spirits in a season of diminishing sunlight. Once the province of children's dress-up fantasies, Halloween now ranks behind only Christmas in overall retail sales, and has become the most popular national adult party day after New Year's Eve and Super Bowl Sunday.

In Collinsville we celebrate both holidays with an anticipation and vigor that make them the public equivalent of birthdays and anniversaries. They anchor the periods of change in the year with an opportunity for each one of us to reaffirm our membership in the community. In spring we find comfort in our connection to the past, and in autumn we celebrate our love of whimsy. Collectively we explore the poles of tradition and innovation that are the engines of any place worth knowing. Ultimately, I'm not sure what can be said for a community whose holidays are at the antipodes of experience, whose public commemorations involve the most somber and the most frivolous of feelings. I know I just want to be part of it.

There is a preserved-in-amber quality to Collinsville's Memorial Day that returns us to a time of innocence and optimism. It is a small-town event in a place no longer so small, and you can briefly fill your lungs with the air of a young twentieth century. Yellowed programs of seventy years past could be used with fair accuracy now, and newspaper clippings of the 1940s match today's event with uncanny detail.

On Memorial Day, bearing flags and ceremonial rifles, veterans and their auxiliaries step off from a school yard where many of them played decades ago. Years have not stolen all crispness from their march, though uniforms have grown tight. Antique cars sporting running boards and bulbous headlights carry some of their number. In gold-braided, brass-buttoned suits and plumed hats the high school band plays lively and patriotic tunes, periodically halting to perform for clutches of people lounging on the grass, sitting in folding chairs, or perched on porches draped with red, white, and blue bunting. Girl Scouts and Brownies, Boy Scouts and Cubs carry banners, walking proudly through the applause of parents and friends as their leaders work like border collies to keep them in order. With fellow firefighters, I feel self-conscious and slightly uncomfortable in my uniform, intently trying to stay in step on the sun-warmed pavement. Modest cheers of thanks erupt. We tell jokes when the band pauses, complain about the heat, reminisce about members no longer with us. Behind us, diesel pumpers rumble slowly down the street, every ladder and axe gleaming, strobes flashing, an occasional air horn or siren blast drawing smiles and shrieks from children.

Celebration on the Collinsville Green, 1906. The author's home is first on the left. (Courtesy Canton Historical Society)

The parade goes by in five minutes, but the route is remarkably dense with spectators, some of whom pack up after the march passes and, taking short-cuts, watch again from another vantage point. And if you're not watching the parade, likely you are in it. Indeed, if you grew up in town it would be hard to avoid marching at some point with the scouts, the band, or a school group.

We start down a quiet residential street grateful for shade, and turn onto broad Maple Avenue. At the mill pond the parade follows Main Street. The crowd thickens in front of the coffee shop and the Collins Company's three-story masonry office building. Soda, potato chips, cookies, and candy bars sell briskly at LaSalle Market, and the crowd is several deep in front of Town Hall and the Eaton Hardware building. Red, white, and blue banners hang from the bank. The lawns of The Green are neatly trimmed, the gardens on its triangles freshly planted and mulched as they have been for this day for as long as anyone can remember. The marchers trudge uphill with groans and sweat until they reach the cemetery, where fresh-cut grass sits thick among the stones.

Standing before a silvery microphone on a grassy rise, Mr. Kilburn, a white-haired World War II veteran, calls for quiet as a clergyman gives an invocation. An audible breeze moves through overhanging maples until a burst of brass begins "The Star-Spangled Banner"—a fair but slow and ponderous rendition, better some years than others.

A few remarkably poised children recite "In Flanders Fields," the Gettysburg Address, and "The American's Creed." Each year the conjured visions of crosses row on row, poppies, and government by the people mingle in my consciousness with the smell of fresh-turned earth from a near-by garden. My neighbors' grown children have recited these sanctified words over the years, and I picture Josh and Bekah someday at the microphone.

Veterans stand at attention as they listen to the annual speech, given by a local dignitary, that seems somehow longer when the weather is warmer. The words can be thoughtful and philosophical or laced with bombast and knee-jerk patriotism. Always the oration is punctuated by calling mock-ingbirds, whistling cardinals, and twitching children.

Taps is dolefully bugled, and an even sadder echo replies from up on the hill. A rifle salute pierces the quiet. A final stentorian order is barked to the military men standing rigidly at attention: "Parade dismissed!" And as if a spell had been broken, the crowd files away, chatting, eager to picnic on grilled burgers, potato salad, and chips.

Within the flat grassy area where children huddle and speeches echo is a little-noticed, rusticated chunk of granite. A bronze plaque embedded in the stone bears the names of thirty-nine men whose remains were lost to distant Civil War battlefields. Each year a floral wreath is laid at the monument's base. When the monument was unveiled on Decoration Day in 1903, the event drew a few thousand people. Hundreds of children, women, and men marched through streets bedecked with patriotic bunting, streamers, and flags as a band played stirring tunes. There were religious blessings, speeches, and the cheers of school children to commemorate the sacrifices of the uniformed veterans. That day was the origin of our yearly parade and ceremony, and neither the form nor the sentiments have changed much since.

Josh and I approach the monument as the crowd disperses. I run my fingers over a bronze-cast name and he reads in a first grader's halting pronunciation: "Thomas Sessions."

I lean against the cool granite. "He was the first person from town killed by enemy fire," I tell my son. "A skirmish at Rappahannock Station, Virginia."

"Did he have a blue uniform?" Josh asks. I nod. "Did he shoot a Confederate first?" No one knows. "Did he have a sword?" No: he wasn't an officer. "What did he do in Collinsville?" Sessions was a fireman on the locomotive to Plainville, I explain. He often treated boys to a lesson on the valves and levers when he wasn't busy shoveling coal into the firebox as he switched engines in the Collinsville yard. A cloud comes over Josh's face. "That was sad that he couldn't give boys a ride on the train anymore." I am quietly pleased for a slight tarnish on his Hollywood image of Civil War heroism.

I pointed to another name. "Emery Mosman," Josh reads.

"He lived around the corner on South Street."

"A real Civil War soldier lived near us? Did he shoot in battle?"

"He was very brave. He agreed to scout enemy territory alone. He never came back. Some say he was hung from a tree as a spy."

"Did it break his neck? Did his face turn colors?" The romantic notion of spying has him hungering for more vivid details than I can conjure.

We climb the cemetery's terraced slopes. Buried among bankers, lawyers, grinders, electricians, doctors, and machinists are veterans not just of the Civil War but of the Spanish American War, World War I, World War II, Korea, and Vietnam. The Collins Company made bayonets, knives, and machetes for each conflict. A flower in his hand, Josh and I approach a pink granite stone high above the village. Here rests William Edgar Simonds, the only Congressional Medal of Honor winner from Collinsville. Josh lays down his flower at the modest marker and straightens the small flag set beside it. Sweating from the climb, we sit on the rough grass and look down into the village, which is largely obscured by trees. "Tell me again how he rescued his men," Josh asked.

"Well, it was early spring in Louisiana. A few soldiers were scouting a sugar-cane field ahead of their regiment. Suddenly, enemy fire burst from the woods and the men hit the dirt. Lying among the tall cane stalks and with smoke from gunfire like a thick fog, they became confused and couldn't figure out how to get back to the rest of the troops. Seeing what had happened, Simonds decided to single-handedly go to the rescue. Bullets whizzed overhead as he crawled closer. Simonds was breathing hard when he reached the pinned soldiers. His heart pounded and his face and uniform were spattered with muck. He yelled over the gunfire for the men to follow him. They moved slowly on their bellies through dirt, smoke, and the hail of bullets, but with Simonds shouting encouragement they made it safely back."

"He was very brave to do that," Josh concludes. I nod. "Okay, let's go to the picnic," he says, getting up suddenly. "I want to play army with my friends."

Early in October 1994, as the village maples began showering down leaves like colored confetti, a casual conversation that began among local artists sparked a notion that quickly took on a life of its own. Within a few days a group of painters, glass makers, musicians, woodworkers, potters, and others were busy painting the windows along Main Street in bold cartoon strokes of orange, black, green, and red. Ghosts, witches, and bloody faces materialized where hair spray, plumbing fixtures, and newspapers had been displayed. The staid countenance of Town Hall was splashed with creepy color.

As the week progressed, orange bulbs appeared in street lamps and porch lights. Ghosts made of white plastic bags were strung from trees and between second-story windows across streets. Word of a costume parade spread, of creepy creatures wandering the streets and a trembling "wall of fear" that would strike terror into both the most sensible minds and the bravest hearts. With each new decoration, excitement grew among the neighborhood children, who gathered to plot and plan their costumes and tricks as the day grew closer.

Around six o'clock on the appointed evening the streets began filling with people—many in costume, most eager to see what would materialize from this hastily organized event. No one knew what to expect, but everyone wanted to be involved. With help from a couple of neighbors, I had placed 125 luminaries along The Green and around the triangular islands that flanked its ends. Recorded wolf howls, funereal organ music, and dement-ed laughter echoed through downtown like the soundtrack of a grade-B monster flick. Bizarre and bloody papier-mâché heads hung from light posts. Green and orange theater lights cast an eerie glow on Main Street and smoke machines breathed fog into a crowd that swelled to two thousand in number.

Among the milling denizens sharing a break from reality was a surreal and cacophonous rank-and-file: Frankenstein monsters with bulging elec-trodes; ghosts; witches with long noses, lavender faces, and long black capes; baseball players with enormous gloves; doctors with maniacal grins teamed with patients carrying IV bags; Mickey and Minnie Mouse; bloody-mouthed vampires; walking leaf piles; sword-carrying knights; tigers; gorillas; ghouls with bloody faces and tire-tread marks across their bodies; kings; soldiers brandishing weapons; a Collins axe with a silvery wedge-shaped headpiece and clothing fit to resemble a handle. These were lawyers, store clerks, engineers, truck drivers, doctors, machinists, teachers, physical therapists, secretaries, accountants, carpenters, merchants, and plumbers, all fleetingly cut loose from their workaday identities. Four-year-old Bekah clung to my leg as these strange apparitions worked their way through the crowd. "Everyone's someone else tonight," she whimpered.

That first year I wore a wizard's robe Sarah had sewn. It was patched with moons and stars. I went about turning noisy children into frogs with my broom-handle wand. Sarah was a witch in a glittering dress, Bekah a princess, and baby Josh a black bat whose pink wings spread when, much to his delight, he was held upside down. Everywhere smiles were born of the pleasure of staring and of being stared at, in the sheer size of this sudden Mardi Gras.

Oddly enough, the serious and sedate historical museum with its broad, double-tiered balcony at the foot of Main Street was the epicenter of this wild and spontaneous event. Scores of people gathered there, drawn by the music, the colored lights, and the machine-generated fog that issued from it. The theme from *Ghostbusters* played, gradually growing in volume until it enveloped us. Dancing erupted and then gave way as the crowd, of its own volition, moved off in an impromptu parade. Few were watching from the sidelines, principally because there was no way to escape becoming a part of it. Strobes flashed, mist thickened, and the laughter of a demented tape loop echoed. The crowd turned onto The Green, where the white paper bag luminaries flickered, the candles outlining the street like a dim landing strip. Pumpkins with triangular eyes, round mouths and expressions of pain and torment were lit on dark porches. A flickering strobe light at one house cast spidery shadows. The face-painted, cone-hatted "goon squad" threw candy and small toys to children who scrambled for every piece.

At the corner of South and Front Streets, in the shadow of Sam Collins's church, fog rose and drummers steadily thrummed at "Voodoo Island," a mock graveyard of wooden tombstones and crosses surrounded by the odd-ball images of fierce pagan gods painted on plywood. People stopped to dance and in the colored smoke a party within a party took hold and grew. The parade came full circle to its starting point at the museum, where the cartoonist John Squier, who was decked out in a lab coat and whiteface as the horrid "Boosolini," stood on the balcony addressing a mass rally of the weird while cider was ladled below. He urged and taunted the crowd to cry "boo" ever louder, threw packaged cookies into the throng in the first annual self-proclaimed "cookie toss," and invited contestants to the microphone to howl for dollars. Music blasted. Monsters danced. Costume-competition contestants joined Boosolini on the balcony, and an eager crowd raised dole-ful cries to indicate their choice for such awards as the scariest, most original, and funniest outfits, and the coveted best-in-show. Following the contest, something like an impromptu Halloween ball began, a grim and gleeful masque in which ghosts danced with witches, President Nixon twisted with a Swiss cheese wedge, and a policeman twirled Dracula.

A fevered excitement gripped neighborhood children following the parade, as their preparations for trick-or-treating a few days later grew more elaborate and their anticipation of an evening of adventure height-ened. When that night of candy and spooks came, the streets were teeming with the typical half-pint goblins, but costumed adults were common too. Houses were more elaborately adorned than ever with ghastly trappings: more strobes, meticulously carved pumpkins, ghoulish dummies, and eerie music. And so with such spirits has each subsequent parade amplified our sense of wonder and fun.

Though the Memorial Day parade seems as inevitable as the equinox, tradition is fragile. The march, the speeches, the rifled salute do not simply materialize. Each year the proud, uniformed men standing at attention have grown grayer, more stooped, more frail. When they are gone, who will tell the various contingents when and in what order to march? Who will contact a speaker, find children to recite the Gettysburg Address, lay flowers at the Civil War monument, or plant flags by the cannon at River and Bridge Streets?

Each year the Halloween parade crowd slowly disperses, disappearing as gradually and mysteriously as it assembled. In the dark and over the course of several days after, volunteers pick up street barriers, collect spent luminaries, wash store windows, and strike the graveyard set. Hundreds of people—some years over a thousand—enjoy an evening of childlike fun, but only a few make adult time to arrange for smoke machines and lights, buy the goodies that will be tossed to children, solicit donations of cookies, paint store windows, or screw in orange light bulbs. The colors and the raucous sounds fade. A once-memorable 1950 Halloween parade eight hundred strong had been wholly forgotten until recalled by a brief note in the 2000 historical society calendar. How easy the relapse into civic amnesia!

We depend on public ceremonies. They imbue our everyday places with meaning, join us together, and kindle a sense of connection to those who have gone before. But beyond all these, we depend on the volunteers who labor to keep events vibrant year after year. They, not a May or an October parade, are a community's glue. Yet few realize that happenings do not "just happen." A good place to live is built with shared effort. A community may exist where community happens, but it happens because people take the time and put in the effort to make it so.

Collector's Items

How will we know it's us without our past?
—John Steinbeck, The Grapes of Wrath

Six Guns, Fountain Pens, and the Uses of History

Some will rob you with a six gun
and some with a fountain pen.
—Woody Guthrie, *"Pretty Boy Floyd"*

Like most Saturday mornings, this one mixed frenetic activity with reassuring routines. At our house, breakfast, peppered with conversation and paragraphs of the *Hartford Courant*, was leisurely after a late start. But between the paper's coverage of a subdivision proposal on Huckleberry Hill, Bekah's description of new Pokémon cards, and the details of the Civil War play Josh wanted to stage with his friends, we had lost track of the minutes. Carrying my sticky egg-coated plate to the sink, I announced the time as I glanced at the clock. Suddenly Sarah was out the door for a haircut. I had less than half an hour to make the bank and the post office.

Abandoning the breakfast dishes, I hurried to wrap a package of outgrown children's clothes to mail to my sister, and a pair of catalog-ordered shoes to be returned. As usual, scissors, tape, boxes, and marking pens were not where I'd expected and I grew frantic glancing at my watch. The scissors were under the newspaper where Sarah cut coupons; the tape sat where

Josh had been building a cardboard airplane. I finished up the packages with a mixture of speed, dexterity, and strong language. Then, dashing from bureau to dining room table to kitchen counter I wrote several checks to be cashed at the bank, to fill our wallets for a week of small transactions.

In the short time it had taken me to get ready to head out to the bank and post office, the children had become engrossed in a Bugs Bunny cartoon that, with the briefest glance, I recalled from my own childhood. "Say yur prayers, yuh long-eared varmint," Yosemite Sam threatened with drawn revolvers. I interrupted the program—my words far less welcome than a commercial—to get the two of them up and out before the bank tellers left their windows and the postmaster locked the door. They looked up at me as though I had asked them to run naked in the snow. I checked my watch; I had less than twenty minutes to make the bank a couple doors down and the post office at the other end of Main Street. With bold determination, I turned off the television to an ugly grunt from Bekah and an exclamation from Josh that his affections were now only for his mother. Such assertions did not deter me, but the children continued complaining and dawdling with shoes and jackets as the digital VCR display ticked away another minute.

"We have to hurry," I kept reminding them with increasing annoyance. Then I had a cartoon-inspired idea. Maybe a tale, one of those morsels of history some people find so dull and useless, could be put to practical effect and motivate them both to move faster out the door. Forget noble notions of history providing a common identity to inspire care for the community. I needed feet in motion.

Thumb up and forefinger extended, I formed a pistol with my right hand and shouted like the rabbit's nemesis: "This is a stickup! Get down on the floor!" Suddenly I had their attention. "I know it sounds like TV," I added with an enticing smile, "but those very words were once shouted by men with guns at our bank. Hurry! I'll show you exactly where it happened."

Five-year-old Josh was out the door in an instant, firing a string of questions about guns and loot and blood. Hands on hips, nine-year-old Bekah acted too sophisticated for such a simple ploy, protesting a story with guns, clearly reluctant to go along with anything that produced such enthusiasm in her brother. "Did you know," I told her, "that the bank was once robbed with a pen?"

"Funny."

"It's true. Hurry!"

With a skeptical roll of the eyes she stepped outside and plodded down the driveway in distracted annoyance while her brother jumped eagerly at my side like a puppy. "It was a lazy May afternoon in 1935," I began as we made our way toward the stolid masonry building, "and you could smell blooming lilacs. The brick walls of the bank were covered with thick green ivy back then. Sunlight came in through the big windows and made all the oak woodwork glow. Lamps hung from the tall ceiling and the thick, steel vault door lay open just behind the teller's counter."

"That's just the way it looks now." Josh exclaimed.

"But there's no ivy," Bekah corrected.

Despite the lack of ivy and the presence of such technological conveniences as an ATM and electronic deposits, the bank evokes a sense of changeless security. There is a hushed formality to the small lobby with its high ceiling and heavy woodwork. Many tellers have been there for years, and in a passbook savings account the interest is still penned in red, regardless of the wonders of the electronic age.

Just shy of closing, the lines were long. My friends and neighbors clearly had the same idea. Rhett was making a deposit and getting change for the hardware store; Colleen and John had checks to cash. I got talking to Leslie about her new fence.

Josh tugged on my arm. "What about the story?"

"Yeah," his sister chimed in. "Don't just make us stand on this boring line."

"Unlike today, the bank was quiet that afternoon," I started to explain while Leslie and John half listened. "The clerks were catching up on their work and the bank's president, an older man named Charles Farnham, stood at the teller's window preparing checks for Herbert Terry, who owned a gas station. Mr. Terry leaned against the counter in oily work clothes."

In these days when bank names change faster than you can finish up a package of checks and bank presidents are ensconced in high-rise glass offices in distant cities, the steady habits of the Collinsville Savings Society seem curiously refreshing. The bank has not changed its corporate structure in a century and a half, and chit-chat between depositors and the president is still commonplace. If you don't see him—Mike Langer, fit and athletic—behind the counter, you might run into him in the supermarket, or helping out at the fire department jamboree. Rarely do people address him as Mister. After all, he grew up here and started as a teller over thirty years ago.

"Terry was the only customer in the bank when three men walked in. A short, heavy guy with fat red cheeks got in line. He wore a gray suit and seemed like an ordinary businessman. But as Mr. Farnham looked up from his desk, the guy in line pulled out a gun. 'This is a stick up! Get down on the floor!' the man shouted as his hand trembled. Suddenly the clerks in the bank noticed that each of the robbers held a revolver. A short, skinny man guarded the door, while a tall guy with dark hair tried pulling off the bars that were in front of the cashier's counter back then."

In mock menace I gestured with a fist at Bekah as our line shuffled forward. "'Get down or I'll knock you down,' one of the robbers yelled at a person who hesitated." Her eyes widened. A few people around us quieted. I could sense them listening, cocking an ear, softening their own conversation. Though the practical mechanics of time travel have not advanced much past Jules Verne's imagination, clearly a story of the past told in its place has the power to transport. History need not be a stuffy school lecture nor as flashy as the glitz of an amusement park attraction.

"Finding he couldn't yank the bars off the cashier's counter," I continued in a hushed but fierce voice hinting at danger, "the tall man cursed in frustration." With a sweeping arm gesture I described how he leapt onto the counter and, grabbing a chandelier, swung over the oak barrier.

"Did they shoot someone?"

"No, but holding old Mr. Farnham at gun point, the bandit grabbed $1,000 from a drawer. The banker was forced into the vault, where the thieves dumped over $1,000 in silver into a white canvas bag. They demanded that Mr. Farnham open another safe inside the vault, and when he couldn't because it was on a timer, they shouted and waved their guns. The bank workers were afraid they might be shot." We shuffled forward in line. Gently I laid a hand on each of their shoulders. "Keep your eyes open, children," I warned. "You never know when it could happen again."

I watched as they slowly scanned the room. I suddenly applied more pressure to their shoulders, and they jumped as I resumed the story. "'Get down on the floor,' the tall man yelled at Mr. Farnham. But the old man would not be bullied even when the crooks pointed their guns at him. Afraid his weak heart would give out, Mr. Farnham shook his head 'no.' Instead, he sat in a chair. 'Regardless of what you fellows do,' he told them, 'I'm going to sit here and take one of these pills.' He pulled a small box from his pocket, opened it and swallowed the medication.

"The tall man got red with anger and slammed the heavy vault door. He swore under his breath and then all three gunmen ran out of the bank."

"Good morning. May I help you," came a kind, soft voice as distant in tone as in time from the desperate tale of the thieves. Grandmotherly and bespectacled Muriel LeGeyt took my checks with a smile and some small talk about the weather and how big the children had gotten.

"Were you here when the bank was robbed?" Josh asked, his soft brown eyes wide with curiosity. Mrs. LeGeyt shook her head "no" and smiled.

Though no one now working at the Collinsville Savings Society witnessed the robbery, a number of people have heard me tell the tale, and an event once all but forgotten has gained some measure of notoriety and currency. I have heard the story referenced occasionally, as people try to enliven the routine of cashing a check or having their pennies counted. Such stories grow and strengthen what we share about a place by the very act of retelling. The usual, taken-for-granted locations where we live our lives become more vivid as we hear and pass along what happened there.

"Dad, you've got to finish the story," the children implored, tugging on my arms as we walked down the bank steps. "The robbers got into a dark getaway car parked right there on River Street," I said, pointing to a spot on

Corner of River and Main Streets. The Collinsville Savings Society is on the right, the Fireplace is behind it, and the Valley House is across the street. (Photograph by Walter Kendra)

the west side of the bank where a green minivan full of children was parked while their mother was inside. "The car peeled out with a screech toward North Canton. Police arrived about fifteen minutes later and took off after them in an old, beat-up cruiser."

"Did they catch the bad guys?" Josh asked, skipping beside me as we made our way down Main Street toward the post office. At Eaton Hardware a paint-sale poster caught my eye, reminding me that the living room ceiling needed work.

"They never did. They lost the trail in Massachusetts."

"They never found them?"

"Months later a bootlegger named Nathan Boverman was killed by a police detective in Montreal. He was wanted for murdering a bank clerk in Quebec. Employees at our bank identified his picture."

"What about the other guys?"

I shrugged my shoulders.

"Mr. Farnham was a real hero," Bekah said. "He didn't let himself be bullied." Bullies at school had been a recent dinner-table topic.

Bill, one of my fire department buddies, hurried toward us after stepping out of LaSalle Market with a coffee. His glasses were set on crooked, drawing attention to his soft blue eyes. "I've got to make the bank," he said without skipping a step, "but I need to talk to you about the ladder drill at Canton Station on Monday." The last words were uttered over his shoulder as he passed. A leading voice at the firehouse for all kinds of training, from incident command to cold-water rescue, he wasn't someone who liked to be unprepared. Being late for the bank probably bothered him more than it would most people.

We are single-minded and focused on our own needs as we rush to Saturday morning chores, yet the act becomes a community activity. For the moment we fix on the bank and post office; later our attention will be drawn to the transfer station and the hardware store. Cashing a check, buying stamps, dropping off the recycling, or purchasing a tube of caulk at Eaton just before they close at five o'clock: this is how I catch up with many of my neighbors. The most trivial private transactions afford us many such opportunities.

Bekah hopped onto one of the stone steps in front of Town Hall. "Maybe that's kind of a cool story, but you said the bank was robbed with one of these," she challenged, taking a pen from her pocket.

"A fellow named Seth Norton did it in the 1850s and 1860s," I began, as we passed the barber shop where Nancy was clipping an anxious little boy's hair as his mother watched. A group of skateboarders congregated next door at LaSalle, and several people lingered over breakfast at tables under the awning.

"What he did was kind of like cheating on your homework. He was hired by the Collins Company as a bookkeeper in 1847. He learned about the company finances, and Samuel Collins soon trusted him with all sorts of private information. The company was only about twenty years old, and the big stone building along the river was just being finished. Back then there was no bank in town, so people deposited their money with the company. But Sam Collins wanted to get out of the banking business.

"Norton was a hard worker. Like you, Bekah, he was pretty good with figures." My math-wizard daughter brightened at the compliment, giving a toss of her long brown hair. "There's a picture of him in the museum.

He had wavy hair and a beard around his chin. He looked like a serious businessman, someone you could trust. He helped start the bank in 1853 and was the first treasurer. Of course, he didn't have to go too far to do the bank's work because their first office was in the Collins Company headquarters.

"Everyone seemed to like him. The town meeting asked him to join a group studying how to provide help to the poor, voted him the animal pound keeper, and put him on a committee to distribute money to Civil War soldiers who volunteered. He was elected to the state legislature.

"Even the U.S. government trusted him as Collinsville postmaster," I said as we entered the rectangular brick post office erected during the Eisenhower administration. In Norton's day, of course, the post office was housed with the Collins Company.

"Hi, Donny," I said to a burly truck driver as he pulled mail from his box. A long time firefighter and former chief, he lives right next door, but seems to enjoy the ritual of the post box. He nodded as I walked to the counter where Patricia, a tall, dark-haired woman was rushing to get things wrapped up just a few moments before closing. Even on the busiest day she has a smile and a good word for kids who shyly say hello with a bit of prodding. She knows to get out the baseball commemoratives to catch Josh's attention.

With the package weighed, stamped, and on its way, we headed back up Main Street. As we passed the Collins Company office building, whose tenants now include a yoga instructor, frame shop, and therapeutic massage practice, I explained that Samuel Collins made Norton the company's agent with the power to sign checks.

It wasn't just the business community that trusted the ever-helpful bookkeeper. He was respected with even the most deeply personal matters of life and death, and had been elected president at the first meeting of the Collinsville Cemetery Association. When Eliza Crane died in 1858, Norton became guardian of her four children. His judgment in such matters was so highly valued that in 1859 he was elected judge of probate, responsible for the financial welfare of villagers from cradle to grave.

"He was a nice man to watch out for those kids when their mommy died," Josh said as we rounded the corner of Main Street onto The Green.

"He was very generous, and lent money to many people."

"Okay," Bekah demanded, "if he was such a good guy and everyone loved and trusted him, why did he rob the bank?"

"No one knows. In October of 1867 he suddenly got sick while at the Collins Company annual meeting in Hartford. When business was done he went to his hotel room with a fever and chills. The next day he came home," I said, pointing to the mansard-roofed house across the street from ours. "But he got worse, and just before the end of the month he died.

"There was a fancy funeral attended by Samuel Collins and many important people. Soon after that, the bank's trustees found that not only was there money missing, but the books Seth Norton had kept as treasurer were so confusing that it was not clear what had happened to much of the funds over the years. In addition, Norton had borrowed a lot of money, including about $6,000, from his own bank, which was against the law."

"So everybody who trusted him got ripped off because he added things up wrong," Bekah said.

"It wasn't just that the numbers weren't calculated right. It was like he didn't do his homework. The accounts he should have kept were never done or were missing. It was a crime."

"You can get arrested for not doing your homework?" Josh asked. Bekah rolled her eyes. "Norton was worse than the robbers with guns because he cheated people who trusted him."

"Did he buy a lot of stuff with the money?" Josh asked.

"No one knows what happened to the money. When he died he didn't have a lot of fancy stuff. The whole thing was hard for people to believe because everyone thought Seth Norton was a great guy and trusted him." I paused for a moment pondering whether I should play the parental Aesop. "What's the lesson of this story?"

"People aren't always what they seem," Bekah volunteered, a more sophisticated answer than I'd expected

"Something like that. But don't forget there were also very good people who straightened out the bank's records and helped depositors get a lot of their money back. Today this is one of the best run banks in the state," I said, recalling from somewhere that Collinsville Savings Society had earned the top five-star rating for strong fiscal performance from Bauer Financial Reports.

"Our bank is really a neat place. I'm going to tell my friends. I mean real things actually happened there," Josh said, as if the bank had the mystery and romance of a far-off castle.

"Yeah," Bekah agreed. "It's like stuff that happens on TV."

The Terrible Saint
on Main Street

Just before one o'clock on a Sunday afternoon in March I was preparing lunch for the family. Josh was parked on the couch. The television blared a Rugrats cartoon at a volume approaching the OSHA limit. Bekah and Sarah were in the basement, planting tomato seeds under lights.

I'd mixed the tuna and mayonnaise, sliced the celery, and washed grapes. Juice was poured, coffee brewed, but on opening the refrigerator I found only three slices of bread. Josh wanted peanut butter with jelly, and Bekah and Sarah asked for tuna sandwiches. Since breakfast, I'd been craving a slice of toast with the cranberry-raspberry jam we'd bought on vacation. Clearly there would be war among four hungry people if I had to somehow split three bread slices among us. Fortunately, a battle with forks and spoons was easily avoided with a trip down the street to LaSalle Market.

I crossed The Green and walked along Main Street, wrapping my scarf tightly against a biting wind that spit a few frozen flakes. Under the pewter

LaSalle Market building in the late nineteenth century. (Courtesy Canton Historical Society)

sky, lawns seemed almost gray. Way down the street, over the long brick facade of the old Collins packing department, Sweetheart Mountain loomed, a brooding presence, its top merging with the clouds at some undefinable point.

As I entered the market I was greeted by the familiar tinkle of a bell hung on the plate-glass door, a warm and moist burst of air, the hum of conversation, and the smell of bacon and eggs frying on the grill. About half of the ten tables were occupied, and a few customers waited at the register holding gallons of milk, the *Hartford Courant,* and cups of coffee to go. I waved to Tim, who sat at a nearby table. A gentle man with spectacles and an interest in history, he has a law degree and teaches grammar school. At the moment he was in a heated discussion with one of my neighbors over plans to renovate the old elementary school and turn it into a library. As I watched, someone brushed me from behind; I turned and saw David, a soft-spoken man who designs kitchens and installs cabinets. About a decade and a half ago he built the ones that grace my kitchen. Later he set up shop in a storefront opposite Town Hall. He asked about the children as he headed out the door with a newspaper and coffee.

Larry sat at the table beside the bread display. A banker with a lilting laugh, he was trying to get two tow-headed children to finish their bagels. As I bent down for a loaf of wheat bread, he wondered aloud whether the board of selectmen was ever going to replace a tree around the corner that was cut last fall. A staccato conversation about the education budget, the sugaring season, and baseball spring training ensued, interrupted by admonitions to "have a few more bites of bagel" and the scraping off of excess cream cheese. One of the kids whispered in his ear and they headed quickly to the bathroom out back.

On line at the register with sprightly Bev, whose face seemed one great smile, I got the latest on the yoga classes she teaches on the third story of the old company office building. I asked if she'd heard the forecast. If the snow continued, did she and her daughter want to join us sledding? She agreed cheerfully, putting a few dollars on the counter and dashing out with her groceries.

There were two other people ahead of me. I was growing impatient as the first, a heavy, dark-bearded man, debated at length over which cigarettes to buy. I'd seen him before. He drives an ancient Ford pickup and frequently fishes from the Farmington River Bridge.

From behind I heard a deep baritone voice pitched in normal tones which nevertheless carried over the general hum of conversation. Turning my head I saw another vaguely familiar man, tall and lanky, with a farmer's weathered features. He was standing halfway across the room near the doughnut tray, one hand holding a coffee cup and the other gesturing for emphasis. He appeared to be emphatic about some issue and several people were listening to him. I seemed to know that lean jaw and those piercing eyes, but could not place him. Another of the bridge fishermen? Perhaps I'd seen him at the bar in the Fireplace or at a coffee shop concert. Did he say something about a trip to Kansas with his family? Complain about someone with a rifle? Allude to a hunting trip with his sons? Suddenly a voice close by startled me.

"'Morning. How's it going today?" John, laconic proprietor of LaSalle, punched up the price of the bread on the register.

"Fine. Bit chilly out there," I replied, still preoccupied with where I'd seen the bearded man before. John asked me how the maple sap was running, and I said something pro forma—"okay," "good," or the like. He handed me my change, and I turned for a last glance at the tall man, but he was gone. I grabbed the bread and, with a few waves goodbye, left with a feeling of slight, undefinable discomfort.

The wind seemed to have picked up, blowing hard in my face as I made my way down Main Street's steep hill. I squinted at the mix of gritty snow and sand that whipped up off the pavement. Reaching my driveway, I scanned the lawn for sticks and limbs that might have fallen in the gusts.

Looking over the forsythia hedge I caught sight of the handsome Italianate house next door with its decorative brackets at the roofline and its wraparound porch. A funeral parlor a generation ago, it still has plumbing for draining fluids and spaces designed for storing coffins in the basement. In the mid-nineteenth century it was the home of Charles Blair, a longtime Collins employee and public-spirited man who rose to be superintendent of the works, was elected to the legislature, and held other public posts. Charles Blair—somehow I sensed he was the key to the man I had half-recognized at LaSalle. Looking at the house had established the connection, as if the handsome building were a Rorschach blot that would enable me to free-associate the answer.

Obviously I could never have seen Blair or anyone else from his era, and yet the man in LaSalle seemed somehow connected with him. Maybe I hadn't had a good look after all. Perhaps I'd barely glimpsed him out of the corner of my eye as I was talking with Bev. With so many distracting conversations going on around me any number of misidentifications were plausible. What seemed certain was that I couldn't possibly have spotted John Brown, the radical abolitionist whose raid on Harpers Ferry, Virginia, had been the most violent and telling prelude to the Civil War. He had been hanged before an angry crowd a century and a half earlier.

In my effort to learn more about the village, had I been up too late reading about the Collins pikes that Brown had stockpiled among his munitions in a Maryland farmhouse to fuel a slave uprising? This kind of fact-induced fancy had hit me before, like a waking dream. I was discovering that the more I dug into history—not its grand sweep, but simple everyday events of community life—the more I found the line between past and present blurring. Unearthing the details of the things that had occurred nearby seemed to bind me more tightly to this place. I came to realize that the past was not dead history confined to old photographs or the dusty prose of textbooks, but something organic that was all around us at every instant. Even at that moment, with the reality of daylight, cars, electric lights, and telephone wires close at hand, anchoring me firmly in the here and now, the pictures I'd seen and the newspaper accounts I'd read so stoked my imagination as to call forth the spectral image of the hawkish-looking Blair on the lawn next door. He was partially obscured by the bare hedge, rigid in a black suit and high collar, lips pursed tightly below a blunt wedge of nose. A big gust tore down the street and the massive maple branches groaned overhead. Empty sap buckets banged against tree trunks. I looked up quickly.

When I turned back to the hedge the image was gone. I walked swiftly back to the house and continued making lunch without saying a word of Blair or Brown to anyone.

Such moments occur more frequently as I delve more deeply into Collinsville's past and discover that even this small village is too large to know completely. It's not that I see ghosts, at least not in the manner of Hollywood ectoplasm or graveyard monsters. Nevertheless, I do occasionally encounter something that so strongly draws forth what I know of the past that I can see it vividly, like an archeologist imagining a long-dead civilization from objects troweled and sifted from the soil.

Blame it on the weather and the strangely coincidental time of year. It had also been a flurried, blustery day early in March 1857 when Charles Blair met John Brown. Like me, Blair had walked out of the wind and cold into the warmth of a Collinsville shop—in his case George Polk's "family medicine" store, which once stood at the corner of Main and Market streets, three doors down from LaSalle Market. I pictured the scene plain as day.

As Blair stepped into the store he shut the door behind him, shook off the cold and let his eyes adjust to the dim light. Master of the Collins forge shop, he had a commanding presence and was used to people in the village taking notice when he entered a room. But this time he got hardly more than a passing glance. Several neighbors were gathered around the warmth of the stove, listening in rapt attention to a tall, clean-shaven man with a leathery face and haunting eyes who told of a hard-fought battle beneath the blazing Kansas sun. Blair had heard John Brown's impassioned speech the night before in crowded Tiffany Hall across the street, where a hat was passed to fund the abolitionist struggle to keep Kansas a free state. Brown's appeal to "all honest lovers of liberty and human rights," still echoed in his ears. Blair squeezed into the circle as he looked around the store, shelves and counters crowded with bottles of patent medicines, perfumes, cigars, toys, stationary, and painters' supplies.

The square-jawed Brown told how he had captured Captain Henry Pate, a newspaper man turned deputy U.S. marshal who led Missouri militia troops attempting to take him into custody for killing pro-slavery Kansas settlers. His voice rose and fell dramatically: "moved through a wooded ravine . . . flanking the enemy . . . a rifle crack . . . counterfire . . . crawling on hands and knees . . . hold the lines . . . close quarters . . . a white handkerchief tied to a ramrod."

Collinsville had endured a rough winter in 1857. The church had burned on a freezing night in January, a flood had swept through the village and left large ice cakes blocking the road north, and now a fatal sickness was carrying off those living closest to the ice. Weary of these troubles, the men were spellbound by Brown's enthralling account of a more exotic place.

As his story came to an end, Brown suddenly reached toward the floor, and his startled listeners jumped back. From his boot he drew a broad, double-edged knife with an eight-inch blade. The polished steel glinted in the low light as he turned it over meditatively. "If I had a lot of these attached to six-foot poles they would make capital weapons that the free settlers of Kansas could keep in their log cabins to defend themselves," he announced. His piercing gaze settled on Blair. "What would five hundred or a thousand of these cost me?"

Not prepared for the question, Blair let Brown's query hang a moment. With fourteen hundred tools produced a day the company had never been busier, and *it could hardly keep up with sales. A small order of pikes was clearly not crucial for business, and the forgemaster quoted a stiff price he was sure the cash-strapped Brown would never accept. "Offhand," Blair shrugged, "maybe a dollar twenty-five apiece for five hundred, though I could probably let you have a thousand for a dollar each." But Brown was not a typical customer. "I'll have them made, then," he said matter-of-factly.*

It's not uncommon for me to hear someone boast about the Red Sox, or describe a trout lurking in a pool below the falls, or recount the outcome of an election while I'm buying a candy bar or drawing coffee out of a stainless steel carafe at LaSalle. Sometimes deals are cut to have houses built, firewood split, or cars repaired. But could a few such words once uttered beneath the pressed-tin ceiling really have changed the course of the nation's history? I imagine that few things professed in the old building had boasted a half-life much beyond the cup of coffee over which they were said. Undoubtedly Charles Blair felt much the same about John Brown's offer as he left Polk's Drug Store that raw, gray morning in 1857.

Never expecting to see Brown again, Blair was startled when he later appeared at the forge, in earnest about the proposed thousand pikes. "I am a laboring man," Blair told him over the din of hammering, "and if I engage in this contract with you, I want to know just how I'll be paid."

"That's all right," Brown replied calmly, as if it was the reaction he'd expected. "I'll make it perfectly secure for you with five hundred dollars within ten days and the balance thirty days later."

Not long afterward, Blair shipped a dozen samples to Brown. He liked them, but asked for cast- rather than wrought-iron ferules. He also noted that he preferred the heads to be screwed rather than riveted to the handles, for easy disassembly. By month's end Blair had received three hundred fifty dollars, signed a contract, begun forging the heads, and engaged a handle-maker. In April he received another two hundred dollars.

Even with money in hand, the pikes troubled Blair. With Kansas full of settlers toting firearms, what good were these forged weapons? And why have them made in Collinsville when work could be done closer to the action? Was Brown not telling him something?

As it was, Blair had not heard from Brown for almost a year when he got a letter asking him about the pikes. Five hundred blades were made, he replied, but with no further payment forthcoming work had stopped and the materials were in storage. Brown acknowledged Blair's reply, but sent no payment. The forgemaster considered the matter ended—indeed, the matter of bleeding Kansas was shortly concluded—but Brown would be back.

At about six o'clock on the evening of June 3, 1859, over two years after Blair's first meeting with Brown in Polk's store, an old man with a long gray beard appeared in the forge shop. "I have been unable, sir," he said softly, "to fulfill my contract with you up to this time." He paused. "I have met with various disappointments. Now I stand ready to complete the bargain." The bearded face was only vaguely familiar, but the voice was instantly recognizable.

Blair cleared his throat before speaking. "Mr. Brown, I consider our contract at an end. It will be very difficult for me to make the pikes now. My men are fully employed at other work, and I don't see how I can do it." Indeed, there was a new shop under construction solely for the manufacture of hoes. Besides, there was something about the pikes, the oddly timed payments, and Brown's mysterious air that Blair wanted done with.

"Don't worry," Brown answered him, "you won't lose a cent."

"That's right," Blair said. "I've been careful not to spend more than I had in hand, and I won't lose anything by dropping it right here. If you want, you can take the steel and the handles as they are."

"They're no good for anything that way," Brown responded testily.

"What earthly good can they be to you now that things in Kansas are settled?"

"I don't know, but at least if they're finished I might be able to dispose of them somehow."

An exasperated Blair repeated that he was too busy to finish the work, but for four hundred fifty dollars he'd try finding someone else. Brown agreed. He left the overheated forge to the sound of pounding trip-hammers under a dimming sky, walked through the village and took a room in the rambling Collinsville Hotel that stood at the foot of River Street near the mill pond.

Sometimes at dusk I imagine the proud and determined abolitionist, striding through the village styling himself a soldier of God: the rhythm of his strong, old man's gait; the determination in his eyes; the breeze lifting his long beard. As before, the distinction between past and present slips, and makes me uneasy. (Or, as Bekah once observed in perhaps the clearest terms when I described it to her: "It's creepy, Dad.") Yet the history of these events, if somehow intangible, is no less a fact than the things we meet each morning, like the river or factory buildings. For those who know of Brown's place here in time, his presence is real.

At seven the next morning Brown appeared in Blair's shop, hurriedly peeled off fifty dollars in bills and handed over a check for one hundred dollars, promising three hundred more in a day or two. He left in haste, walking swiftly uphill from the riverside forge to catch the New York train. It was the last Blair ever saw of him.

Brown paid the remaining amount within a few days. Blair had the pikes finished and shipped to one J. Smith & Sons in Chambersburg, Pennsylvania, as Brown had asked. On a cool morning in mid-October, news reached Collinsville that John Brown and twenty-one others had seized the federal arsenal in Harpers Ferry, Virginia, and taken sixty hostages in an effort to instigate a slave rebellion. The Hartford Courant *gave extensive coverage to the incident. Reading the close type, Blair may have felt a chill or his stomach tighten as the reason for Brown's interest in the pikes finally hit him. The rebellion's untrained slaves might not be skilled with rifles, but the knives on six-foot poles would be especially deadly in those hands so used to cutting crops.*

Over the next several days accounts of Brown, who was trapped in the armory fire-engine house under a barrage of rifle shots, filled the papers. Armed farmers and militiamen poured into Harpers Ferry thirsting for the old man's blood. Spectators cheered the soldiers under Colonel Robert E. Lee's command who smashed the building's heavy oak doors while the raiders fired through a haze of powder smoke.

In thirty-six hours Brown's war for slave liberation ended dismally, with seventeen lives lost. Among those who died were Brown's twenty year-old son Oliver, who bled to death on the engine-house floor. The boy's slow, tortured end hit Blair hard, for only two summers earlier he had given him a job in the shop. He was not the strongest youth Blair had ever met, so when the hard work in the August heat proved too much, the forgemaster found him a job haying instead. Despite Oliver's death, the papers observed that Brown was cool and defiant in captivity. How was it, Blair wondered, that Brown could set himself so detached from what he had wrought, and lead so many law-abiding citizens to assist him without the slightest remorse?

All the talk in the shops, on the porches, and along the streets of Collinsville was of Brown and his raid. Blair lived in fear that his dealings with the out-law would be made public. The story was already being whispered around the stove in Polk's store and elsewhere in town.

Shortly thereafter, the papers reported that Collins pikes had been found among the insurrectionists' cache of papers, pistols, and rifles. A business-like but friendly letter Blair had sent Brown appeared in the press. It was not unlike many other business letters he had written, but to a country rife with finger-pointing and talk of subpoenas and indictments and grave charges of conspiracy and treason, it looked like more than it was. Blair knew that the notoriety was bad, both for the company, which had a thriving southern busi-ness in planter's hoes and other tools, as well as for Charles Blair.

Not two months after Brown swung from the gallows, Blair was in Washington answering questions fired at him by angry senators. He was never accused of illegal activity; nonetheless, despite a long and successful career as a busi-nessman and public official, he came to be best known for the few moments he had spent with John Brown. For Blair it was an embarrassing black mark that he carried to his grave.

Was it thus an apparition from the past I encountered in LaSalle, or merely someone whose impassioned words over a contemporary issue called to mind the "terrible saint?" It doesn't matter. Events simply don't occur and disappear; they remain layered around us in the present, waiting to recount their larger truths much as soil strata tell the story of natural occur-rences. To know the past and to keep it alive with such vivid tales makes one a partner to what has gone before, and fixes one in the continuum of human events that sustain a community. And like pools of oil or seams of coal below the surface, what happened long ago often fuels contemporary circumstances and disputes. Collinsville is not unusual in that regard. Many small places are large in the fourth dimension.

But for his visit to a Collinsville store that March morning in 1857, Charles Blair might be unknown to American history. Instead, he was caught up at the edge of a defining national moment. Collinsville was clearly a small village then, and it remains so today. But I always listen carefully when dropping in at LaSalle Market, the Collinsville Savings Society, the Center Spirit Shop, or other downtown businesses. In the echoes of such encounters, perhaps Collinsville is not as small as it seems, and a walk to the market can be a long journey if we know not just where we are, but where we have been.

Deeds in Time

Nothing ever dies in this town. It is like a
bottle of wine, just gets older and better.
—Tony Horowitz, interview from
Confederates in the Attic

It was a warm and languid evening after a day of scraping and house painting. Bill had been doing the same at his place on Torrington Avenue, and so had Rich next door. In the fading June light the three of us sat on my front stoop, letting the energy run out of us as we discussed the progress of our projects over a second round of beers. Rich's house, with its inviting wraparound porch, sparkled with the fresh paint and the new clapboards that had replaced asbestos siding.

"Sam Collins himself would like what you've done to that place," I told him, pointing the long-neck bottle toward the house.

"He sure wouldn't like what we're sipping now in plain view," said Rich taking a swig as he stretched his long legs.

"Better watch out," Bill added, rubbing his mustache, "or Sam's ghost will take your house back."

We laughed. One thing new Collinsville home buyers learn early, generally from the bemused lawyer examining the deed before purchase, is that a clause prohibits the production, sale, and sometimes even the consumption of alcoholic beverages. It's one of the first hints any Collinsville initiate has that he or she is buying in a place that's a little different.

Given my fascination with historical characters and my penchant for storytelling, it was probably no surprise to Rich or Bill that I was able to quickly locate a copy of my deed. Returning from inside, I read aloud to them with as much pomposity as I could muster the lines regarding the prohibition on "manufacture, sale, or other disposal of spirituous, malt, brewed, vinous, ardent fermented or intoxicating liquor, drinks or beverages."

"I think we qualify under 'other disposal,'" Rich said with a sip.

"Just don't go back to home brewing," Billy added.

Rich whistled. "Must have been a real straitlaced place."

Billy, who grew up in town, shook his head. "Not when I was a kid. Downtown was a little rough, and the Valley House," he said, pointing at the stately brick Victorian, "was kind of the red-light district."

"Strange how that's changed. Now the Valley House is divided into condos and filled with professionals," said Rich.

"Stranger yet," I added, "when you consider it was built after the Civil War as a hotel for visiting salesmen in the South American machete trade. It had an international flair and you were as likely to hear Spanish or Portuguese spoken as English. They served fancy meals and hosted theatrical performances."

Still, relaxing with a beer and looking down narrow Main Street with its small masonry and clapboard buildings, it isn't hard to understand Collinsville's reputation as a relatively uncontaminated remnant of the past. Some say Collinsville is a kind of picture postcard, and certainly you could crop and frame your vision to make it so. Such an image lures artists to set up easels along the river, photographers to wander the mill complex, and visitors to stroll the streets and point.

It is all an illusion. There is no more reality to this nineteenth-century island refuge of small-town values than to a Frank Capra movie set, and a postcard created now no more fully reflects today's village than might one taken a century ago. This is not the "town time forgot" that is written up in magazines and newspapers for consumption by a nostalgic public craving authenticity. Such a fixed image is about as accurate as a timeless depiction of the Valley House as a hotel, or a flop house, or a condominium for professionals. It was and will always be all those things. Collinsville, like any place, is about change and rediscovery, and the village of today is constantly being shaped by these forces. Such has always been the case.

Samuel Collins's clause, the private Eighteenth Amendment that we laugh about and defy today, sprang from the founder's original vision of the town as an extension of the factory. "The welfare and happiness of this village can only be promoted effectually and permanently by such judicious management of our business as will enable us to meet all our engagements," he wrote to his workmen during the company's first decade. Back then, Collinsville was not a staid and settled place. It was a rough village of dirt streets, factory haze, crowded living accommodations, and half-finished buildings. Men labored long hours in dim light beside smoky fires, subjected to continuous and deafening grinding and pounding. The company was undercapitalized and faced fierce competition. An inferior shipment of axes, whether the result of inadequate materials, poor workmanship, or bad luck, could lead to the company's demise.

Collins did not want Collinsville marred by the unwholesome reputation characteristic of other manufacturing villages, but even more than that he wanted work to get done. Hard-working men engaged in backbreaking labor often drank equally hard, and then failed to turn up for work or, worse still, showed up drunk. For practical reasons Samuel Collins the factory owner and town founder began a lifelong moral crusade against drink, though as a partner in his uncle's Hartford dry goods business years before he had sold wine, rum, and other spirits. He did not stop at deed provisions when molding an image of sobriety and industry. Collins is said to have bought up two hotels and a drug store in order to stop liquor sales, and supposedly paid a drunk to promise never to come within ten miles of town. Of course, his purchase of the riverside Tim Case Tavern in 1836 was also good for business, since it allowed him to raise the dam and flood the site the next year.

Despite becoming a major industrial corporation with all the ensuing legal battles over trademark and patent infringement, materials specifications, nonpayment for goods, and other commercial matters, the company's only Connecticut Supreme Court appearance involved the village rather than the factory—specifically, shopkeeper Bradford Marcy's defiance of a no-alcohol deed clause. Although the deed's validity was upheld, a lack of compelling evidence allowed Marcy to escape the charges and left Samuel Collins bitter in defeat.

By the mid-1850s, when the factory owner and the shopkeeper battled over liquor before black-robed judges in Hartford, Collinsville had been transformed from a backwoods mill site to a modern manufacturing center. A single stone factory building had grown into a cluster of shops for forging, tempering, grinding, and packing. Burning coal fires darkened the air and trip-hammers boomed rhythmically through the valley. Collins pursued innovations and new technologies such as drop forging, shaving axeheads, and using anthracite coal even when they were not immediately profitable. This approach not only produced a continually improved product, but did so more cheaply. The company made whatever customers wanted and had produced over one hundred fifty axe and machete patterns in the years before the Civil War.

Buoyed by military contracts, Collinsville was a boom town by the time Lee surrendered at Appomattox. It was as close to the center of the universe as a small town could come, in the very heart of the industrial revolution that was implacably changing the world. Its products were history's touchstones: The company's axes felled trees for lumber, its plows tamed the Great Plains, its picks hacked gold from California hillsides, its hoes tended southern cotton, and its machetes planted and harvested the bounty of Latin America—cocoa, rubber, bananas, and sugarcane.

The village grew with the company. Bustling with commercial activity, Collinsville offered most anything a buyer could want. Harnessmakers, blacksmiths, attorneys, bootmakers, and insurance agents set up shop. A telegraph office, the *Collinsville Star* newspaper, and a printer traded in words. Hawks's Collinsville Retreat, a basement saloon, offered oysters, pies, beer, and "seegars," while the Collinsville Hotel near the mill pond advertised "Good entertainment for man and beast" in somewhat unsettling terms. Several dry goods merchants stocked clothing, crockery, and blankets. At the corner of Market and Main Streets, T. C. Bodwell sold stoves and hardware for cash or "country produce." A prize pumpkin could fetch some tin roofing or hinges in trade. Jewelry was sold, clocks repaired, and clothing tailored. Drug stores offered medicines, paint, coal oil, tobacco, stationary, and "Yankee notions." In a building that once stood where the Town Hall parking lot sits today, you could have your hair cut, your teeth pulled, your watch fixed, and your trousers repaired, and then grab a bite to eat—all without leaving the premises.

By the 1880s Collins was a world-class manufacturer. Over twenty-five hundred people depended directly or indirectly on the company for their livelihood. The rhythm of life was marked by steam whistles, and son succeeded father in the plant, each sometimes working for forty or fifty years. Collinsville had a permanence, a mission, and place in the world. In 1928 the company was deemed "the greatest plant of the sort in America," and during the Great Depression a scribe from the Federal Writers' Project observed that Collins tools were "known wherever men struggle with nature."

Prosperity during and immediately after the Second World War resulted in record machete exports and steady dividends for six hundred and fifty Collins Company stockholders, and recruiting skilled workers became the principal challenge. But success was ephemeral. Management failed to keep up Samuel Collins's commitment to innovation, and a 1946 *Fortune* article noted that "the layout of the plant at Collinsville would discourage the most persevering efficiency engineer." By that point machinery was old and outdated, and the article observed that "no money is wasted on unnecessary modernization." The Collins Company came to be seen as provincial and old-fashioned, and increasingly the village projected an aura of antiquity. The company established plants in Latin American to reduce costs, and business in Collinsville declined. In a near-fatal blow, the river rose to a raging torrent in the summer of 1955, and twenty percent of the company's buildings were destroyed.

By the early 1960s both the company and the village were dying. Only one hundred seventy-five workers remained, and many plant buildings were vacant. The company lost faith in the village as a vital, growing concern and sold off commercial property and houses for fear of the costs of sewer assessments. Factory buildings were demolished to avoid taxes. The village grew derelict with the company's tortuous retreat, hemorrhaging retail business to Albany Turnpike, the commercialized highway strip two miles distant. The turnpike offered what the village could not: acres of parking. More than half the storefronts on Main Street ended up vacant, and space was so cheap it was used for storage. Only Eaton Hardware, the bank, and the barber shop remained. The Valley House hosted a decrepit saloon that boasted few visitors. Even at midday, Main Street was all but deserted. Weeds grew in the railroad tracks and plywood covered the freight station windows. Charred remains of the Hurly Manufacturing Company moldered on North Street. Peeling paint, cracked and broken glass, boarded-up windows, and untended plantings were common. Collinsville became a desolate place, a small industrial slum.

Eager for renewed vigor, many thought that the old mill town needed to be brought into the twentieth century, and so in 1963 plans were made to apply for a federal grant to demolish the area around Main Street and replace it with a shopping center and garden apartments. The village was deemed a blighted area, and wrecking balls and bulldozers were to be accordingly dispatched to eliminate substandard buildings and generate the increased taxes to fund public works projects (such as the building of sewers to eliminate pollution of the Farmington River). Collinsville seemed destined to be recreated in the image of an ordinary suburb until, after angry debate, a town meeting narrowly defeated these plans for urban renewal.

Early in 1966 the Collins Company gave the village a six-month closure notice. It was a crushing blow. Men were thrown out of work as the town's largest taxpayer evaporated, and a place synonymous with making tools lost its purpose. Resentment and anger flared and spread as shipping clerks and machinists searched for new jobs and higher taxes loomed. Pensioners felt cheated, and those who wheezed with grinder's lung or lost their hearing to the drop forge honed their bitterness on the sharp and unwelcome news. Residents parlayed a sense of abandonment into a morose animosity at management. But the final act, the sale of the factory buildings themselves, inspired a new beginning.

While the company was selling off inventory, machinery, and equipment like old household items at a rummage sale, Thomas Perry stepped in. A local manufacturer of precision aerospace parts with a strong entrepreneurial spirit and sense of history, he asked John Meconkey, the company employee reluctantly in charge of liquidating the factory's assets, if he could buy the old factory bell. The veteran Collins man paused a moment with a finger to his lips before a wry smile appeared. "You can have it," he teased, "if you buy the whole factory with it." Perry just laughed, but the idea stuck with him. Rounding up a handful of investors, he created the Collinsville Company, put up $64,000, and walked away with the deed.

Perry, an intelligent and athletic man with boundless energy, saw the old buildings as a crucible for new and emerging enterprises. He suffused the cavernous spaces with the same innovative business spirit that had made him a successful manufacturer, the very drive that had motivated the young Collins boys when they first began making axes along the river. In a few years the premises boasted a range of new tenants: printing and welding companies, an operation applying new techniques for making metal moving parts more abrasion-resistant, an innovative packaging maker, and a company producing plastic compounds for polishing optical surfaces. Following a tour of the plant, newspaper writer Stephen Davenport Jr. remarked that everybody "exuded that kind of excitement and enthusiasm that only people with enough guts to go out on a limb with something new seem to have. Everyone was hustling, everyone was proud, everyone was hopeful."

With modest rents priced solely to cover taxes and maintenance, the old factory attracted new companies looking for good start-up conditions. Though there was still some empty space ten years later, Perry's vision proved prophetic, and the old Collins buildings wound up housing fifty-six small concerns employing about 160 people. Metal stamping, toy making, and glass blowing, as well as an auto repair shop and warehouse space, filled the expanse where once axes and machetes had been forged, ground, and packed.

Perhaps as an indirect result of Perry's tenacious effort to keep the factory complex part of the community, Town Hall was renovated in 1975 after bitter controversy and expanded into old storefronts on Main Street. First Selectman Ray Bergeron, a wiry and lively fellow with the nickname "Beans," fought off fierce opposition mounted by the partisans of new development to get the project funded. Bergeron, who spent twenty-five years in the Collins heat-treating department, saw Town Hall as an anchor for village revival. By investing over one million dollars in Main Street, he finally defeated the urban renewal plans that would have destroyed the village. Townspeople were invited to bring their picks and sledge hammers and help demolish the building interiors to make way for renovation. The community had thrown its lot in with Collinsville for good.

By the early 1980s tenants in the old factory included manufacturers of cigar wrappers and security systems. A maker of clutch and brake systems with the oxymoronic name of Inertia Dynamics became so successful that it built a new factory elsewhere in town and became one of the locality's top-ten taxpayers.

When Perry died in 1987, his young wife Barbara took the reins. As the twentieth century drew to a close, tenants renting the factory spaces included more and more artists and artisans. Barbara envisioned space for microbreweries, a jazz club, a state heritage park, and the performing arts, and occasionally she circulated an artist's rendering or site plan. But the cost of code compliance in the aged buildings and the complexities of development left her grand plans stillborn.

As it had in the past, activity at the mill spilled over into the village. Formerly vacant Main Street storefronts eventually housed a used bookstore, a coffee shop, art galleries, and even a caterer's kosher kitchen. Some of these concerns survived and some didn't, but for the first time in decades businesses were interested in Collinsville. Young professional people from out of town, like myself, began to buy and renovate houses. The factory's brick shipping-department building was reborn as an antique center, reinforcing the community's historic image.

Main Street increasingly bustled with people, especially on Saturdays, and artists not only had their studios in the factory but lived in the village. Local musicians played at downtown spots and for community events. A new theater company in the Town Hall auditorium produced the works of Shakespeare and Neil Simon, as well as original plays.

Customers flocked to a canoe and kayak store established in an old lumberyard along the mill pond. The fertile trout waters below the dam and above the impoundment lured a fly-fishing shop to Main Street. Conversion of the old railroad right-of-way into a bike trail brought small crowds to the village on warm weekends, and a bike shop opened in due course. The desolate community abandoned by the Collins Company found a new meaning and way of life.

By the mid-1990s newspaper and magazine articles were referring to the village as a "Norman Rockwell sort of place," with an "All-American Main Street." Film crews and actors occasionally appeared to shoot brief movie or television scenes. Soon wider public opinion held that Collinsville was "unspoiled" and "quaint." It was enough, as one of my neighbors—a lifelong resident—opined, "to make you puke." The transition from factory town to blighted community to picture postcard was complete, but the consequences left many a little uneasy.

From his perch on my front stoop, where we remained breaking the literal words of my deed, Rich stared at the Valley House, now restored to nineteenth-century elegance and neatly maintained. It is part of the new tourist-brochure image, as are the homes in which we have invested dollars and sweat. We have tried to rebuild them in the image of what we think they were meant to look like, rejecting the run-down look that characterized the dejected community of a generation ago. Have we, I wonder, straightened and buffed away too many of the rough edges that make the village interesting and different—even real?

"So, what's your take on the Tilney project?" Rich asked after a swallow of beer, referring to the developer under contract to buy the factory complex from Barbara Perry and the Collinsville Company. Rusty Tilney's prospectus called for converting the factory complex into "a village within a village mixing residential, office, street-level retail, artisan, recreation, hospitality, and light-manufacturing uses." It seems in keeping with the dream many of us have had, of restoring the buildings and more fully integrating them into the community.

Still, anxiety haunts Collinsville; there are concerns about potential uses, traffic, historic appearance, public access, open space. Neighbors have met with Tilney and without him. Where is the money coming from? What if the project is left only partially completed? Though the company closed over a generation ago, the same questions that greeted that momentous change echo today. The fate of the village still rests with the factory, as it has for one hundred and seventy-five years.

"Something's got to be done," Bill interjected. "The place is falling apart." A building inspector in a nearby town, he knows what he's talking about.

I nodded in agreement. "If only things could stay the way they are. Decrepit buildings are interesting, like abandoned forts or ruined castles. Besides, that's what's kept rents low and allowed the artists to stay. I hate to tinker with that." I stretched my legs and leaned back on my hands. "But Bill's right. Some of those structures are in real trouble."

"Fixing the place will cost a fortune," Rich acknowledged in a tone usually reserved for his role as financial officer of a large construction company. "How can they afford market rates for spaces that meet code? The project is bound to change the way of life around here. I guess the changes we've made to our houses have as well. It can't be helped."

"We've got to work with him to avoid a yuppie Disneyland of Starbucks, Victoria's Secret, and upscale condos," I added. "If things are going to change we might as well have a hand in it."

During this exchange I am struck by the full implication of Samuel Collins's deed provisions: development and change in Collinsville remain social and moral issues, not just a matter of zones and tax ratables. Development governs who lives here and what the town looks and feels like. Our passionate concern with what happens to Collinsville comes from exploring and growing to know more about it. I suppose this is true with any place people care about.

"Something's gotta give one way or the other," Bill said.

"For sure," Rich said, taking a last swig of beer as he stood and cast a glance down Main Street. "Who knows what Collinsville will be like five years from now?"

ycles

The year has many more seasons than
are recognized in the almanac. . . . Live
in each season as it passes; breathe the air,
drink the drink, taste the fruit, and resign
yourself to the influences of each.
—*Henry David Thoreau,* Journals
(1851, 1853)

Maple Fever

Boiling maple syrup is a distillation of place. . . .
The activity and the outcome are distinctly
regional, a marker of home.
—*Brian Donahue,* Reclaiming the Commons

Village living need not mean sacrificing an awareness of planting
and harvest, of seasonal change and hospitable sharing that is touted as the
touchstone of rural life. In fact, the neighborly values and attachment to
the earth's cycles that are the hallmark of an agrarian society can survive
and flourish in a village, city, or suburb if people practice the rituals and
routines that bind us to the seasons, sky, and soil. We can do this without a
self-deluded nostalgia about "living off the land" or the theme-park fakery
of barn-like garages sporting cupolas and weather vanes. There are many
ways to tap into these endless cycles, but nowhere have I found a more direct
connection than in maple sugaring.

I am a farmer without a farm. Despite the fact that I live on less than half
an acre, the town assessor considers my buckets and evaporator farming
tools, and the federal agriculture census lands in my mailbox every few

years. You do not need vast acreage with a tractor, pasture, or barn to be a sugarmaker; all that is required is what many people have in their back-yards—a tree. Unlike the romantic scenes depicted on syrup containers, my sugarbush is not a mountainside, but the narrow, hilly streets and cramped lots of Collinsville.

Late in winter I tap twenty to forty maple trees, overarching the street in front of my own and my neighbors' homes, in backyards, at the church, and behind the phone company building. As the sun's angle steepens with lengthening days, temperatures inch into the high thirties and sap starts rising. I become fanatical about weather, entranced by sudden spikes, busi-ly tracking trends. I monitor the sky like a child hoping for a school snow day and become a Weather Channel zombie. At last tapping day comes— sunny, warm enough to draw sap out of the roots and into the limbs, and perhaps to melt a little snow but not soften the ground much. A sensible per-son might set forth for adventure on a pair of skis, or relax with a cup of tea and seed catalogs. I gather my tools and get to work.

At first tapping intoxicates me with a sort of Currier-and-Ives romance. I size up each tree, reintroduce myself as if to an old friend I'd not seen in some time, check to see how much last year's tap hole has healed, and find a smooth patch of bark in which to drill. My old carpenter's brace bites into the tree, and squiggles of blond wood curl along the corkscrewed drill bit. Into the hole I hammer a spile, or tap, from which I hang a dented galva-nized bucket that I've broken free from a stack of others with equal mea-sures of banging and swearing. Soon the metal container pings with the pulse of dripping sap.

As I make my rounds, neighbors stop and chat about spring's advance, tree health, the sun's warmth, and other verities. Like the groundhog and his shadow, I've become a harbinger of the season. By the time I finish in the cold dark, I'm sore and sobered of romantic notions and Foxfire cleverness, and sometimes left to tap the last few trees by the glow of a flashlight.

I came to sugaring not through some philosophical notion of getting in touch with the earth and seasons but because the grand old maple in front of a friend's house had succumbed to the ravages of road salt and carpenter ants. Unwilling to face spring without simmering a pot of sap on her wood stove, she'd turned her attention to the pillar-like maples growing on either side of our front walk. Sarah and I watched the clear sap drip from the spiles and discovered that a drop on a finger was slightly sweet with a woody, almost nutty tang. Fascinated, we thought we might try it. Syrup seemed simple enough: all you had to do was boil.

By that season's end we had four dripping taps of our own. Despite a range fan and open doors and windows that chilled the house and tempted stray cats, the steamy kitchen atmosphere grew as thick as Grand Banks fog. Thirty to forty quarts of water must steam into the air to make a quart of syrup, and the room seemed to sweat feverishly, condensation sliding down walls and puddling on countertops. By April we had almost three gallons of syrup—and some badly curled wallpaper held fast with thumb tacks—to show for our efforts.

We gave sugaring little thought over the following summer, but shortly after New Year's Day we were gripped by the sort of excitement that seizes children as the December holidays approach. Would it be six taps, or eight, or perhaps ten? Gluing the wallpaper had been tedious, so we purchased the most powerful hotplate Eaton offered and moved operations to the garage. With our harvested bucketfuls boiling like a witch's cauldron that March, we made just over five gallons of syrup, burnt two pots dry, and quenched a fire with a few gallons of sap and some snow.

It wasn't enough for us. The next fall we bought a barrel evaporator, a fifty-five-gallon drum cut lengthwise and fitted with a flat pan over the opening and a firebox door on the end. With the garage transformed into a sugarhouse for two months, wood fires produced ten gallons during this first serious season, and almost fifteen the next. We expanded to sixteen taps, and then to twenty-five. Finally we bought a smaller but more efficient evaporator to handle even more sap. Our expanding efforts required additional storage tanks, buckets, pails, filters, and hoses. Fitted with firebricks, cement, smokestacks, and fans, our garage would never hold a car again. But far more disorienting than the loss of space was the change in our sense of time.

Toss the calendar and forget the tyranny of numbers: The year begins with rising sap. Anywhere from four to six weeks we are at the weather's mercy, constantly attuned to the warm sunny days following freezing nights that make the sap rise. Sometimes I after work to catch buckets before they overflow, or set out before dawn to prevent the gathered liquid from freezing in the shifting temperatures of the sugaring season. Sarah might dart out in the afternoon to tend to the fastest taps. Rain, snow, or fog, dripping sap is impatient. Sleep, meals, housework, and the usual social obligations are neglected. I begin sniffling and chain-suck cough drops, and when I'm not out collecting I worry that I should be.

As with so many of my Collinsville excursions, I run into my neighbors while I'm out attending to the taps, stopping to catch up with Alan on a recent planning commission decision or to talk with Colleen about the primary school math curriculum. Occasionally I'll chat with Joe, who appears red-faced from a run along the river, or waylay soft-spoken Walter as he carries a loaf of bread and some eggs from LaSalle. Surely politicians would abandon campaigning at the transfer station and start sugaring if sap ran at election time.

The gathered liquid is emptied into five-gallon pails that I carry to a collection tank in my Ford Explorer. The pails weigh about forty pounds apiece and I quickly find myself hunched over in a simian posture as I go about the business, knuckles practically scraping the ground. But the routine of emptying buckets is also soothing, providing the sure pleasure of physical rhythm without thought. It is especially so in the quiet of night as I steal around houses in the darkness while televisions flicker blue-gray in the windows. Occasionally a police cruiser slows down to have a look, so the officer can assure himself that I'm not a Peeping Tom or a burglar.

From the truck, sap is pumped into tanks and barrels alongside the garage-turned-sugarhouse. Generally this is sufficient storage, but when the sap flows fast we search madly for more containers. Old carboys, a washtub used for apple bobbing, and kitchen pots are hastily pressed into service, and many an evening Sarah and I have had to search long and hard for an empty sauce pan in which to cook dinner.

Maple sugaring is much like gold mining, where tons of rock are pulverized for a few ounces of metal, since the object of sugaring is to rid yourself of almost all of what you've broken your back carrying. And like mining, the task calls for time-honored tools and dedicated effort. Our small evaporator is something close to a wood stove topped with a rectangular stainless-steel pan. Early on weekend mornings, or in the icy dark after a workday, I open the cast-iron firebox doors, strike a match to a nest of newspaper and kindling, and warm my hands as the fire crackles. A few more sticks of wood and the metal evaporator and chimney flue begin to ping and groan with heat. Soon pinprick bubbles rise in the pan. The fire roars when I feed it larger chunks of fuel, the furiously churning cauliflower mounds of foaming sap erupting as sweet maple steam rises, lingering in ghostly clouds before dissipating out the roof vent.

As the sap boils I move restlessly about the sugarhouse, fidgeting with the fire, adjusting evaporator valves, and adding fresh sap. Impatient as a five-year-old helping to bake cookies, I ladle the boiling liquid, checking to see if it's become syrup yet. Always I keep an eye on the evaporator. Turn your back and the syrup thickens and threatens to caramelize like the coating on a candied apple; let the sap level drop too far and the metal pan goes into meltdown.

Eventually the boiling liquid darkens and grows slowly viscous. A hypnotic single-mindedness overtakes me then as the steam wafts from the eaves and billows out doors and windows. Though an observant passerby once raced up the front steps and frantically urged Sarah to call the fire department, neighbors now know that the vapor is an informal invitation to stop by and visit, to have a beer, a cup of coffee, a pretzel, or a donut. This is time set apart from the frenzy of business, family, and housework. The steam is like an old and familiar welcome mat: It says come up—I have time.

On a typical Sunday afternoon last season, my best friend Alan wandered down the hill from High Street and breathed in the sap steam as eagerly as a lung patient might gulp oxygen. He sat thumbing through the *Courant*, punctuating my fussing about the evaporator with comments regarding the town's budget or the current power struggle in Russia. He mentioned that rumors he'd read on the Internet indicated that the New York–Penn League franchise in Pittsfield, Massachusetts, might up and leave. We reminisced briefly about the battered wooden and corrugated-metal ballpark whose poor westward orientation blinds fans and batters alike with the afternoon sun.

Not long afterward a big "Hello!" boomed through the sugarhouse as Rich, accompanied by his three sons, arrived from next door. The cramped building soon filled with noise and chaos, and we quickly sent the boys out to play with my kids. I got some beers from the house and we gossiped with Alan about the rumors for the planned redevelopment of the Collins Company buildings. Where was the financing coming from? How loudly would the money talk? Willie, a young firefighter, stopped by with his little dark-haired daughter, who stared moon-eyed at the evaporator as speculation about the old factory bounced around the room. He left shortly with a restless child, briefly mentioning as he departed that Engine 4 was out for repairs again. Others came and went, drawing in the fragrant steam and stopping to chat about things at hand: vacation plans, children, office politics, gardening, home repair, baseball spring training.

Sometimes sugarhouse conversations turn personal and serious, especially after dark. Late one night I spent hours with a usually cheery woman, talking through the steam about her divorce and an insensitive supervisor at work. In an awkward conversation punctuated by nervous pauses and uncertain, measured advice, we achieved a rare if fleeting intimacy. During a lull she took a deep breath and remarked how the sound of boiling sap reminded her of surf battering the shore, each with a similar soothing power. Ever since, I too have sought reassurance beside the evaporator whenever I have felt troubled.

The evaporator is a lit hearth, a ready setting for conviviality. Here time is measured in sap boiled, syrup ladled, and sticks of wood burned. At day's end I have a pot of syrup, sore muscles from chopping wood, and a sensation of friendships strengthened.

But sugaring is not always the easy labor of a languid weekend. March—

our prime sugaring month—is a constant tug of war between seasons. One week I fret over frozen trees that don't yield a drop; the next, temperatures soar into the sixties and sap runs through the night. The gathered bucket-fuls spoil if left too long, so I often race home from the office and gobble down dinner in the sugarhouse with Sarah and the children to keep pace. Past midnight and well into the quiet calm of morning I watch the sap boil, the radio and a pile of old magazines for company. Outside the wind may be frigid and the snow may be falling, but in this Yankee Turkish bath I feel feverish. My back aches, and like a late-night couch potato I can barely keep my eyes open. When I stoke the hot firebox, beads of sweat well up on my face. I'm like a train fireman, or Hawthorne's half-mad Ethan Brand tending his hellish lime kiln alone on the dark slopes of Mount Graylock.

One might imagine that the backbreaking work of collecting thousands of gallons of sap, keeping a fire stoked, and chopping wood would not typically elicit volunteers, but I have frequently had assistance from my neighbors. Alan generally joins me in setting up and tapping; Scott has gathered sap while I'm away; and Steve and wiry Bill A., who runs marathons despite approaching the age of sixty, help chop wood. The year that a back injury forced me to take a sabbatical from sugaring, many people told me they missed the familiar sight of the buckets on The Green and hoped I hadn't given up.

After they have been ladled off the evaporator, we carry gallons of syrup from the sugarhouse into the kitchen, where samples are tested with a thermometer and hydrometer to ensure proper sugar content. We filter, refilter, and filter again. The hot liquid is tediously poured into containers, and caps are tightened. Counters are covered with a chaotic scattering of metal, glass, and plastic jugs. Every surface grows sticky, and the sweet moist air lends a foretaste of spring.

Prior to sale, we label the containers with our Crown and Hammer Sugarhouse logo—the old Collins trademark superimposed on a maple leaf. This somewhat nostalgic effort—to brand a Collinsville-made item with the once-familiar image of a muscular arm wielding a smithy's hammer—may indeed recall the town's heyday, but the fact is that Samuel Collins might have welcomed neither the syrup nor the sentiment: We are manufacturing and selling a product in violation of a clause in the deed he signed in 1847.

And then toward the end of March I find myself collecting sap late at night, tiptoeing around houses with full pails sloshing. The air is heavy and still, and a little foggy. Temperatures do not dip below freezing, and drops of sap seem to measure time like a ticking clock as they fall into the buckets. Going about my routine, I note a faint sound like distant sleigh bells coming from the swamp across the river: spring peepers. The end of sugaring is near.

A few more days of warmth bring redwing blackbirds and robins. The trees begin to bud and the sap turns bitter and as yellow as urine. Sugaring began in the depth of winter, when the ground was hard and snow-covered and I wore a heavy coat. Now I work in shirt sleeves and sweat beside the evaporator like a ballplayer in August. It's time to yank spiles and collect buckets. I hurry to boil off the last sap before it turns cloudy. Relief mixes with sadness as the frenzy and grueling routine suddenly come to an end. The year's first garden crop is in.

With sap no longer flowing, buckets, pails, tanks, and barrels are washed and left to dry in our driveway. Most years Alan helps with the cleanup, just as he visits the sugarhouse and assists in tapping. While there may be some romance in being an initiate to the time-honored harvest, washing the equipment is pure dishpan drudgery. But Alan joins me, both to share the company of a friend and for the same basic reason I'm drawn to it: Cleaning the tools has become a ritual of the season.

One year's sugaring does not end before the next starts. I begin chopping wood purloined from utility roadside cuttings or gathered from the remains of a shade tree felled in a neighbor's yard by a winter storm. There is value in exchanging syrup for broken limbs or a chainsawed trunk. Sarah shakes her head as the driveway comes to resemble a lumber camp, but is philosophical. There will be no syrup next year without the dry, splintered old bones of the trees to serve as fuel.

Backyard sugaring is too hard and exhausting to pursue for anything other than the sheer love of it. Though we have sold as much as forty gallons in a year at eleven or twelve dollars a quart, I doubt any true accounting would show us in the black once all expenses were factored in—even if our time was valued at the staggering rate of five cents an hour. Labor is at once our principal investment, operating expense, and profit. The work is its own reward.

Our syrup has been sold at LaSalle Market and other nearby shops. There is some pride in having a local product on the shelf in these days of world-wide distribution. It has, like other things made in Collinsville, become part of the community mystique.

Neighbors take tins of our syrup as gifts when they travel, leaving a taste of their home to be savored in far places. In suitcases it has gone to as many countries as have Collins axes: Russia, England, Norway, Japan, Austria, Australia. The sweet essence of Collinsville has thus made its way far from The Green, and graced breakfast tables around the world.

Naturalists Scott and Helen Nearing believed sugarmakers could eke out an existence of Thoreau-like simplicity. I dream of no such utopia. But sugaring can enable suburban dwellers to connect with seasonal cycles, refresh their sense of community, and steep themselves in something elemental, antique, exotic, and yet as practical as a backyard vegetable garden. One need not have a farm to feel some of agriculture's rhythm. Just find a tree.

Cultivating

By the time the last spile is pulled and the evaporator fire is banked for the season, green shoots are bursting through our garden's dark, moist soil. Nodding snowdrops, bright crocuses, and delicate bloodroot flowers have bloomed and gone. Horn-like daffodils and tulip cups open to the sun, and in some years lilacs burst forth at my sugarhouse windows by the last boil. Spring brings new life swollen with energy and power, but when maples bud the sap sours and sugaring season ends.

Time is more accurately marked by the appearance and growth of buds and shoots than by the transit of the sun though the sky, or by the phases of the moon, or indeed by any calendar. There are cycles within cycles such that no one can quite say when a year begins. Spring is the obvious choice for a starting point, but as Karel Čapek observed, "October is the first Spring month, the month of underground germination and sprouting, of hidden growth, of swelling buds . . . while the gardener's autumn begins in March with the first faded snowdrop."

Perhaps a gardener's year begins with the gardener. Newcomers to Collinsville often are as likely to begin planting as they are to paint their new home, clean the windows, or wash down the porch. The outside of the town's houses look much as they have for over a century, as each new occupant establishes ownership with a new tree, foundation shrubs, or a bed of salvia. Winter arrivals brim with questions about what grew where. They know by sight what sort of house they have purchased, but the grounds remain a mystery shrouded in snow and hardened soil. Spring teases them cruelly with the anticipation of hidden plantings slowly revealing themselves.

We arrived in July, and Sarah and I put off planting, patiently watching the weedy margins of the house, the vines growing through the picket fence in back. Here and there we spotted the fluted foliage of worn-out tulips or the gangly remains of daffodils that had bloomed before we arrived. Among the crab grass and plantain beside the garage stood orange daylily trumpets. Not far away were the tall, wandlike stems and spotted cups of their cousins, the tiger lilies. Carefully removing a tangle of bittersweet and yanking up a smothering mat of goutweed, we uncovered a few anemic phlox, a lone aster, and a tomato plant that marked an abandoned compost pile. We were horticultural archeologists tracing the pursuits of past gardeners. A small greenhouse built where cellar bulkhead doors once opened suggested that our predecessors were serious enthusiasts who started their plants inside.

Between the painting, sanding, and wallpapering that absorbed most of our time that first winter, we drank vast quantities of tea and pored over seed catalogs and garden design books. Novels at bedside were replaced with tomes by English horticulturists like Gertrude Jekyll and Christopher Lloyd, as well as company catalogs from White Flower Farm, Johnny's Seeds, and Burpee.

As soon as the earth thawed—and a few times on crunchy frozen ground—we began to move soil in prodigious quantities. Using an old pitchfork with bent tines I turned over a patch of grass on the south side of the lot for a vegetable garden. It was painstaking work, digging in the compacted earth and pounding soil out of clumps of grass, but the smell was intoxicating. I removed sod for a brick terrace and walkway with a rusty spade. Along one side I turned soil for a perennial border, and then for a rose garden at a bend in the walk. Before the plants were purchased, we mentally arranged and rearranged them in their new beds, picturing them as portrayed in catalogs and books without so much as a yellowed leaf or drooping petal. On a gentle slope in back we cleared a jungle of brush and built a retaining wall, an operation that required us to move, shovel, rake, and smooth wheelbarrows full of soil. A weekend's worth of dirt would stay wedged beneath the fingernails well into Wednesday, and often longer as the urge to get my hands into the ground again proved overwhelming— strong as that which once drew me to suburban dirt piles with my toy tractors and trucks.

After peat moss, fertilizer, lime, bone meal, egg shells, and banana peels were folded into the soil, we began planting. Around the foundation we dug out yew bushes with clear ambitions to be trees and planted rhododendrons, holly, and a skirt of pachysandra. Sarah laid out the vegetable plot in neat bean rows, mounds of squash, tomatoes, peppers, and eggplant. Along the fence separating the vegetables from the lawn she dug deep and planted asparagus crowns with layers of compost and sand set beneath .

The perennial border gave me pause, as I considered Gertrude Jekyll's charge to "place every plant or group of plants with such thoughtful care and definite intention that they shall form a part of the harmonious whole, and that successive portions, or in some cases even single details, shall show a series of pictures." It seemed easy enough, this painting in time with changing living things. But I wondered whether the tiny coral bells would clash with the purple columbine. Would the small daisy-like flowers of boltonia on such tall stems shadow the low-growing asters? Would they look awkward side by side? Perhaps the grassy foliage of spiderwort would cover the forget-me-nots. Could I expect waves of blooms in neat succession, or would it all flower at once, leaving the garden barren for most of the season? I had to separate sun- from shade-loving plants and tall back-border from low-growing species. And what about securing delicate flowers from aggressive and invasive ones?

I laid plants out on the newly turned soil as if I were organizing the pieces of a puzzle. After much fretting, planting, digging, and replanting I gave up and let the bloom come where it would. And then, despite a satisfying succession of color among a variety of foliage tones and shapes, I found myself shuffling plants around for better effect late in that season and early in the next. So it has been every year: plants are shifted, new ones placed, and winter failures removed.

Neighbors watched as our yard was transformed with rhododendrons and laurel, yellow coreopsis and spikes of delphinium, brick paths and stone steps. Conversations about pruning, watering, and sunlight begun over the fence with Karel and her bearded husband Howard led to discussions about work, the school system, sports, and child-rearing. Our friend Alan frequently stopped to watch our progress with hoe and trowel. Jim, who asked for our grass clippings after my first haying of the overgrown lawn, told us we were "turning the yard into a showplace." The elderly Houghs began making their secret forays into our garden. Although working the soil provided a rich harvest of companionship and conversation as well as flowers and vegetables, most hours in the garden and backyard were quiet, the greenery a welcome retreat from a noisy world. I felt the lure of suburban security, an inward withdrawal into the psychological fortress offered by owning a small parcel of real estate.

On a sticky June afternoon I was bent over the perennial border, among flower spikes of fan-leafed lupine, bright-eyed daisies, and fragrant peonies. Sweat streamed down my back, and my hands were rough and dry from working the soil all morning. I'd been deadheading coreopsis, pulling weeds, smoothing mulch, and filling a bare spot with a tuft of low-growing dianthus. Stooping down with handfuls of mulch, I felt a presence hovering above me. I turned and saw that it was Walter. "Please don't feel you have to get up," he told me. "I can see you're busy and I don't mean to interrupt, but I've been watching your garden all spring and just thought I'd extend an invitation to come up around the corner for a cup of tea and to see what Max and I have been planting."

"Sure," I said, getting slowly to my feet, easing the stiffness from my back and brushing dirt off my jeans. "Would now be all right?" Perhaps I was more eager than was polite, but Walter and Max's property lay just up the hill near the back corner of our lot, and the big gray barn they had converted into a studio loomed above our garden. Max was a pianist, and all spring we had heard him practicing a Brahms concerto and a work by Rachmaninoff while we turned soil and planted. What would a garden planned and planted by a painter and musician look like, I wondered? I dashed into the house to get Sarah.

Surrounded as it was by a board fence, I had never had so much as a peek at their yard, though I had walked around the block many times. Walter opened the gate, warning us not to expect too much because they had been busy with so many other projects in the studio. We entered a tidy and understated outdoor room, a small and civilized space. Beside a glass-topped table on a maple-shaded bluestone terrace sat Max, a gangly Australian with a warm smile and infectious laugh who rose to show us around the garden. Walter went into the house with a promise to quickly return with a pitcher of tea. Rhododendrons grew all along the fence, faced down by pachysandra. In small raised beds and terrace pots were massed a gaudy profusion of impatiens, geraniums, nasturtiums, and other shade-tolerant annuals. Though their space was very different from the larger and sunnier one that Sarah and I worked, I felt a sudden kinship with their labor, and overflowed with ideas for new plantings and notions for paths and foliage combinations. Walter hinted at all of the secret gardens behind the fences and buildings of Collinsville, and those hidden along its walls and terraced into its slopes. "You find swatches of color and clever combinations of greenery in some of the least expected places," he added.

I'd been so busy with my own yard that I'd hardly noticed. But as we walked home the long way around the block I saw a village I'd not seen before. In the haphazardly drawn lots, and on uneven ground and around the oddly shaped houses and outbuildings were small bursts of bloom, twisting vines of wisteria and grapes, thickets of shrubby andromeda or holly, and redbud and dogwood trees that suggested a bonsai garden. Not every space was carefully cultivated, and some even enjoyed a picturesque neglect, but the plants generally spoke of a passion for gardening both in the here and now and in years past. To my awakened senses the town was alive and ablaze with gardens, both cultivated and accidental.

Gardening had always seemed a solitary task best suited to the quiet company of plants. But if gardening in Collinsville is isolated and done off-the-cuff, this fact might not be readily apparent to a visitor. One person's work stimulates another's, and the gradually accumulating beauty benefits the entire village and encourages more planting. How odd that gardening, with its essential individuality and privacy, should be instrumental in building community. Next to home repair, gardening is the activity Collinsville residents share most in common. I have discovered neighbors who like talking about their plants as much as they do about their children. We exchange bulbs and seeds and swap catalogs and advice. Though we are governed by modest plots of land and early valley shadows, our flowers and greenery brighten narrow alleys, tiny backyards, window boxes, steps, and out-of-the-way corners.

This wealth of shadows and paucity of space, however, makes vegetable gardening truly a rare pastime in Collinsville, and produce perhaps all the more highly prized. Each year there are passionate over-the-fence discussions about asparagus with Eric, each of us jealously monitoring who has the initial spear nosing out of the soil, and thus who gets to savor the first meal. It doesn't matter that Rosemary has only a few potted tomato plants on the terrace of her apartment next door: She will fiercely defend them against insects and fungus, spending hours researching remedies despite a career in landscape architecture that might easily incline her toward a more callous familiarity with the plants. Sarah is a gentle and compassionate soul when it comes to animals, but all-out war is declared and no remedy seems too extreme should a woodchuck mow down her beans. "The exhilarating anxiety about crops," wrote Gustave Stickley, "comes only to the man who planted them and means to use them to best advantage." As with so many pursuits, nothing ties us so tightly to the place we live as the investment of time and hope that vegetable gardening embodies.

Few of us have plots or patches large enough to supply all our needs, save for August's inevitable avalanche of zucchini and tomatoes. Our harvest pales beside the glamorous pyramids of produce piled under florescent grocery lights. But it is not so much the garden as the gardening itself that matters. Growing and eating our own food, in however small a portion compared to the easy abundance of the supermarket, awakens in us a direct relationship with our plot of ground. The home-grown foods we enjoy at our kitchen table are alive with the flavors of the soil we see from the kitchen window.

The fertility of a small, developed area can be surprising. Collinsville is between forty and seventy percent built-up and paved, but all about The Green one finds a prime agricultural soil known as Gloucester gravelly sandy loam. Our third of an acre is taken up by a house, driveway, and garage, with most of the remaining space lawn. But in a ten-by-fifteen-foot plot we have grown a variety of crops to rival a greengrocer's stock: broccoli, aspara-gus, tomatoes, potatoes, peas, sunflowers, Jerusalem artichokes, cabbage, brussels sprouts, parsnips, radishes, eggplant, lettuce, Swiss chard, beans, zucchini, pumpkins, summer squash, chives, and more. Currants, blueber-ries, and raspberries thrive in corners of the yard.

A vegetable garden may be small, but the act of gardening is large and grows the gardener in unexpected ways. Nothing inspires us to follow the old adage of thinking locally and acting globally as a vegetable garden. It spurs passion for the smallest places while stretching community space across vast expanses, embodies a stand on global issues and heals the plan-et. It is a political act, and our lives and our communities are the better for dirtying our hands.

Excepting the person bearing a baseball-bat-sized zucchini on a humid August day, is there any neighbor more welcome than the one bringing a bag of fresh-picked produce? Generosity grows naturally among gardeners since the payoff is not what you take out but what you put in. Even with this shared measure, our yield is such that occasionally the bounty of our small plot makes its way to town via the cash economy. Our produce has been sold at LaSalle, and the berries from our lot have been made into jams hawked at various fairs. As with the sugaring season, in growing a garden we grow a community and tie it to the world.

If the odd lots and awkward slopes of Collinsville promote creative planting around homes, the quirky geometry of streets offers unusual opportunities for us to garden together. At either end of The Green—at the intersection of South and Center Streets, the corner of Main and East, and the
junction of High at the top of Main—are little islands of soil surrounded
by pavement. They are anomalies in today's macadamed world, and in most
places would have been blacktopped long ago to improve traffic flow and
limit the need for constant maintenance. But in Collinsville these relics of
nineteenth-century dirt streets and slow-moving traffic have survived.
Some of them boast flowers and tropical foliage planted by nearby neighbors. Others are given over to unruly tufts of weeds and unkempt grass. All
are opportunities for beauty and community initiative.

The soil triangle set where the north end of The Green meets Main
Street features a tidy plot with a few well-chosen rocks and miniature
shrubs inset with daffodils and annuals. Maintained by a clutch of sisters
in remembrance of their father, the former proprietor of Eaton Hardware,
it is vaguely reminiscent of a Japanese garden. On the hot July day we
moved into the village, we found this spot a soothing oasis of color in the
middle of the street. As we unpacked, hung pictures, and painted over the
next few months, I watched curiously as the ladies stopped by to water,
weed, and rake this small and public patch of ground. Occasionally I'd spot
one of the sisters, Babe, and take leave of my indoor tasks to walk over and
chat with her while she stood with a hose that ran from my neighbor's
house. She patiently answered my steady barrage of questions about the village and my new house, and the following year she invited us to watch the
fire department fireworks display from her lawn. I was taken with her devotion to keeping this small spot in bloom, a personal memorial that made the
heart of the village look so nice. Each year it was harder to bend and dig,
she said, but she was not about to abandon the flowers to the plantain and
crabgrass. Always buoyed by her matter-of-fact community spirit, I'd walk
back to the house, eyeing the triangle covered by weeds and an overgrown
yew bush at the other end of The Green.

The next spring one of my neighbors, who had also observed Babe and her sisters at work, suggested that we attend to the desolate south triangle. The idea emerged during a spontaneous sidewalk gathering in front of my house, the happy result, as is frequently the case, of a string of impromptu meetings: two people on their way to LaSalle crossing paths with another person walking a dog while Sarah and I raked thatch from our lawn and Howard played stoop ball next door with one of his girls. A sudden contagious excitement erupted, not just because we could all imagine enjoying the color and orderly foliage of a garden in the street, but more tellingly at the thought of working together. All of us had recently moved to Collinsville, and having mostly grown up in the suburbs were unfamiliar with the idea of neighbors associating for much more than an occasional backyard barbecue. Coordinated action to produce something immediate and tangible was attractive to us. I volunteered to get permission from the selectmen. Sarah said she would go to the farmer's market for plants. Someone else offered the spare plants he was thinning from his yard, while another person agreed to buy peat moss, and yet another neighbor would work to get a local nursery to donate mulch.

Within a few weeks we were busy turning over the dry, compacted dirt. Both a pick axe and a pitchfork were needed, but eventually we worked enough moist peat moss into the soil to give the plants a reasonable chance of survival. More folks from town lent a hand. Karel carried over rakes and trowels. Nancie, who at that time lived to the north of us, came by cheerful and full of design ideas, a couple of shovels in hand. Walter brought more trowels and a bucket, while Sarah and I lugged over our garden fork, bulb planter, and several small rakes with sharp tines. There were nine of us pitching in at various times over the course of more than four hours, but we had tools for three times our number.

We filled a red wheelbarrow with rocks and tufts of discarded crab grass. We transplanted daylilies to the center and popped red salvia and blue ageratum into the ground around them. An instant sense of accomplishment spread through the neighborhood, and over the summer we watched color come to The Green, with the occasional casualty lost to the reflected pavement heat. In the fall we planted tulip and daffodil bulbs. We shared a sense of common ownership, looking out at someplace that belonged to all and to none of us, and it felt good.

Within a year flowers were flourishing, but our view from the triangle had changed. The bank added a boxy vestibule of smoked glass that obscured its grand masonry entry, and a nearby house newly converted to offices had its facade chainsawed for air conditioners. While there might have been some private grumbling and a few words of disappointment over the fence, the success of our joint effort on the triangle encouraged a small cadre of us to gather neighborhood support and petition the selectmen for a historic district. Not long afterward it also pushed us to campaign against a large Huckleberry Hill apartment development above High Street that threatened to force the widening of roads and pour traffic into the village. Gardening together sparked no magical inspiration or organizing genius, but a few of us did get to know each other, and discover that we could work together, and learned that we care about the place we live.

As we continue to fathom what grows best, the triangle garden has changed. Marigolds now bloom most years where the salvia and ageratum once did, and the initial excitement of new planting has been replaced by our accustomed yearly drudgery of raking, weeding, watering, and dead-heading. A few of our neighbors have gone and new ones have come, but each year a handful of us spend time together in the dirt. Now and then the inevitable, quiet resentment over who has done what surfaces, but it passes. Each year cars, bicyclists, and pedestrians stop and marvel at the effort, surprised that tending the garden is not a municipal function. Nothing makes us smile more.

In the course of a walk one afternoon, tree expert Ed Richardson and I discovered over thirty species within a two-block area without venturing into a single backyard. Ed marveled over the large kousa dogwoods along The Green, and found a twenty-four-inch white spruce along Bridge Street that he felt confident could rival the state champion. Downtown Collinsville has a small arboretum's worth of trees: Black walnuts, gingko, copper beech, catalpa, black and honey locust, aspen, elm, hawthorn, horse chestnut, European larch, and several types of maple and oak all flourish here. Though planted haphazardly, these trees, and our separate plots, and that triangle on The Green, give us the sense that we reside together in something like a large garden. And each and all of them make Collinsville a better place to live.

Gardening provides the creative energy to transform the places we live. A cultivated space, whether a solitary backyard affair or a common effort, is not a casual frivolity but the very foundation of a community.

River

The river created Collinsville. It permeates our lives in more ways
than we realize. The Farmington sustained Native Americans, who caught
and ate salmon and used alewives to fertilize beans and corn. In times past
it turned wheels, drive shafts, and webs of leather belts to stamp out blades
and sharpen edges. For a number of years it generated electricity. It now
dilutes our treated sewage. Photographers and painters are lured by its
beauty. Beavers, muskrats, great blue herons, stoneflies, and water striders
find it an ideal habitat. An enemy in times of flood, the river befriends
swimmers on hot days. It draws trade for a canoe store and fly shop, and
beckons children eager for adventure to mess about with a paddle or a set of
oars. Toddlers thrill to the ducks that gather for a few tossed bread crumbs
at the water's edge. Winter brings the joys of skating as hearty souls dash
across the ice with sticks and a puck. Summer finds water skiers zooming in
broad arcs across its gleaming surface.

We often gauge our moods by the river as it mirrors or provides a counterpoint to our daily frame of mind. It can be low and lethargic or charged with water and truculent energy. Sunlight sometimes makes it translucent, or glances off busy riffles, or creates the sort of bloated cloud reflections that invite introspection. At other times it appears waxy and dark. As temperatures plunge in autumn a fog hangs low over the watercourse, and in winter it can become our newest roadway—flat, open, hard as pavement, a straightforward physical fact. The river imperceptibly wears through our lives much as it has channeled through the bedrock, now and in ages past.

Many's the day I am drawn to the river, whether for the chance of seeing an otter, or by the practical need to cool off, or to fulfill a spiritual urge, or simply to hypnotized by the water's constant movement. It was for one of these reasons, or perhaps for all of them, that I stole some time from gardening on a Sunday afternoon one past June and walked about half a mile downstream to the lower dam. Pea plants were climbing their trellises and the spiky horns of yellow columbine lit the dark foliage of the perennial bed. On that brilliant cloudless day, the rote tasks of pulling weeds and laying down mulch, however useful and therapeutic, were simply too domestic, not enough of the out-of-doors. It was an easy walk down The Green and Spring Street to New Road, which parallels the east bank out of town. Away from my usual pursuits, it was time to see how nature's gardening was coming along.

Across New Road from the southern tip of the factory property, Ed sat on his concrete porch. He joined his trademark wave to a hearty "hello." A former Collins man with thick gray hair, a florid face, and a big smile, he is a sentry of good cheer at this prime gateway to the village, greeting passing cars and pedestrians whenever the weather is warm. Like LaSalle Market or the falls, he is a Collinsville fixture. Most visitors, not knowing his name, simply refer to him as "the waver."

Just beyond Ed's house, I cut across a small unpaved parking lot and slipped past a locked gate onto a dirt right-of-way. Built in 1912 for a narrow-gauge train that carried tons of bricks, cement, and other materials from the factory down to the site of the new dam, this rough-hewn path set in a long and irregular parcel of land hugging the river became the access road for the long-since abandoned hydroelectric station. It remains a hard-working bit of property, with electric transmission lines above and the forty-eight-inch aqueduct from Hartford's two-billion-gallon reservoir buried below. I once considered the poles, wires, and manholes—not to mention the herbicide and bush hog treatments—a scar on the landscape, but I have since come to marvel at the way in which the pipes and wires make vibrant connections from distant reservoirs and power plants to our homes. This "scar" has also saved the shoreline from the crowded addition of houses that would have formed an impenetrable barrier to the river.

As I headed down the dirt road I looked across the river at a couple of fishermen casting fly lines into the riffles below a small island. Sunlight danced on the water where they waded, their bright green lines looping and rolling out behind them like molten gold as the flies settled gently below. Catching fish means knowing fish, and the men, clad in baseball caps and khaki vests, figured a big one might be resting where the island stemmed the current. This watery habitat generally forces fish to work hard merely to stay still; the eddy would provide them a respite from the relentless flow.

A casual observer might find the right-of-way barren, irreparably dam-aged by regular trimming and clearing. But the man-made disturbance pro-vides a ready home for a wide range of wildflowers. Walking here every week or so during the growing season heightens my awareness of the year's progression, as one species fades and another blooms. Along the hardened, sun-scorched path bright blue-eyed chicory, Queen Anne's lace, and plumes of goldenrod each take their turn in the fullness of summer. Even in the cracks of ruined pavement, jewelweed flourishes. As fall draws close, asters bloom beneath the trees, the last flowers before the first frost.

But on this particular trek it was barely summer, and I was heading for those damp soils along the water's edge that had once been inundated when the Collins Company set a higher water level behind the dam. Here the mottled leaves and nodding yellow flowers of trout lily can be found, and the white, five-petaled star flower seems to float over a whorl of foliage even into the warmer weeks. The clearing required for the transmission of water and electricity has not only provided a public way along the river—it also harbors a greater variety of wildflowers than any other spot within walking distance of Town Hall. This open space is an artifact of other intentions, a recycled space ripe with possibilities rather than a pristine habitat. Such places exist not only in tired mill villages, but in scores of other settings, from abandoned urban waterfronts and derelict factories to forgotten rural roads and overgrown pastures. They await discovery.

Although I was soon in the trees, shade offered no relief from the day's humidity. I rolled up my sleeves and opened a couple of buttons on my oxford cloth shirt, grateful for the soft breeze on bare skin. This foretaste of deep summer brought to mind those warm mornings when stalks of mullein stand like rockets ready for launch and viny nightshade twists back upon itself in strands. Swallows, flycatchers, and purple martins worked the water, darting erratically like bats feeding at dusk. A kingfisher perched on a branch overhanging the river suddenly took off with lunatic screams that echoed down the water. I looked skyward for the osprey that often cruises high above the river. A flotilla of mergansers swam among the riffles, resting in eddies and dipping their heads down regularly for a snack.

About two-thirds of the way to the dam I came to a ledge outcrop that is obscured in summer with raspberries and red-stemmed pokeweed. A good part has broken away, as if some rock-eating giant had made fast work of it. Drill holes and chisel scratches mar the remains and a few angular pieces of stone litter the ground, perhaps quarried during construction of the dam. No doubt it has found its way into the foundations of some factory buildings. Though it bears the marks of man's upheaval, this tiny quarry poses numerous questions—historical, geologic, and engineering—that more than compensate for the appropriation of the stone and the loss of the natural ledge.

Immediately beyond the quarry the path is covered with coal cinders— the spent fuel from the factory's boiler. Josh likes searching here for glossy pieces of slag and gobs of rusted, misshapen metal. "Do you think this was left over from making an axe?" he will often ask me of a quarter-sized piece of iron. Often we sift through fifty years of decayed leaves and woodland detritus on the river side of the trail. Here the Collins Company piled not only cinders but broken slate shingles, odd pieces of wood, and rusted sheet metal from which machete blades have been stamped. Occasionally we find that most coveted of items—black phenolic plastic machete handles. Of all the company's manufactured materials they were probably the lowest in value, but to Josh they are pure gold. Finding them is like uncovering arrowheads in a plowed field—Collinsville arrowheads.

Beyond the cinder piles I passed a slender sapling growing out of a ledge. It would have escaped my notice were it not for the fact that several Thanksgivings ago my father-in-law and I found a large garter snake hanging in the crotch of this young tree about three feet off the ground. Though the snake was alive, it was torpid with cold and barely moved when touched. When I returned early the next day, it was gone. Had it slunk away to the safety of a decaying log or ended up as dinner for a winged predator? I never go by without thinking of it, the image as mysterious to me as the leopard found high on the mountain in Hemingway's "Snows of Kilimanjaro."

Trees along the path are tall, mostly common species—red maple, red and white oak, sycamores, black cherry, tulip poplar, white pine, ash, and hazelnut. Not far from the quarry I entered a low-lying area along the river where relatively young trees grow in damp organic soil. Black locusts, trees-of-heaven, and red and silver maples less than twenty-five feet tall are typical, their understory made up of multiflora rose, honeysuckle, blackberry, and staghorn sumac. Willows, alders, and elderberry take up the dampest spots. Early in spring, the ethereal sounds of spring peepers emanate from this area.

Leaving the path, I wandered through this tangle of small trees and brush, some of which were leafed out in a bright, newly minted green. The ground was spongy underfoot, and each step brought forth a fragrance like garden compost. Here again I found starflower and a blanket of mottled trout-lily leaves, but no blooms. I couldn't find a single trillium as I snaked my way through the area where I had seen several the year before. Skunk cabbage was thick in boggy places, and a few Jack-in-the-pulpits grew nearby.

This nursery of spring flowers with its young trees and rich, damp soil is not naturally occurring. It exists because for over half a century the five-foot flashboards from the concrete dam just downstream inundated this area. They backed water up to the factory and drowned an additional five acres, though steep banks kept most of the water within the river channel. When the company went under in 1966, this land burst forth into the sunlight, where its alluvial soil nurtured species of plants not commonly found nearby.

I heard water crashing over the dam well before I spotted the long-abandoned brick gatehouse which squatted at the edge of the falls, its broken slate roof patched with moss and covered with sticks and pine needles. I stepped onto the concrete apron that extends in an upside-down L along the side and front of the building. Leaning on the rusted pipe railing above the rushing water, I looked across the river and, through a sparse curtain of trees, saw cars on Route 179 making their way into and out of Collinsville. Though they whizzed by at fifty miles per hour, I could not hear them over the roar of the water as it slid dark and glossy over the dam before crashing down in a curling froth of white foam.

Between the road and the river I spied cyclists, parents pushing strollers, and a couple of skateboarders on the old railroad bed that was now a paved trail. Once an important commercial corridor, this level right-of-way enables everyone to get close to the river, from toddlers taking their first steps to wheelchair-bound seniors. Since the trail was built, more people than ever have waded the Farmington's cool water, fished its riffles, and contemplated its history from a perch on the dam. The trail keeps up the railroad's role of bringing business to the village by drawing visitors vital to retailers and restaurants, enlivening the small downtown on warm days. I like biking this path near dusk on summer days, when dank odors waft over the banks and I am besieged by the myriad flying insects that hatch on the water. It sounds bizarre, disgusting even, but it is at such times that I feel the raw procreative power of the river.

I turned back to the shore, glancing at the wall of the gatehouse which is visible from the highway and so serves as a billboard upon which each high school graduating class paints their year and their slogans in bold, gaudy colors. Layers of accumulated paint haveobscured the rough texture of the bricks and have given a new purpose to the long-derelict structure.

Back on the path, I peered inside the gatehouse at four giant metal gears meshed with a vertical shaft. Turning the gears used to raise or lower gates housed below the concrete floor, controlling the flow of water into a huge concrete canal 650 feet long, 50 feet wide, and 17 feet high. The water was channeled to a downstream power house, spinning two turbines that together generated a combined 700 horsepower. Below the gatehouse the path parallels the canal with its cracked and crumbling walls. It is an impressive structure, a weathered, New England version of a Roman aqueduct. A couple of teenagers were fishing along the top of the outer wall, which forms a dike along the river. They cast and retrieved their lures in regular rhythm, taking swigs of soda as they reeled in their lines.

On reaching the end of the canal I ducked inside of the squarish two-story brick powerhouse, stepping over broken pieces of wood, roof shingles, leaves, and other sodden material. About a decade ago vandals set fire to the building, and all that's left now is a roofless shell. The windows and doors are long gone; beams have crashed to the floor and broken electrical connections dangle from high walls. Two large, round concrete basins take up most of the floor. They once housed the turbines that generated electricity for blowers, rollers, grinding wheels, and trip-hammers. This forgotten place, open to the stars, was once a temple to the twentieth-century dynamo. Now it is a hazard in danger of collapse. Peering into the empty turbine pits where water once rushed, I saw pieces of rusted gates, sticks, and leaves decaying in muck.

I stood a while inside the forsaken structure, eerie light pouring down from above. There was a romantic, overgrown aspect to it that called to mind decaying pyramids in Central American jungles. All the while I was mindful of the lingering possibility that this building could be restored to its former use. The price of oil and the call for renewable energy conspire to keep hopes alive. The latest application for hydroelectric development was approved in 2001 by the Federal Energy Regulatory Commission after more than a decade of environmental, historic, scenic, and financial scrutiny, as well as scores of letters and reams of studies. I admit to a certain excitement at the possibility of restoring this site and the plant in the village to their former glory, producing power to once more light houses and turn machinery. But there is also value in their slow decay, and the air of mystery and time's inevitable passage that they provide. Would a Mayan temple be more enticing if the rainforest were cut away and religious rituals resumed? Yes there is a beauty in the practical harnessing of falling water. Of course the power was significant one hundred and fifty or seventy-five years ago. But the two dams together wouldn't even generate 2,500 kilowatts compared to the megawatts of electricity by which we measure the capacity of modern power plants. Would such a plan amount to merely toying with the river, riffing on its past with no real compensation for the loss of the free-running habitat?

On the downstream side of the powerhouse a bar of muck and sand beckoned to me. This little spit of land is sandwiched between the river and a narrow creek that trickles from the tail race where vast quantities of water were discharged after they spun the turbines. I used to fish from this bar frequently before we had children. Back then there was less gear to haul up and down the trail. Occasionally I still cast my line here where I caught my first brook trout on a dry fly, and remember how the water sparkled around the rocks as I reeled in the eleven-inch fish with a blue-wing olive hooked in its lip. My smile that day was as wide as the trout was long, but quickly faded as I watched the subtle shades of cream, brown, and green stippled with orange dots fade as the fish drowned in air. You can never possess what is most beautiful in a fish, and its sweet savored taste is little compensation.

Turning to regain the bank, I heard a loud "plop" in the stagnant pool of the old tail race. A bullfrog larger than my fist squatted at the mucky edge of the water. At the opposite end of the pool I spied a stick that on closer inspection proved to have eyes and a mouth. A two-and-a-half-foot-long water snake was sunning itself. It was here for the same reason as the frog and the fishermen—to soak up some rays and perchance to catch a meal.

The latter pursuit is humankind's oldest use of a river, and in that way it has perhaps the most to teach us about our relationship to the world around us. Long before the first and long after the last Collins Company trip-hammer fell, fish have been caught on the Farmington. Massacoe Indians camped at the site of what would later become Collinsville to spear salmon and shad negotiating the stepped ledges. Fishing continued even after dams curtailed the salmon runs and industrial wastes and sewage from businesses and villages polluted the river. On June 3, 1858, a local newspaper reported that S. V. R. Barnes caught a sixteen-and-one-half-inch trout just below the upper dam. Around 1870 the Collins Company reportedly released bass in the mill pond. The state's longest-lived trout hatchery was established in 1923 on a tributary a few miles away as part of a plan to stock pollution-resistant brown trout.

Today the Farmington is Connecticut's most popular trout-fishing stream. On opening day in April restaurants and fraternal organizations serve predawn breakfasts and the banks and bridges are crowded with anglers. From that chilly spring day through the mayfly hatches of summer, and into the months when rocks are laced with ice, the river is fished by all sorts of anglers: boys with coffee tins of worms, retirees with cane fly-rods and wicker creels, corporate executives from the suburbs, and immigrant laborers from Hartford. All share a common bond with the place.

Fishing is a way of looking at and peering into the world, a means of honing acuity and understanding. "A good angler," wrote Izaak Walton in the 1650s, "must not only bring an inquiring, searching, observing wit, but he must bring a large measure of hope and patience and a love and propensity to the art itself." So motivated, anglers fret about changes in temperature and the barometer's movement. They read how water runs around rocks and eddies along the shore. They assess color and clarity. They learn the habits of fish lurking in slack shadows, or congregating at the feeder streams where cool, oxygen-rich water and food wash down. Are fish rising to feed on flying insects, or are they slashing at the surface as if drawn by baitfish? Serious anglers learn about midge pupae, caddis larvae, and stonefly nymphs; they scoop bugs from the water with nets and examine them with a hand lens, and use binoculars to watch distant feeding activity.

Fishing is a process of endless exploration that ties people to their environment, forces them to understand their relationship with other creatures, and so invites involvement in the politics of development, water quality, and the stream habitat. People fish, writes journalist Howell Raines, "because it seems like magic to them, and it is hard to find things in life that seem magical." This enchantment has less to do with catching fish than with the unstated, ethereal connections whose mystery frustrates as many people as it enriches. The river that runs through Collinsville and beckons us to fish lures us into piecing together the varied elements of life and landscape.

Reconnecting with nature does not necessarily mean living in the woods like Thoreau or wandering the mountains like Muir. It merely requires the constant search for the beauty of simple facts and the consciousness of what is around us. Forget the fishing rod: just spend an hour outdoors every day. Familiarize yourself with the night sky; learn cloud patterns; bring outdoor objects like shells or stones inside; grow to know the trees in your neighborhood. Climb a spreading oak, or figure out where your trash goes. Keep a list of animals that you spot in your yard. If you can't go outdoors, learn about refrigerator molds, or shower-stall mildew, or the dust mites in your bedding and the spiders weaving in your basement. Get a few house plants and figure out their requirements for sun, water, and fertilizer. Find a nearby hiking trail, or organize the clearing of a vacant lot. Tend a municipal tree or garden. And remember that you can always follow a river and see where the water and your thoughts take you.

Next Door Wilderness

I only went out for a walk and finally
concluded to stay out till sundown, for
going out, I found, was really going in.
—*John Muir,* John of the Mountains:
The Unpublished Journals of John Muir

No place worth living should be difficult to get away from. As much as I enjoy the company of neighbors and the village's modest bustle, one of the great joys of Collinsville is the ease with which I can walk away. It takes but a few minutes to leave the houses, shops, traffic, and pavement behind and find myself where trees reign and deer and turkey are more at home than I am, where mica-flecked ledges and humus-leavened soils provide a rugged contrast to the angular regularity of lawns. The best places provide chances to challenge the body and refresh the spirit. Such opportunities are not unique to rural areas or fortunate villages on suburban outskirts. Our most crowded urban areas offer the chance to stroll beyond the usual confines. Even in New York City millions of people are an easy walk or subway ride from the greenswards of Central and Prospect Parks, or the beaches of Gateway National Recreation Area, or the islands and ragged wetland shores of Jamaica Bay Wildlife Refuge.

Often we are insensible to an entire undiscovered country of woods and waters a short jaunt away simply because we cannot imagine anything interesting so close nearby. We have been trained to think that we must travel to find places worth discovering, and thus a visitor from the other side of the country is more likely than we are to explore a vacant lot down the street. But fascinating natural phenomena are not just in far places or designated parks. There is a Yellowstone of spaces for each of us to explore just beyond the door. "Mysterious and little known organisms live within walking distance of where you sit," observes conservation biologist E. O. Wilson. "Splendor awaits in minute proportions."

Within half an hour of my house, and no doubt of any other, is enough nature for a lifetime of inquiry and retreat. Encountering the natural world nearby not only reveals undiscovered creatures and places, but makes us more at home. Ecology, broadly understood, is the study of home, since "eco" is an abbreviated form of the Greek *oikos*, meaning habitation. Practically every house bears evidence of the desire to tie nature to home, in the rocks, driftwood, shells, and bird nests collected and displayed like sacred objects. A shelf in my library holds pieces of iron ore, dolomite limestone, and red sandstone proudly displayed near a stick chewed by a beaver, a snakeskin, a turtle shell, and deer and caribou antlers. Some of these treasures were gathered from down the street, others in the wilds of Labrador.

Within a month of moving to Collinsville, I framed my restlessness in the form of the local USGS topographic map and hung it above the toilet. Each time I gaze at those carefully printed features, my mind spans the 35,500 acres they chart, wandering along the narrow blue line of the Farmington, tracing the black squiggles of tributaries to their origins in green-shaded areas, and scrambling along the tight brown contour lines that indicate ravines and ledges. I float on the blue surface of Nepaug Reservoir and explore the swampy shoreline of Secret Lake. "Maps are a way of organizing wonder," Peter Steinhart notes. I get organized and go.

At the map's center is Sweetheart Mountain, the dominant natural presence in Collinsville. A long, beaver-backed ridgeline whose 820-foot summit looms 500 feet above Town Hall, it forms the western wall of our narrow valley and is visible from my front porch and most other places in the village. I've never spent a day in town without contemplating its thickly forested slopes. Clear days begin when sun illuminates the ridgetop while the village is in shadow; sunset is measured against its darkened form. A rainy-day fog can be gauged by the opaqueness of its slopes. Subtle greens and reds mark spring's progress, and summer thunderstorms often come rumbling over the top. Autumn is a wall of red, yellow, and copper. Winter ice turns the mountain and its trees into crystal sculpture, and the rate of snowfall can be determined by the slopes' visibility.

From Dunne Avenue on the village's west side I walked up a narrow driveway between two houses and into a meadow. The grass was tawny from the hard frosts of November. From this tight opening between backyards, the Hickory Trail rises steeply, winding through a maze of pole-sized trees running in a swath up the hill. The climb was strenuous, making progress slow and providing me an opportunity to look around. Here and there among the trees were abandoned utility poles, some fallen in a tangle of wires, others with light fixtures still attached. This may be a nature preserve and perhaps a future slice of wilderness, but it was put to very practical purposes at some time past.

This patch of Sweetheart Mountain once boasted a downhill ski area with two rope tows powered by automobile engines. There were several trails, one a third of a mile long, and the lower slope was blasted and bulldozed to soften a steep descent. The ski area was built by volunteers who wanted to enjoy the outdoors near home. At its zenith in the 1960s, the Canton Ski Club, which got its start after the Second World War, boasted over six hundred members—some one hundred adults and five hundred children. Though the area is quiet now except for the chatter of chickadees, this used to be a busy place, bustling with expert skiers taking jumps and children learning to shift their weight and make turns. Shouts and laughter once mingled here with the swoosh of skis biting into the snow. Conditions permitting, the club operated seven days a week, as many as fifty days a year.

Beyond these old ski trails, Sweetheart Mountain is dominated by substantial oaks with tangles of glossy-leafed mountain laurel growing beneath them. Hickory, birch, beech, and maple are abundant, and dark clusters of hemlock huddle in cooler spots. Although the large trees seem to have been here forever, this is not the forest that greeted the first settlers. Within a few years of the Collins Company's founding, all of the hillsides roundabout had been clear-cut to make charcoal to heat its forges. Only after nearby wood supplies were exhausted did Collins turn to Pennsylvania coal, a change that helped keep the company competitive. It also gave this area a respite. Sweetheart's trees slowly grew back and were felled over the years for firewood, with portions of the slopes kept as pasture. But as small farms with a few cows lost their economic viability, even the grassy fields were given over to woods.

Today there are more trees here than at any time since the first settlers arrived. The forest continues growing back, and with a few minutes of determined hiking a person feels deep in the woods, isolated from the village, automobiles, and buildings. The area is alive with deer, turkey, fisher, and coyote—animals unseen by skiers a generation ago.

But this resurgence owes more to large economic and social forces than to an environmental ethic. Pipelines that reduced the cost of oil, thermostats that rendered wood-cutting unnecessary drudgery, and cars that took the place of horses and thus eliminated the need for hayfields have done as much for the trees as the legions influenced by Thoreau and Muir. We may be in the woods, but we are still in the world.

And though saplings have grown big, we will never again encounter the forest of Samuel Collins's time. As permanent as these protected woods seem, with trees that far exceed human scale in size, strength, and life span, the forest world is as much in flux as our own. American chestnut, a grand tree once as common as oak, has been reduced to no more than a short sprouting shrub since the blight of the 1920s. The dark evergreen clumps of hemlock, threatened by the woolly adelgid, a miniscule sap-sucking insect, are fading to gray and losing their needles. Soon they will be only a memory. These sylvan glades, as much as the village, are both moment and lens, and through them we can peer, Janus-like, at past and future if we know how to look and learn.

Pausing for breath a second time at the top of the ski trail, I wandered a few yards off the path to the ruins of the upper towhouse, a pile of twisted metal, rotting boards, and roof shingles. On a concrete pad a car engine rusts in peace along with a set of large wheels where the rope tow was threaded. The date "1964" is scratched into the cement. This must have been a noisy place, with the rumbling engine and grunt and squeak of the circulating rope. It's hard to believe volunteers groomed trails, maintained machinery, organized work parties, operated the tow, and kept up a ski patrol. But that same spirit of community effort continues today as volunteers mow the meadow, maintain hiking trails, and put up signs. Looking at the rusting engine, I recalled a story from the early 1970s of a girl who caught her long hair in the tow. Though the safety gate at the top stopped, it was mistakenly restarted and she was practically scalped, left to wear a wig the rest of her life. This mishap, combined with competition from a newer and much larger commercial ski area in the next town, forced the operation to fold in 1975.

Beyond the towhouse, I followed the trail through a twilight of thick hemlock and along a contour below the ridge south, until it turned up hill at a jumble of ledges and boulders that formed small caves. At the trail's edge was a concrete water trough, a reminder that this dense rocky woods was once pasture land.

On the cusp of winter the ground was not yet obscured by snow nor armored with ice. Light dappled the forest floor through bare trees, revealing bony ledges and roots grasping at stony soil. I felt the very bedrock; I sensed the tilt and folds of the landscape. The wind picked up with December's bite, and not yet acclimated to the cold, I caught a chill. Hemlocks, glossy Christmas ferns, and laurel thickets were the only green set in this bronzed November landscape. With little vegetation to block the view, my eyes were drawn to the lacy splotches of faded olive and yellow lichen tattooing the rocks. These tenacious patches of life were the first to colonize this area after the glacier retreated. They preceded mosses and grasses and even soil, taking up residence thousands of years before the first oak tree. A symbiotic partnership of fungus and microscopic green algae, lichens thrive in harsh arctic and desert climates; here they make do on the building foundations along Main Street, on stone walls along High Street and the Collins canals, and on cemetery headstones exposed to winter winds and blazing summer sun. The fungus provides a structure and absorbs water, minerals, and nutrients while the algae is the engine of photosynthesis.

Despite occasional glances across the valley to Huckleberry Hill, my focus was on small things, and I discovered that a few square feet of ground encompassed a miniature wilderness. On a log I found a massed approximation of British soldiers, tiny red-tipped gray-green stalks of lichen standing like Lilliputian matchsticks. Pixie-cup lichen on nearby rocks reminded me of tiny golf tees ready for an elven game, and leathery crinkled lobes of dog lichen clung to a ledge beside a clump of moss. Though tiny and primitive, these species have been used as a measure of air pollution, monitoring one of the most intractable modern problems as they rely on rainwater and fog. The acids they secrete dissolve boulders and help produce the soil on which civilization depends.

My inspection of this strangely familiar miniature world was suddenly interrupted by a loud pounding. It combined the energized bursts of a jackhammer with a hollow resonating sound that penetrated far into the quiet woods. I darted quickly up the twisting path and into the brush, plowing through barberry and laurel thickets as dry leaves crunched underfoot. Suddenly I stopped about seventy feet from the dark hulk of a huge decayed tree whose massive limbs had long ago fallen away. Wood chips and rotten pieces of bark were flying. I walked closer; the sound stopped. I halted again. My chest heaved from running, and I had to struggle to calm my breathing and keep quiet. When the hammering resumed it was so loud that I jumped in surprise even though I'd been expecting it. Sneaking closer, I spotted a bright red crest and dark back just as a crow-sized bird lifted off, a flash of white navigating effortlessly through the dense woods. The red, white, and black face reminded me of the painted ceremonial mask of an African chieftain. It was a piliated woodpecker.

The dead trees from which these flashy birds harvest insects interest me as much as healthy ones. The broken branches, sloughing bark, and decaying trunks host entire worlds of feeding, mating, and pupating insects. The insides of their trunks are easily carved out by nesting birds like chickadees and woodpeckers, whose carpentry work may later be enlarged and taken up by squirrels and eventually opossums and raccoons.

As the din subsided, I discovered that the woodpecker had made several rectangular holes roughly three inches deep by two inches wide and four inches long. It had blasted open a soft area cut by carpenter ants—a favorite snack. These industrious insects swarmed around the trunk like a panicked crowd during an air raid, darting into the elaborate honeycombed galleries that housed and protected eggs, larvae, and pupae.

Pulling one of the last patches of bark off of the tree, I found bark-beetle egg tunnels lightly etched on the smooth surface below. These tiny canals radiated, or forked, or potholed, or squiggled. The hatching beetles eat their own tunnels through the wood, the size of the passage increasing as the larva grows. When nearly mature, they hollow out a chamber to pupate, forming a snug cocoon for the winter. Adults emerge through the bark and fly off to new trees.

It's not necessary to go far into the woods in order to understand the ecological importance of dead trees: we encounter such spectacles all around us as we go about our daily chores. Carpenter ants, bark beetles, and scores of other fascinating creatures are hard at work along the street, in vacant lots, or in the backyard. I sometimes break apart the spongy center of ant galleries and watch the insects scurry as I'm splitting wood for a dinnertime fire, and the bark falling off a dead branch that has crashed to the lawn during a storm often reveals a delicate network of beetle tunnels.

Even late fall and winter, generally nature's downtime, are full of marvels: abandoned papery combs left by wasps; large football-size hornet's nests hanging from branches; tent caterpillar webs; abandoned birds' nests; trees spotted with bracket funguses, galls, and cankers. Shrinking one's focus creates a wilderness of things to see in the compass of a few yards.

I'd stood beside the old woodpecker-pocked tree long enough. The cold once again pierced my jacket and compelled me to move. I could tell from the groan of a nearby tree sawing against its neighbor that the wind had picked up. At a brisk pace I bushwhacked uphill through towering oaks and skirted laurel tangles. Soon I'd left land-trust property and crossed a narrow parcel held in private hands. Crossing a high point I entered the domain of the Metropolitan District Commission (or MDC), a regional water utility. With long strides and uneven leaps, I descended the densely forested and rugged terrain, crossed a dirt road, and shortly reached the cobbled shore of Nepaug Reservoir. No comparable opening in the landscape exists anywhere nearby, and reflected light makes the vast plane of water—all 950 acres of it—seem larger still.

Even more remarkable is the long, uncluttered shore. Most Connecticut lakes, regardless of their size, are hemmed in by cottages and by roads teeming with cars. However, except for a large storage tank and filter plant near the high concrete dam, there are no structures along the reservoir. Even these are not visible from where I stood, nor from most places along the water. In fact, a short stretch of abandoned paved highway at the north end notwithstanding, people are not welcome at Nepaug. While I may take all the water I want from my tap at home, here I am a trespasser.

I pulled binoculars from my battered blue backpack and scanned the water carefully, focusing on a few dots bobbing near a forested point in the distance. They turned out to be a couple of darkly silhouetted black ducks floating in the blue-gray water. Just beyond them was a hooded merganser, its head solid black save for a dramatic fan-like white crest behind each eye. A group of long-necked Canada geese swam just at the edge of my sight. Nepaug is an oasis for water fowl seeking food and rest during spring and fall migrations. Loons, green-winged teal, ring-necked ducks, buffleheads—and occasionally greater scaup, black scoters, and horned grebes—bring the colors, shapes, and sounds of Florida, Mexico, the Gulf Coast, and other distant places to our shore.

The lake is surrounded by thousands of acres of commission- and state-owned forest. Hundreds of bird species nest or pass through these expanses of mixed hardwoods and evergreens. In the spring ruby-crowned kinglets, pine warblers, solitary vireos, flycatchers, and blackpolls are numbered among the migrants. Nesters include scarlet tanagers, red-breasted nuthatches, wood thrushes, red-eyed vireos, veeries, ovenbirds, chestnut-sided warblers, and yellowthroats. The doleful calls of great horned, screech, and barred owls haunt the woods. In fact, most forest species of wildlife, from fox and bobcat to mink and muskrat, wander here. Deer are abundant and bears occasionally lumber through. Only people are posted.

Though few Connecticut places are as wild, Nepaug is not a vestige of primeval wilderness purposely saved from axe and pavement. It is an accidental, providential wilderness whose origins date to the early twentieth century, when the reservoir was built to slake Hartford's thirst. Nepaug's construction required a 113-foot-tall, 600-foot-long dam that diverted a river, drowned wetlands, destroyed productive farmland, uprooted old families from their homes, and required the excavation of cemeteries. The project had environmental and social consequences that would today be unacceptable, but if city officials had not coveted a clear-running stream to water lawns, flush toilets, and clean industrial metals, this nearby wilderness would be veined with roads and divided into house lots, like so many other rural landscapes devoured by sprawl.

The sudden appearance of cumulus clouds entranced me as I watched their mirrored movement across the sky and water, but once more the wind's chill reminded me that it was time to start walking. Besides, an MDC police patrol was likely to pass by any time, safeguarding my drinking water from the various intrusions of fishermen, and swimmers, and lovers. For that matter, neither walkers nor bird watchers are above suspicion or immune from summonses.

Turning from the lake, I regained the road, cut back into the woods, and climbed the steep grade until I reached the summit of Sweetheart Mountain. A series of sun-bleached rock outcroppings at the edge of a precipice offered a panoramic view east, north, and south. Here among the stunted oaks and bonsai-like pitch pines the arch of Nepaug's shore and the vast expanse of pewter water came into view. Ridgelines rolled in every direction like ocean waves, and below me the village was cradled so naturally between the hills that it hardly seemed man-made.

Above the village, the cemetery was a khaki-colored mound, its sides dotted with white, gray, and brown stones rising toward the forested dome of Huckleberry Hill. Poking above the trees was a huge water tank. Spaces cut for large, elaborate new houses and the roads to service them could be read in the broken canopy. I once spent time wandering those woods, following the old Kings Highway, looking into abandoned cellar holes. Like Sweetheart Mountain, Huckleberry Hill was clear-cut in places for charcoal and for pastured animals. But while the two share a past, the future looks different for the mountain and the hill. The latter is being carved into house lots, and while open space has been preserved, in some places even with connecting trails, it has become constrained and tamed, a mere epitaph for the woods and fields that once were there. Some of the mountain may yet share this fate, but between the land-trust and MDC holdings a substantial portion will remain open.

Stretched out on the ledge, sunbathing in the lee of the breeze, I watched turkey vultures cruise on the updrafts far above. I often see broad-winged hawks with their banded tails and larger red-tailed hawks with streaked breasts kettling here. Broadwings appear quite comfortable nesting in suburban areas, and redtails seem taken with utility poles, from which they track mice, rabbits, snakes, and frogs.

Sweetheart Mountain is not a long walk from the road, and is by no means a wilderness, but you can be as much on your own here as in places that are truly remote. You are likely to see fewer people in a couple of hours spent at the edge of Collinsville on a summer day than you might in the Great Gulf Wilderness of New Hampshire's Presidential Range or on the trails of Maine's Mount Katahdin. Though this is not a wilderness far from the frenzy of people, you can get a sense of wildness if you make the effort. Ecotourism begins at home.

From my perch I looked down on village, forest, patches of field, a huge lake, the winding river, and distant hills that look like charcoal smudges. What I strained most to see, though, was not an object obscured by trees, or even the distant horizon, but what was immediately before me—the weight and consequence of time yoked to the spaces so clearly outlined in sunlight. The endless pursuits of human life—grazing animals, manufacturing axes, building homes, using water and electricity, skiing, fishing, and hiking—had forever altered the view. Permanence was a great illusion. The density and type of trees, the species of wildlife, the course of rivers, the height and slope of the hills, the balance of water and dry land . . . these were as much the work of man as of Providence.

Our landscape is a garden writ large, a synergy of human and natural forces. Seeing these places in time as well as space awakens us to our power to create tomorrow's countryside. The question before us is not whether there will be places to live, work, shop, and enjoy nature, but what kind of seeds we will sow.

Giants in the Earth

There were giants in the earth in those
days; and also after that . . . mighty men
which were of old, men of renown.
—Genesis vi:4

Just as the living could not exist but for the dead, a town cannot exist without a cemetery. Graveyards are often a settlement's oldest human marker, and are as integral to local life as a barber shop or a grocery store. If we did away with garish Halloween images and horror-film fears, we might make better use of the space where the dead rest to contemplate, observe, and connect to the places where we live.

The Collinsville Village Cemetery occupies twelve acres on the south slope of Huckleberry Hill, a couple of streets up from the Congregational church. Monuments are terraced into the hillside in irregular rows on a slope that rises over one hundred fifty feet. Cemetery Road cuts across the graveyard about two-thirds of the way up, roughly dividing the active from the established portion. The steeper areas are set with retaining walls that are bulging and cracked, having been patched many times over the years.

Collinsville Village Cemetery. (Author's collection)

The green expanse is well-clipped, though, and a line of decrepit sugar maples mark the vertical stripe of an old wagon road, now covered with grass.

With other nearby hillsides thickly wooded, this "community" of the dead stands out from any vantage point, but it is the view from among the stones that is the most striking. Below is a panorama of houses, churches, offices, and stores from which everyday sounds waft up softly. The river sparkles along a curving belt of trees. On autumn mornings I often take a brief detour on my way to work, driving up to the pinnacle of Cemetery Road for the view. On my way home on many a winter evening the same stop beckons, a Milky Way of village lights twinkling below.

The relationship of the village of the living to the village of the dead also struck Rose Terry Cooke while visiting her sister Alice and brother-in-law Howard, Samuel Collins's son, a century ago. Sitting at a window facing down into Collinsville, and looking across to the cemetery from a big house halfway up the long hill that is Torrington Avenue, Cooke penned a verse for each settlement.

Over the river, on the hill,
Lieth a village, white and still
All around it the forest trees
Shiver, and whisper in the breeze;
Over it sailing shadows go,
Of soaring hawk and screaming crow;
And mountain grasses low and sweet,
Grow in the middle of every street.

Over the river, under the hill,
Another village lieth still,
There I see in the cloudy night,
Twinkling stars of household light,
Fires that gleam from the smithy's door,
Mists that curl on the river's shore;
And in the road no grasses grow,
For the wheels that hasten to and fro.

A graveyard reveals much to those who stop and wonder. In Collinsville's Village Cemetery the headstones roughly mark the date that the village was established, and while there are older interments, the sheer number of graves reveal that the town had a substantial population by the 1830s. Monuments speak of increasing wealth too, in their growing size and sophistication. But they also speak to a measure of equality, as members of the Collins family are buried alongside factory workers, and the differences between simple and elaborate headstones are minimal. There are no pharaonic catacombs here. The only substantial structure is a modest granite-walled building in which lawn mowers and hand tools are kept.

Whether granite, brownstone, or marble, the gathered monuments call our attention to all sorts of forgotten details: the range of materials available locally and those shipped from afar, the changes in carving techniques and technology, and the shifting fashions in inscriptions, images, and design. Embedded in stone are clues to our predecessors' views on death and commemoration. Today's bulging retaining walls, broken and faded monuments, and missing fences and railings also tell us something about how we define our responsibility to the past. Though the graves of those within living memory are lovingly tended, the cemetery as a whole is losing its battle with time. The budgets and priorities of the living are vividly apparent; the non-profit Collinsville Cemetery Association has resources inadequate to its task, and the minimal response to their financial appeal to the townspeople a few years ago suggests that few view the cemetery as a vital part of the community. Indeed, a huge monopole cell tower has been proposed at various times for the high point of the graveyard, begging the question of whether rent from idle chatter should serve both to mar and to repair this silent village.

Names and dates mark families that have been here since before the company's founding, and others whose time in Collinsville lasted a life span or less. The stratum of immigrant forgers, grinders, and shipping clerks—Germans, French Canadians, Irish, Scandinavians, Poles, Slovaks and other eastern Europeans—is set in stone. Some monuments herald the deceased's country of birth: Julius Pajunen was born in Finland, John Doolen in Limerick, Ireland. A few inscriptions, like Louise Screiber's, are written in native tongues: "Christus der ist mein leben / Sterben ist mein gewinn / Dem thu ich mich ergeben / Mit freud fahr ich dachin." All these clues, taken together, also give a rough census of Catholics and Protestants. If names are an easy guide, Moses and Abraham Wise, who lived and died here back in the nineteenth century, may have been Jews.

Dates recall the tragic loss of stillborn children and women who died in childbirth, and mark the sadness visited upon both the humble and the powerful. Three of Samuel Collins's five children never lived to celebrate their second birthdays. Elisha Root, the mechanical genius to whom Samuel Colt would one day pay the highest salary in all Connecticut, lost his wife on October 28, 1838, just days after their sixth anniversary. Their son Jophet died at eight months, on March 5, 1839. The harrowing math of these dates is terrible to contemplate. Though more than a century has passed, I wince at family plots crowded with infants and school-aged children. Perhaps one parent can feel another's grief across time. The graveyard lays to rest complaints about the dangers of childhood in the twenty-first century: At least there are fewer tiny graves as the years draw closer to our own.

But if the shift in infant mortality is heartening, the threat of wartime's early grave holds for every generation. Men who wore the blue kepi of the Union, charged the enemy in Cuba, endured the muddy trenches of France, hit Pacific island beaches under Japanese machine-gun fire, and suffered the icy winters of Korea are buried here. Some lived to march through decades of Memorial Day parades; others returned in caskets from foreign lands.

Whenever I walk these grassy slopes the stones pose questions and conjure stories. Where was First Lieutenant Albert Johnson wounded at the battle of Seicheprey in France, and how long afterwards did he die (age 25, on May 8, 1918)? What of the melodiously named Pleasant Valentine who passed away in 1915 at age 67? What circumstances led to the killing of John Felter, "who died by a murderers hand on the 16th of Apr. 1875 In the 50th year of his Age?" I had particularly wondered about Valentine for a dozen years before an accidental encounter with a retired school teacher from another town filled in the details. The teacher revealed that Pleasant was a black man, a collier who slept beside a fire of mounded cordwood that rendered charcoal. Later on I learned he was born in Virginia. With these facts in mind I walked past his grave one windy autumn day and calculated his birth year from the information on his headstone. Born in Virginia in 1848: Despite his genial name, Pleasant Valentine began life as a slave.

Stories of the dead drift into the consciousness of the living slowly, by accident and by coincidence, so that a graveyard is never the same from one visit to the next. I'd passed the name of James Spencer dozens of times with no more recognition than of a phone book listing. Then one winter day I paused in front of his faded marble marker on my way to take in the view of the sunset-reddened village from the hilltop. Piecing together a bit of recent conversation and a newspaper article I'd read four months earlier, I realized that this man, who had died in 1888 at the age of 73, had lived around the corner from my house. Though blind, he had served for many years as the Congregational church organist. I pictured him with his cane on a Sunday morning, tapping his way slowly and deliberately to worship while the bell tolled with its familiar, deep resonance. I was about to resume my trek to the hilltop when the inscription on the tombstone caught me short. "Thine eyes shall see the King in his beauty," I read. And perhaps he did.

From the age of three, Josh has been a frequent companion in my walks through the precincts of monuments. At first he wondered about ghosts, speculating that the stones were used to weigh them down and keep them in the ground. He wanted to know what was actually beneath the grass. Would the body look as if it was asleep? I explained what happened to flesh under the circumstances, and he asked about the bones and how long they would last. Were there skeletons underground? Did they wear clothes? Could we dig them up and see? We talked about coffins and funerals, why people die, what heaven was like, and what part of the person went there. Without a cemetery, how would these issues be raised with such natural ease?

On our first visits, Josh ran around and rolled down the hillside, picking buttercups and hawkweeds that grew too close to the stones to be clipped by the mower. When he realized that the markers bore words, he asked me to read them to him. Later he began identifying numbers and letters, and then took to reading inscriptions himself. Always he wanted to know where the people had lived and how they died.

Seeking out characters whose stories I knew, I stopped at the graveside of Leonard Hough, who had been our neighbor on The Green. I described the tall and kindly gentleman who had lived quietly behind a high hemlock hedge, and Josh was in awe that I actually knew someone buried here. He was full of questions when we reached the graves of John and Dorothy Meconkey, once I explained they had been the previous occupants of our house. What did they look like? What was John's job with the company? Was the house the same color? Who had slept in his bedroom? When I ran out of answers we moved on to the stone of Jasper Bidwell, the town's first Civil War volunteer, who marched with the initial batch of recruits down Main Street past a cheering crowd and bunting-draped buildings to the sound of a brass band. We stopped beside the plot of John Wheelock, whose nineteenth-century store had boasted "the largest and choicest stock of goods ever seen in this place, at rates positively pleasing to the buyer." I described Wheelock's horse-drawn delivery wagon, how he took produce in trade and guaranteed "to fulfill the most windy promises." My scraps of facts and Josh's imagination transformed the stones from forgotten monuments into a lively thoroughfare of people and tales.

Spend sufficient time at varied hours in even the most urban cemetery and you realize that a graveyard is not merely a place of dead dreams; it hosts scores of living residents as well. I often hear the screaming crows of Cooke's poem as I look from high on the slope toward her grave. Her soaring hawks are here too, as are osprey and bald eagles. Red-tails will perch on lofty skeletal limbs around the perimeter, watching intently for a mouse, vole, or garter snake. Occasionally I witness a dramatic dive and in a blink the bird is aloft with something struggling in its talons. Toads seek shade from the sun, deer come forth into the open at dusk, and skunks dig for grubs at night.

The mowing regime determines which wildflowers grow here among the cut gladioli and potted petunias that are sometimes left in memory of a loved one. Cinquefoil, ground ivy, dandelions, and violets are common. Scraggly asters, the spotted orange horns of jewelweed, and wild geranium with its delicately veined lavender petals grow close to stones or at the edge of the woods. In the midst of the preponderance of typical lawn plants, I'm ever watchful for the odd and uncommon. Maintenance regimens and leftover spaces may favor plants rarely found elsewhere. Sandplain gerardia, a small, unassuming, and unusual snapdragon-like plant with light-purple flowers and little narrow leaves, was found by ecologists in a small town cemetery several years ago. With a minor change in the mowing schedule, it has done well.

Cemeteries have reputations as quiet places, but they can be noisy too. Birds sing and whistle, wind rustles through the trees, late-summer crickets chirp, and the rolling whoosh of passing cars echoes to the furthest stone. In winter, the screams and laughter of sledding children occasionally break the silence. But the noise I most often hear is the gentle hum of conversation. It is not the hushed tones of mourners or the respectful speech of visitors. When the moment is right I hear many voices engaged in earnest discussion and disagreement and gossip, like a large and unruly family around a dinner table. These speakers are the dead, of course, recalled to life by the names and dates on cracked and tilted stones. They awaken me to a community existing both in time and space. Buried here are not just individuals, but relationships.

Just below and to the side of the Collins family plot is a brownstone obelisk taller than any monument to the company founder. Here lie the remains of Bradford Marcy, who was pursued by a litigious Samuel Collins all the way to the Connecticut Supreme Court for selling liquor in violation of a deed restriction. And if I listen intently, I can hear the stones speak.

"You tried to ruin me, you bully. I was just a poor shopkeeper. You were like a king."

"Liquor was an evil, dangerous to society."

"You sanctimonious hypocrite. Before you became a titan of industry you sold all sorts of strong beverages in that grocery business you ran with your uncle in Hartford."

"Back then I didn't know the effect of drink on the productivity and moral fitness of laboring men. You did the devil's work in that basement shop."

"I was not selling intoxicating liquors. You lost the case, remember? I am in heaven now because you put me through hell. I was publicly embarrassed. My family was left uncertain of their future, and the costs almost broke me."

"I lost the case on a technicality, not because you weren't selling."

"You never went after the obvious purveyors of brandy and wine. You picked on me because I accidentally built a few feet over on your property."

"You worried only for yourself. I had to take care of a whole village."

The argument fades as I walk downslope. I often catch it in this part of the cemetery. It is one of many dialogs I tune in, as if I were listening to a cosmic radio and came in range of the Collins-Marcy broadcast. As I learn more about the village, I hear many such conversations.

Just beyond the range of the Collins-Marcy argument I near the obelisk of Dr. R. H. Tiffany, who built a three-story frame building with a grand piazza and a large third-story hall on Main Street in the years before the Civil War. In the deep baritone of a man comfortable with himself, Tiffany holds forth with tales of the first-floor merchants—a watch repairer, boot maker, clothier. He recalls the Nash brothers, who flew a red flag to advertise their medicated soap. He has a hearty laugh for the antics the stores used to lure customers. There was the story of the pumpkin traded for watch repair: The vegetable was rotten and went bad in less than a week, but that was all right because by then the watch had stopped as well.

As Tiffany's voice fades I pick up the creaky words of Charles Farnham, who as an old man stood up to robbers at the Collinsville Savings Society in 1935.

"Hoodlums. They were just three cheap hoodlums. With my dear wife Sarah gone just a few years and my heart bad, I had nothing to lose. They weren't going to scare me."

Rollin Humphrey talks about his 1858 appointment as agent for the North American and Merchant's Insurance Companies and his partnership in Polk's Drug Store after George Polk died. John Lawrence tells someone how the 16th Connecticut was flanked by Hill's Division at Antietam.

"The dead lay in a jumble everywhere, and the moaning of the wounded haunted us through the night."

I often pass Seth Norton's grave, an obelisk set in a neat family plot with a low railing. Always I hear the half-scolding, half-pleading voice of Charles Blair, company vice president, legislator, pillar of the community. His stone is somewhat distant and his words are always a little faint:

"Why did you do it, Norton?

"Do what?"

"You can't fool me—I was executor of your estate."

"Of course. I trusted no one more."

"And I you. But when they opened the books of the bank after your death it was a mess. It was hard to tell at first that there was money missing."

"I may have been a little sloppy as treasurer, but always I had the best interests of the village in mind."

"Everyone trusted you. You were judge of probate, postmaster, state representative."

"And couldn't I be trusted? Couldn't I keep a confidence? Wasn't I liberal in lending out of my own pocket?"

"Yes, you were always generous. And with your modest estate everyone always wondered . . ."

"And about you, Charles: didn't people wonder about your dealings with that treasonous John Brown? Of course, I always defended you. Never let anyone believe that you would trade your loyalty to our country for a few pieces of silver . . ."

"You know there was nothing to it. I never wanted to make those wretched pikes. I even sent them out to be finished because. . ."

The voices trail off to a whispered cadence.

"Oh, well, let's just forget it all, shall we? Isn't this a perfect place for our final rest? When I became first president of the Cemetery Association, I thought about the public trust in my hands, and I did right by us, didn't I, Charles? The wind is pleasant, the view is good. Calm down and take just a moment from eternity to enjoy this place. When I was alive I never imagined the cemetery would be such a lively place, did you?"

Geography of Imagination

*For each home ground we need new
maps, living maps, stories and poems,
photographs and paintings, essays and
songs. We need to know where we are,
so that we may dwell in our place
with a full heart.*
—*Scott Russell Sanders,* Staying Put

Factory Creations

*With Iron Force, and Coal Force and the far
stronger Force of man, are cunning affinities,
and battles and victories of Force brought about.
—Thomas Carlyle, Sartor Resartus: The Life
and Opinions of Herr Teufelsdrockh*

Collinsville has always stirred creativity in its residents. Perhaps the tireless rush of water pouring over the ledges awakens imaginative energy. Maybe the surrounding hills, training the eye to look toward the horizon, nurtures inspiration. Romans believed places were imbued with a characteristic guardian—a "genius." If so, creative expression is the genius of Collinsville. When this has been fully engaged the village has flourished; when forgotten, it has suffered.

Creativity is most directly associated with the fine arts, but practical necessity inspired Collinsville's greatest burst of genius. In the 1820s and 1830s "Yankee streams were studded with trip-hammer shops," observed writer Diana Muir. "Samuel Collins stands out because he had a knack for selecting mechanics of genius and the vision to fund their work, sometimes for unprofitable years at a stretch." Collins succeeded not just because he was an able businessman, but because his creative, long-term vision for factory, product, and village inspired others. Despite the fact that Collinsville was a rough and out-of-the-way place, he lured the most able mechanics and machinists, men with an intuition about mechanisms and gears and wheels and metals who could bring together raw materials, falling water, and clever ideas to produce the highest quality products quickly and cheaply.

In 1832 David Hinman built cost-effective machines that formed and welded axe heads, enabling the company to resume the defaulted debt payments that could have meant bankruptcy. In 1860 F. F. Smith invented a cast-steel plowshare that combined medium weight with great strength and thus turned over Nebraska sod more easily. But the company might have gone under in its first decade—and the town might never have existed—were it not for the towering creative genius of Elisha K. Root.

It was high summer in 1832 when twenty-four-year-old Root first stuck his head into the Collins Company machine shop. An eager young man with piercing eyes and a long chin, he'd had a knack for repairing machinery since childhood, and shortly after coming to Collinsville he signed a two-year contact for "building and repairing gearing and machinery, keeping polishing wheels in order, etc., etc." Beginning as a lathe hand, Root eagerly threw himself into the work, undoubtedly assisting Hinman in the installation of the new machinery. In 1849 Samuel Colt would lure him away by offering him the fabulous salary of $5,000 per year—two and a half times his Collins pay as plant superintendent—but not before his improved methods and inventions turned a primitive trip-hammer shop into a modern factory. Root's death in 1862 was deemed "a public calamity" by the *Hartford Courant*, which noted that the Collins Company "now enjoys a world-wide reputation, [whose] success is largely due to the inventive genius he displayed."

When Root arrived, Collinsville was a bustling if crude place. More than two dozen houses were under construction along the rough dirt streets, and church services and school classes were held in the company office building. On the first floor of what was then a simple clapboard structure, Samuel Collins fretted over the fact that city merchants peddled competing products. Indeed, the company's weak financial position would lead to a reorganization and the assignment of property to trustees within a year. While sales declined, workmen protested "stringent and illiberal contract" provisions, the company's "temperance principles," and rigid rules. Unconcerned with management's troubles, Root tinkered with levers, wheels, gears, axles, pulleys, and other mechanisms. Like other machinists, his oil- and grease-creased hands were nimble and skilled. But Root also had ideas about new ways of doing things, from labor-saving methods to techniques aimed at cutting the wear on parts, reducing breakdowns, and generally improving products.

He completely reinvented axe making, eliminating the time-consuming process of flattening wrought iron, folding it around a steel pin, and forging the pieces together by pounding them with a trip-hammer. His new method used a series of dies and rollers that formed an axe head by applying pressure to a mold. Such "die-forging" produced a hot wrought-iron axe head with an eye already punched for the handle. Root also reduced labor in tempering by introducing a machine that carried axeheads on a rotating wheel through an oven. Another innovation—the addition of a shaving machine—reduced the tedious labor of grinding a sharp edge, thereby solving a labor shortage caused by the fear of "grinder's lung" among prospective employees.

One summer afternoon I strolled through the hodgepodge of factory buildings sandwiched between the village and the river. I passed a couple of long-abandoned turbines—massive devices with oxidized vanes and pipes—and followed a series of canals whose dark water rushed between collapsing walls. I found myself drawn to an imposing three-story stone building completed in 1847, the last one left from the days when Root was a Collins man. The walls are chipped and bowed now, stuck together with crumbling mortar, and here and there the iron tie-rods are broken. I tried to picture Root toiling away setting up the new machinery: his hard, intense gaze; the broad forehead below the receding hairline; the close cropped Vandyke. In this sorry state, the factory complex is a confused morass, but no doubt a man like Root could straighten it out.

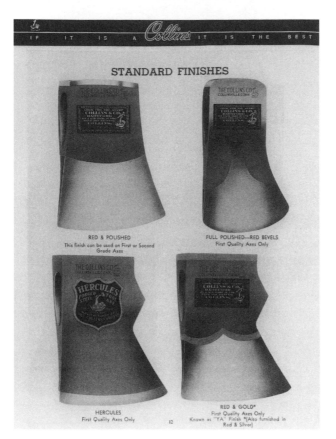

A page from the Collins Company catalog, 1936. If you didn't see what you needed in these pages they'd fabricate it for you. (Courtesy Canton Historical Society)

I walked back toward the smokestack and waved to Doug—an inscrutable bearded bear of a man, the principal obstacle to nature's relentless attempts to return the buildings to dust. Always ready with a paintbrush, a wrench, a hammer, or putty knife, he was glazing a window in the brick boilerhouse, his valiant, solitary efforts a losing battle given the forces he faces.

A patchwork of business signs announce that the buildings are occupied, rotten siding, peeling paint, crumbling brick, and cracked windows notwithstanding. But even with a range of tenants, the complex conveys a certain loneliness. This place seems mythical, like the ruins of an ancient civilization, or the work of a race of giants. Of course, Root himself became the stuff of myth when, a generation after his death, Samuel Clemens used him as the model for the hero of *A Connecticut Yankee in King Arthur's Court.* A mechanically inclined genius, factory superintendent Hank Morgan is described as being able "to make anything: guns, revolvers, cannon, boilers, engines, all sorts of labor-saving machinery." Morgan asserted that he could devise anything, "it didn't make any difference what; and if there wasn't any quick newfangled way to make a thing, I could invent one." It would have been an intemperate boast for a great many fictional characters, let alone a living man, but none could dispute how well it fit Root.

The complex haunts me with its stillness and solitude. This was clearly once a noisy place full of pounding, grinding, banging, and clattering machinery. What happened to the muscular men whose sweat and swearing and vision and guts made this place? Are the buildings their last monument? A power and presence remains in this prosaic collection of structures, something like a kind of creative magic—romantic, almost mystical, akin to the sort of intuition that even the most practical and dispassionate engineers or mechanics bring to their best work. Root embodied this mechanical instinct. Midway through his tenure with the company a heavy, complex piece of machinery failed. Work came to a standstill. Samuel Collins demanded a quick repair, and a stumped company mechanic called Root. The great man tinkered with various parts of the machine, making several adjustments. Nothing worked. Then he then turned the full force of his attention to the problem. As P. H. Woodward, secretary of the Hartford Board of Trade in the late nineteenth century, noted:

> After an interval of abstraction Mr. Root took a seat, motionless and in silence, before the recusant monster, whose mighty arms refused longer to slave. Returning from dinner he held the same immovable attitude till night. No one presumed to interrupt the vigil. Still the mystery baffled him. The next morning the silent communion was resumed.

Soon the clouds broke. Without a word Mr. Root went to his desk and dashed off a sketch that, while preserving the massive frame, dispensed with a multitude of pieces, and produced the needed motion by a few simple contrivances. The reconstructed machine recognized the genius of its master by the unfaltering precision with which it did its appointed work, till replaced a few years later by a new invention of his own, which is still in use.

Heading toward LaSalle for a coffee, I passed the brick scale-house and walked beneath the elevated bike trail that follows the path of the long-forgotten railroad. Crossing a canal, I slipped past the backside of a garage that once housed the fire department and stopped alongside the massive three-story barn-like structure built in 1865 to store and finish F. F. Smith's steel cast plows. From this angle the building looked simple: the porches and chimney built when it was converted into a recreation hall in the 1920s were out of view. Now home to the town museum, it is our municipal time machine.

Preoccupied with Root, I ducked in for a quick history fix. Carl, the town historian at the time, was holding forth with a couple of elderly women on the use of rhino hide to polish blades. Though in the years before his death he did not always remember what happened the day before, he was almost infallible about anything that was graced with a patina of at least fifty years. I made my way to a room where hundreds of Collins tools are strapped to display boards, the floor creaking with each footfall. The inventory is impressive. There is a dizzying array of machetes—straight blades and curved, blunt and pointed, long and stout, grooved and smooth—with handles of leather, plastic, wood, horn, and metal. A baffling range of axes came in all sizes: double bit, fire, bell poll, box, shingling, lath, claw, broad, flooring, forestry, flat-head, pick-head, beveled, and phantom beveled. Other tools included carpenter's, ship, and Spanish eye adzes; cane knives; bush and pruning hooks; lances; fish spears; hoes; picks; mattocks; and hammers. There were obscure and bizarre blades bearing exotic names: cavadores, macanas, barras, aquinches, bolos, paias, barretones, tarpalas, coas, podaderas, froes, and kurkris. This room holds the soul of the company's creativity. It wasn't just the flowering of mechanical brilliance that led to success; the company's most famous products and their worldwide renown was the result of ordinary, talented craftsmen thinking and working with their hands and minds.

Ship captains sailing from Hartford in the 1840s and 1850s brought Collins implements to the forests and plantations along the Caribbean and South American coasts. Taken with the heft, polish, and sharpness of the Collins blades, the indigenous folk tried them out cutting trees, harvesting crops, and digging. Soon they were sending tool orders north, and Collins workmen transformed verbal descriptions, rough sketches, crude native implements, or wooden models into actual tools. In time, catalogs invited customers to inquire for any pattern or shape that they couldn't find within the company's stated inventory. It's said that the trademark burly arm holding a hammer became so familiar that those who did not know the name Collins would address a dealer, arm flexed and fist clenched, to indicate their product preference.

When finally I emerged from the past into the daylight, I resumed my stroll across Main Street to LaSalle Market and nursed a coffee beneath the awning, content to watch the world go by—kids on skateboards, moms with strollers, the ebb and flow of people stopping by for a loaf of bread, a sandwich, or a soda. I stretched, sipped slowly, and savored the light breeze on a day grown lazy and warm. Burly, crew-cut Glen Griffin waved from the basement of the old Collins office building across the street. "Got a minute?" he shouted. "I'll show you my new manufacturing operation down in the factory."

Glen had started his antique lighting business in this small space, so crowded with fixtures that products were displayed in the Collins Company vault. At first he did repair work on a table in back amid an inventory of brass lamp bases and crystal chandeliers. Now he makes fixtures as well as restoring them, and his business takes up many times that original space. The office basement, which he now shares with Kristen, a picture-frame maker, still serves as a showroom. A handsome sign on the granite lintel over the door reads "Griffin Brothers," despite the fact that he has no brother. If you ask, he shrugs sheepishly and says that he liked the classy sound of the name.

Walking together down Main Street, Glen and I descended the wooden stairs at the south end of the brick Collins shipping building, now a multidealer antique mall. We passed beside a long clapboard building and walked through a set of double doors into a wide hallway, heavy timber painted white and scuffed with years of hard use. A turn took us through several rooms on the first floor of the massive brick building where Collins blades were once polished.

In addition to the legacy of Collins metalworking, Glen keeps alive the tradition of custom design, customer service, and business acumen. Though he's around thirty, he still has the broad, boyish face of a high school football player. As we moved from room to room he was as excited as a teenager showing off his first car. He pointed to brass rods, fittings, canopies, pedestals, and slices of sheet metal piled on shelves and the floor. Braids of cord hung from the beamed ceiling, and electrical fixtures, pieces of colored glass, and shades in various designs and colors were scattered on tables. It seemed like a jumble of several jigsaw puzzles mixed together, but in this flotsam Glen saw elegant finished lamps. "We make roughly one hundred different kinds of floor and wall lamps," he said eagerly, picking up an almost finished floor model, pointing out the fluted stem and turning it in his hands to show carefully joined parts. "If there's something the customer wants that I haven't done before we'll give it a try," he added, his words echoing those of Samuel Collins from more than a century before.

We squeezed past a masked worker who was spraying lacquer on brass rosettes. "We can do any finish a customer wants—polished brass, matte, bronze, black—anything," Glen remarked. He is always in motion, checking the progress of a man standing at a polishing machine, hefting new rod stock, and giving a final check to pieces ready for shipping. But while the lamp manufacturing business is taking off, restoration of antique light fixtures—some dating to the dawn of the electrical era over a century ago—is clearly his passion. "This old factory is a big part of my inspiration," he acknowledged, gesturing into a long room lined with shelves of fixtures darkened with age. All of these had missing electrical connections, tarnished finishes, broken or twisted details, or some other defect. "The heart of my business is restoring history, so I wanted to be in a historic place. It sets the right tone."

Arrayed on a large table were pieces of chandeliers from an old mansion. Glen was carefully restoring metal gargoyle faces to their former luster, repairing the frayed wiring and fabricating missing pieces. "I try to find old metal, cannibalize fixtures too far gone, but I can make something look old if necessary." He reached for a gargoyle and turned it over in his large, rough hand, letting it catch the light from the window. "Sometimes you just can't match what they did a hundred or even fifty years ago." He shook his head. "We've got a thousand times the technology and materials science that they did, but sometimes you just can't imitate it."

Walking back to his office, Glen lamented the difficulty of training people in restoration. "You can't teach this in six months, five years or even ten," he said. "You have to love the material, and understand a time past." We stepped into his cozy office, which was cluttered with catalogs, paperwork, and small pieces of decorative metal. I blinked at a flash of sunlight that shot through large windows overlooking the watery expanse of the Forebay, the dam, and falls beyond. Shimmering water reflected the rays on the buildings and a few nearby trees.

He took in the view. "I'd like to be able to stay, because this kind of business belongs here. I'm carrying on the metalworking tradition and trying to stay true to the arts and antiques scene happening here. But I don't know," he added, shaking his head. "They won't give me a lease because they want flexibility in restoring the factory. Well, it's hard to grow your business that way. Maybe the developer wants to make this a restaurant, or an upscale boutique, or condos. I'm willing to bend, but there should be some space. Some people say the Collins Company went out because the directors lost sight of the company's strengths. What good would it do to restore the buildings and then lose the working tradition here?"

Music Everywhere

The city is built
To music, therefore never built at all,
And therefore built forever.
—Alfred, Lord Tennyson,
The Idylls of the King

      Arriving home from the firehouse one midnight a few years back, I pulled into my driveway, nerves jangling. Exhausted, I wanted nothing more than to crawl into bed and fade away, but there was no going to sleep. I was returning from the scene of a car wreck and I could not rid my mind of the image of a swollen, bloody face framed by twisted metal and shattered glass. I turned off the ignition, got out, and slammed the door. The sound echoed in the still night. The early summer air was warm and moist and vaguely scented with lilies that were blooming in the garden.

      The quiet was suddenly shattered by booming drums and guitar chords pouring into the dark from the Fireplace, a ramshackle bar three doors and a street crossing away. The wail of blues harmonica somehow drowned out the sirens that had been echoing in my head, and with them the sound of sheet metal being twisted and pulled by the Hurst Tool and the tinkle of safety glass falling to the pavement. I turned around and followed this new siren song.

The Fireplace is no fern bar; it's unlikely that even the most hardy plant could survive the nightly haze of cigarette smoke that fills the place. It is proudly and unapologetically a "joint." Built as a home in the late nineteenth century, it appears in old photographs as an elegant structure with delicate moldings and a handsome entryway. Later it housed a jewelry store and other small commercial enterprises. Today, a bulging, boxy addition with wide strips of aluminum siding, featureless doors, and smudged picture windows squats in front of the original structure. Paint peeling, at times it seems the building is rapidly reverting to its original elements, a reminder of the dark days when the Collins Company closed. But its condition is a welcome bulwark against the village's growing gentrification. As long as the Fireplace remains, Collinsville will retain some of its beloved rough edges.

The band had just finished a number as I entered the dim rectangular room through a billowing cloud of smoke. I walked past them as they adjusted amplifiers and tuned instruments near the pool table, and made my way to the bar through the milling crowd absorbed in laughter, conversation, and elbow bending. I ordered a Rolling Rock longneck from Bill, the proprietor. He's a fairly soft-spoken man with a graying beard, his thinning hair drawn together in a small ponytail. He doesn't always warm to strangers right away, but he's got a big heart and once you get to know him he'll spin you a yarn or two.

As I turned to face the band, they started up with a series of bluesy riffs. A televised soccer match flickering above the bar was quickly forgotten and all but a few conversations died. Dancing erupted. The crowd shouted out choruses between swigs of beer. The entire packed room vibrated with the music—both the people and the place. We were not so much an audience as part of an event. I thought of Tom Wolfe's observation about Kesey's acid-test house band, the Grateful Dead—that in the moment the place, people, and music merged and became an organism. The place fit like a pair of old, frayed jeans. The bar throbbed and became the perfect conveyance for the band's sound: a little rough, a little down-and-out. The disturbing images of the crash I'd left an hour earlier had not disappeared as much as they'd been subsumed in the music.

About half the crowd was from the neighborhood, and they ran the gamut—friends who lived on my block, business owners, a painter, a potter, and the vaguely familiar people from the area who hung out down at the coffee shop or did their banking next door at the Collinsville Savings Society. Saturday night Fireplace regulars mingled with people who had never crossed the threshold before. Men and women, truck drivers and lawyers, twentysomethings to sixtysomethings bumped against each other, lost in the music. In that moment we were all together in space, time, and outlook. We were Collinsville.

Most of the band lived not more than a five-minute walk from the bar. Rob, the heavy-set singer who had performed for our block parties, had a house around the corner from me, and our sons occasionally played together. Belushi-like in his dark glasses and black tee shirt, he bellowed out the lyrics to "Route 66" with facial expressions to match. Andy, the wiry guitarist, rented an apartment across the street from the bar. The tall, bespectacled keyboard player, Mark, who had long made his living with a rock band, lived up the hill. The drummer and bass player also lived nearby, and were often seen on the streets of the village. Late in the evening, Erin belted out a few numbers in a clear, powerful voice that belied her small frame. She had been a teller at the bank when I first met her, though she was currently working at a saddle shop down in the factory.

The music was still playing in my mind and resonating in my body later as I walked home in the early-morning darkness, and I wondered whether the spontaneity and sheer electricity of that evening would ever be repeated. I was sure it could not. But there would be other memorable evenings in the bar, and folk music at Gertrude and Alice's, and the Friday open-mike night at LaSalle. I would discover music wherever I turned in the village, in forms and in venues I never expected.

The next morning I was groggy and spaced out, hungover more from lack of sleep and the frenzied expenditure of energy at the Fireplace than from the beers I'd downed. Despite the late night and the welcome prospect of a lazy Sunday, I'd risen early as usual while the family slept. I made myself a cup of tea and ventured out into the cool dewy morning to pull the weeds that had started to overtake my Shasta daisies and bachelor buttons. On my knees, contentedly digging out the plantain and clover, I listened to the electronic carillon chiming from the steeple of the Congregational church. Cat Stevens's "Morning has Broken" and Beethoven's "Ode to Joy" were an arresting counterpoint to the raucous tunes still ringing in my ears. I began humming, and once again, I was caught up in a seemingly perfect moment. There was something there that I'd not heard before. The synthesized concert ended with the church's own bell, the one Samuel Collins himself had heard tolling. I spotted parishioners on their way to morning service: seventysomething Dennis hurrying down the steps of the Valley House and up the sidewalk, headed toward his pew, followed fast by a couple of young girls in soft print dresses.

I turned with renewed enthusiasm to the garden. The soil was dankly fragrant, and bees hummed around me, and the nodding blue and yellow columbine seemed a fitting subject for a still life in oils. As if on cue, church organ music came wafting across The Green as it has on summer Sunday mornings for over a century and a half. Though such ecclesiastical chords are not a part of my background, I found inspiration in the echoing sounds of devotion and joy.

Faith should not lapse at the church door, and in a like manner my day with music did not end when the service drew to a close and congregants filed away. The family awoke. Sarah joined me in the vegetable patch, battling cutworms in the squash and cabbage moths around the broccoli while the kids climbed on the swing set. Josh was dressed as a knight, complete with plastic sword, helmet, and breastplate, and shouted his intent to save Rebekah, an unwilling damsel in distress. After tossing a Frisbee with them for a while, Sarah scrambled eggs and buttered some toast for brunch. We all sat on the terrace awash in the garden's splashes of blue, yellow, and white, taking in the leaf shapes and shades of green even as I fretted over all the weeding, staking, and trimming that remained.

Though a table enlivened by two young children has less dead air than a well-run radio station, I somehow managed to hear a sound rising and falling on the breeze—rhythmic, harmonious, more sustained than the songs of the cardinals and mockingbirds that had been the morning's accompaniment. I realized that it was fragments of a classical composition, and figured at first that somebody must have a dial tuned to public radio. Sarah heard it too and momentarily turned her attention from the children. We looked at each other and both uttered a single word: "Max."

Arpeggios cascaded into our yard from the big gray barn just up the hill. The sound faded and vigorously returned, by degrees as light as a popular song and as tempestuous as a summer thunderstorm. I pictured Max's long frame bent over the baby grand that he had shipped from his mother's house in Melbourne to the converted barn he and Walter shared. Max, too, had been at the Fireplace the previous night, and during a break in the music he'd mentioned that he was working on the Khachaturian Piano Concerto. It was a difficult piece to master, even for him with his long and well-trained fingers, and required many tedious hours of practice. Music was his joy, but artistry, he told me, involved more sweat than revelation. Though Sarah and I had thrilled to many impromptu backyard concerts, we rarely thanked him. He was always embarrassed by mistakes we could never detect, but we knew that he knew we were listening, and I secretly hoped that the presence of a small but appreciative audience helped.

There is nothing extraordinary about the music one hears in Collinsville. No renown artist has lived here; no official State Troubadour has been chosen from among our ranks. We are neither Sinatra's Hoboken nor Dylan's Hibbing. There just seem to be, now and again, a surprising number of folks willing to get together and play for fun or a few dollars. Sometimes the venue is a neighbor's lawn; sometimes it's the Fireplace, LaSalle, the coffee shop, or a grand space down at the factory. Collinsville is not atypical in this regard: there is always some kind of music wherever there are people.

Nowhere is this more apparent than among our neighbors. One door to our north live Rich and his wife Barb, who is a violinist with the Hartford Symphony. David is a public health official who strums guitar at his home on South Street, and occasionally gigs with a band. Other neighbors play piano, pluck at an autoharp, sing, or occasionally pick up a brass instrument: They just need some sign of neighborhood interest to draw them out and embolden them to play. And there are always the sounds of children dutifully practicing flute, clarinet, trumpet, drums, or violin. It all starts out rough of course, but a patient if somewhat reluctant audience will come to listen sympathetically and be rewarded as the children progress from ineptitude to competency and sometimes to mastery. From our south side Ruth and Deb have both gone off to college, but the strains of their piano, flute, and clarinet playing were for many years a pleasant soundtrack to summer yard work and evening meals on the terrace.

Music is in fact a Collinsville tradition, its grace notes attuned to our history. The Collins Company itself sponsored a band for many years. Ruth and Deb grew up in the former home of Harriet Flint, a music teacher and choir director who spent half a century as the church organist. She appears serious but kindly in photographs taken a few years before her death in 1930, an old woman with spectacles and neatly trimmed gray hair who would no doubt have enjoyed teaching the girls. James Spencer, her blind predecessor, once lived around the corner on Main Street. A regional ensemble, the Farmington Valley Band, had its origins in the village. Singer-songwriter Bruce Pratt, several albums to his credit, grew up here, and Collinsville's Memorial Day Parade inspired his best-known song, a tribute to the unknown soldier.

At the close of the 1990s there were in fact so many local musicians that the Collinsville Music Collective was formed to develop and promote music and performing arts in the village. Despite the frustrations of organizing and fund raising, the group spent many late nights practicing and polishing music for a CD, leaving "a record of songs from a time when new and old friendships were blossoming here in Collinsville," according to the liner notes. Wildly eclectic, the disc melded ballads, garage rock, blues, R&B, funk, and psychedelia. Songs penned by local residents Erin Berry, Ed Case, Bill Ihne, and Mark Mercier were played by both the writers themselves and other denizens of Collinsville. The CD was called *Our Big Idea*, and its cover featured a drawing of a couple of spark plugs embedded in a human brain set within an electrified capsule. The group's photo was taken at a factory canal railing with the old polishing shop in the background. The community gobbled up the CD and the collective donated its profits to the high school music program.

But sadly, within a few years the group became inactive, and music was less common on the streets of the village. There were the seemingly inevitable creative disputes, and some people moved away. Erin went to New York to study fashion design, and one of the leaders left for Argentina. Professional musicians turned to other projects, leaving the lawyers, accountants, and shop workers to enjoy their weekends and nights playing free from the hassle of putting together a recording. The sound grew even less audible when Gertrude and Alice's closed, the lease a casualty of disagreements between the parties to the sale of the factory property. And like a final sad coda, Max died of a brain tumor.

True to the intangible quality of the medium, a community's musical flowering is often fleeting, whether in the Beatles' Liverpool, or the Grateful Dead's San Francisco, or in nearby Danbury, where Charles Ives juggled selling insurance with composing. But the sweet sounds remain even though the collective has disbanded. I hear them at LaSalle on open-mike night or at an occasional gig at the Fireplace; now and then as a band blares away in the factory or the church choir raises its voice; in the sounds of children practicing and neighbors playing that echo from homes and backyards. Music is here as it is everywhere. Listen.

Life as Art, Art as Life

Once found it is hard to imagine living
without the company of artisans.
—Kathleen Hirsch,
A Home in the Heart of a City

Before its untimely closure, I typically repaired to the coffee shop with one or both of the children late on Sunday afternoons during the colder months and on rainy summer days. We'd sit at one of the small tables with steaming cups of cocoa or coffee and play cards—the basic game of war when they were little, and then go fish, crazy eights, hearts, rummy, or even poker as they grew older. In this way Bekah and Josh got a jump on their arithmetic and learned about patterns. For an hour or two we'd watch neighbors and strangers come and go, indulging in cookies and pieces of candy while we drank up equal measures of cocoa and the gentle hum of conversation and the aromas of food and coffee.

There were rotating exhibits of watercolors, oils, acrylics, and photographs by local artists in the cozy confines of the old freight station that housed Gertrude and Alice's Coffee Bar and Bookstore for the better part of a decade. The shelves were filled with novels, plays, short stories, and imaginative nonfiction. Locally made glassware, pottery, and sculpture in clay and metal sat alongside the books. Some pieces were abstract and whimsical, while others, mugs and teapots mostly, were more practical.

Attracted by bright colors or an offbeat rendering of a familiar object, the children sometimes paused during a lull in a game to examine a still life with a knife and pear or a bunch of asparagus: "Dad, why would anyone want to paint a picture of a vegetable?" They scrutinized landscapes with practical sense: "Dad, how come the waterfall looks like it's flowing up hill?" But they found portraits most interesting: "Dad, how come those people have blue and purple faces?" Such questions were so simple and logical that I found them difficult to answer, abstract notions being no match for the common sense of grade-schoolers.

Gertrude and Alice's was itself a work of art, the creation of Lilias and Elaine, who were inspired by the 1920s-era Paris salons of Gertrude Stein and Alice B. Toklas. In the 1990s, Collinsville's as-yet-unknown painters, writers, musicians, poets, actors, and artisans supported each other much as their Jazz Age counterparts had at the Toklas and Stein gatherings. Even during regular coffee shop business hours it was not uncommon to spy someone in a corner sketching or jotting notes for a novel while the regular crowd talked about a home repair project or the foibles of a mother-in-law. The place was a simmering stockpot of the creative and the mundane.

On a day of frigid wind-driven snow in 1997 Bekah was adding points to our cumulative crazy eights score, which after more than a year of play had grown into the thousands. Over the rim of my coffee mug I spotted a dark, elongated, and serrated object atop the glass-doored refrigerator filled with orderly rows of soft drink bottles. On closer inspection I saw that the mysterious object was a series of small rusted and battered hatchet heads welded together to form a stegosaurus about two feet in length. The head, body, tail, and legs were entirely of Collins products. Aware of my growing fascination, Elaine walked over with a smile. "Amazing, isn't it," she said. "Everything was salvaged from one of the canals when they drained the water for repairs." Amazing, yes. To this day it remains one of the most perfect works of art I've ever seen—not for its beauty or technical facility, certainly, but because of the way it expresses the genius of this place. The practical art of axe manufacture, of metallurgy and the forge, was transformed into sculpture: Product seconds, tossed into a canal because they were not good enough for cutting campfire wood or roof shingles, were reborn in their battered and corroded state as objets d'art.

On another occasion, an unusually warm November evening during the mid-1990s, I was wandering through the maze of factory buildings, moving in and out of the shadows, puffing on a meerschaum pipe clenched between my teeth. The air was still, and in the quiet I was drawn toward the falls, intrigued by their blustery sound on a windless evening. As I reached the old polishing shop I noticed a light coming from an open doorway and found Ken Carder hard at work as I poked my head inside. Ken was a glassmaker whose work I'd seen in a couple of local galleries. We'd had a few short conversations on the street and waiting in line at LaSalle. It was late, and each of us was a bit startled to see the other.

"This your studio?" I asked him, his spectacles and strawberry blond hair lit by the shop's glow.

His grin was welcoming, and I felt like an old friend. "Heart and soul of it all," he drawled. "It's more factory than studio. Guess that fits this place."

Ken had been out escaping the heat of his propane-fueled glass forge. The large high-ceilinged room was cluttered with strange tools for shaping glass and the long steel poles on which the molten material was wound. There were grinding and polishing machines as well, and all about was a jumble of glass shards, half-made projects, finished pieces, and work that would never be completed. His scattered inventory ran the gamut: heads, trout, clowns, and abstract shapes in colors that seemed peculiar to this place. Some were light and fragile, others as heavy and substantial as stone. Ken described the technique by which each piece was formed—the painstaking heating, reheating, cooling, grinding, and mixing. The best pieces, he said, were accidents left over from other intents.

He showed me three sculptures he'd been up assembling until five the previous morning—eight-foot-tall female figures made of pieces of cracked glass strung together and hung from the ceiling. Their heads and bodies were as oddly formed and strangely colored as anything imagined by Picasso, their facial expressions contorted and their body language at once seductive and repellant.

The night went as quickly as it went late. We talked through a range of subjects: baseball, the tedium of producing works of art, first snowfalls, and the toxicity of certain color-producing materials like cadmium. Ken dipped a pole into a vat of molten glass, twirled it gently, and slipped it into an opening in the brightly lit furnace. The conversation continued on to music, presidential politics, factory rents, and how the quiet of woods nearby were ideal for walking and thinking.

After that first visit I spent many nights in Ken's studio until, having tapped into Collinsville's energy for a few years, he departed for new opportunities down south. "This place is happening," he told me in one of our last conversations before he left, "and we've got to ride it out. Creativity comes in unexpected phases. The scene will grow or contract, but as long as the basic energy is here it will always bloom again."

While Ken worked in the lower part of the factory complex, John Squier, an easy-going sort, created a studio and gallery in a Main Street storefront which had over the years sold clothes and auto parts. He covered the walls of the nine-hundred-square-foot space with cartoon-like drawings of potato sack labels whose brand names bore subtle puns: "Shoot the Moon Potatoes" showed a man with a large gun aimed at the moon; "Square Dance Potatoes" portrayed two boxes dancing; "Rain in Spain Potatoes" depicted a rainstorm over a grounded airplane. These visual punch lines sometimes entertained, and sometimes set you thinking. Taking in hundreds of the ten-inch cartoons simultaneously was a visual kick, like watching endless television images flash by.

John is gregarious, and his presence for over half a dozen years in the center of the commercial district across from Town Hall was just what a staid place needed to invigorate it. The trademark name on his work and gallery, "Jon* Art," became so ingrained that some people call him that. I would often stop when passing by and watch him drawing in the window, at times working as if he were in a trance. Many times he gave Bekah and Josh paper and pencil to draw with, occasionally accompanied by a quick lesson on perspective or shading, when we dropped in for small talk about the weather, or happenings in the village. From his window he could see the comings and goings of Collinsville—lawyers filing deeds at Town Hall, telephone workers grabbing a noon sandwich at LaSalle, kids skateboarding after school—and for a while he kept a diary page for a local newspaper.

Now and then Jon held an opening with new potato drawings, or an exhibition of imaginary postage stamps or pieces that transformed common objects like clocks and cans into playful works of light, colors, and shapes. From his small space chicly black-clad people spilled into the street; some were from out of town, but many others hailed from nearby. Once the show consisted of a series of old LP record jackets transformed by drawing, painting, and pasting. The sultry women on a Johnny Mathis album were overlaid with beards and mustaches; colors and shapes issued from Herb Alpert's trumpet; Frank Sinatra was recast as a gangster. It wasn't just the work of professional artists either: neighbors submitted designs, and their children did too.

Jon closed his storefront studio a year into the new millennium so he could concentrate on building a home nearby. Part of his art became the landscape, but his creative energy continues to permeate the village.

The studio windows of Jon* Art did not stay soaped over for long. Within a few months, two local women opened the Painted Lady, an interior design and painted furniture gallery. Months before, Creative Kitchen and Bath had made its debut in the twin storefront next door. It replaced the Whisk, a caterer, which moved its kosher kitchen into a building out back. David, the proprietor of this new place, lives nearby and frequently stops into LaSalle, and had wanted for some time to move his growing cabinet design and installation business into Collinsville because he feels an affinity with the village's rhythm and characters. It was sad to see Jon's gallery of cartoon art close, but hand-painted furniture, wall hangings, and floor coverings, like cabinet work and catering, continues the legacy of practical artistry emblematic of Collinsville.

Walter, who has worked quietly for decades from his home studio on a sleepy side street, is typical of village artists. His paintings and photographs have appeared in galleries here, in New York, and elsewhere. He's painted abstract acrylics and soft gouaches, large individual canvases and several series of trees and of buildings. His vivid photographs of gardens and landscapes draw from both his travels and from Collinsville. Walter has lived in the village for so long that it's not just the output of his studio that embodies his art. His creative instinct and unerring aesthetic judgment are evident in the practical objects that surround him. His gardens are meticulously designed and cared for, as is the island of flowers he maintains at the road intersection outside his window. Though his home is almost as old as Collinsville itself, the clapboards, shutters, doors, and windows belie their antiquity, and look as perfect as the day they were nailed in place during the Polk administration.

The creative impulse also finds expression in the dramatic arts. During the dog days of 1997 four women talking over cups of coffee began to daydream aloud about a Collinsville performing arts center. The discussion spurred them to action and shortly afterwards the Acts Factory Players was born, just as the town's previous volunteer theater ran short of energy and mounted its last play.

That fall Neil Simon's *Jake's Women* was staged under the old proscenium arch in the little-used town hall auditorium. The performances sold out as friends and neighbors and friends of friends and neighbors flocked to see their fellow citizens on stage. These were not professional actors, but lawyers, nurses, teachers, office workers, students, and shopkeepers, and in that sense performers and members of the audience were as one. After the curtain fell the actors would leave their characters behind and shortly rematerialize on the sidewalk, in a booth at ABC Pizza on River Street, or in Town Hall, going about their daily business.

The Acts Factory Players gave Collinsville folk a chance to explore new things, not least that lifelong nagging suspicion that "I could have been an actor." The repertoire ran as regularly as the seasons: *Return Engagements, Dracula, A Midsummer Night's Dream, Steel Magnolias*. When we had tickets for a performance Sarah and I would make a night of it: dinner out, even if it was only a sandwich or pizza, and a leisurely walk to the theater. During rehearsals I'd occasionally encounter people around town in evening gowns or togas, and catch lines of Shakespeare or a song from a Neil Simon musical. At such times the image of the Town Hall as a stuffy, bureaucratic place weighed down by paperwork and records is turned on its head.

Merry Christmas Mother Goose, an original holiday show for children, lured toddlers and teenagers on stage, testing the patience and straining the voices of the production managers. And December's productions have proved a regular measure of change. We've watched our children grow up in *A Christmas Carol, Christmas on Mount Olympus, Chrismyth,* and *The Knight Before Christmas,* all written and directed by a woman from a near-by town. Josh has been Tiny Tim, an elf, and a jester, Bekah a Cratchit kid and a knight.

A place, like a play, starts with words, and while the earliest writings in the village were such terse business documents as deeds, contracts, and purchase orders, more imaginative works have long played a part as well. As early as the late 1850s the *Collinsville Star* (subtitled *An Independent Family Paper of Literature and News*) published front-page fiction in the midst of ads for clothing and groceries. There were moralistic tales like "Nelly, the Rag Picker," a brief account of a society woman who led a secret life as a beggar. Also featured were instructive and satirical poems with titles like "The Devil and the Lawyer," sporting predictable rhymes like "grave" and "knave."

The most notable writer ever associated with the town—Rose Terry Cooke—is obscure today. Remembered by only a handful of people in Collinsville for her poem about the village cemetery, she was well-known for her short stories, poetry, and children's books in the latter part of the nineteenth century. In 1857 she accepted an invitation to pen the first story to appear in the *Atlantic Monthly,* then as now a venue for the nation's literary lions. Her works are devoted mostly to the natural wonders and hardships of rural and small-town New England life, and the jealousies and pettiness of people "retailing some real or unreal story to somebody's disadvantage," as she wrote in her short-story collection *Huckleberries*. I skim through her work occasionally, wondering how life in Collinsville might have informed her words. Cooke knew the village along the river well: she came here to live after the death of her sister, Alice, and raised the two young children left behind as her own. Now, buried on Huckleberry Hill, she rests in the village of the dead she sketched so well in verse.

Given an opportunity, nowadays Collinsville people are singularly articulate on paper, especially when they are writing about the village. Though a number of journalists have lived alongside enthusiastic amateur writers over the years, it was not until a cold, drizzly evening in 1998 that a bold if brief flowering of literary effort took hold. A group gathered on the couches and chairs in the cozy book-lined loft of Gertrude and Alice's that night banded together to form the Collinsville Writers' Collective. After a few workshop sessions and a public reading, they produced a small book of poems and short prose. A second volume appeared in the summer of 2000. These published works reflect the diverse concerns of their contributors, from political diatribe to sibling love and rivalry, from the death of a friend to a drive in the car on a brilliant day.

Though the subjects and styles vary widely, all of the pieces spring from the shared sense of connection to Collinsville. Constance MacDonald submitted an ode to the bank, where

> tellers hand record entries in passbooks made from
> Blue pressed paper
> Deposits and withdrawals in blue
> Interest in red

Kenton McCoy, an architect, contributed an elegy to our beloved neighbor, Max, soon after his death, in graceful words recalling an evening walk the two had taken full of poetry, music, and warm comradeship with "the snow so new and satin." Annie Barret captured the creative spark of another villager by watching her walk, observing that when she raises her arm "you see stars balanced on her fingertips." And Siegfried Haug wrote that in "that little train station, I first let go and soared beyond all previous reaches," as he described the coffee shop.

The creative impulse of most communities reaches well beyond "art" and professionals, and the more I get to know my neighbors the more I am in awe of their artistic endeavors. I know a landscape architect who makes exotic soaps, a school teacher who grows flowers to create dried arrangements, an antiques dealer who weaves exquisite baskets. Shade-tree mechanics, basement woodworkers, and late-night clothing and jewelry designers abound, workaday Clark Kents whose creative passion is their strength, who aren't bereft without their jobs.

The business of many in Collinsville today is infused with the same impulse as the mechanics and metalworkers who brought the creative essence of art to the task of making axes and machetes. Michael practices "holistic law," attempting to understand the spiritual needs of his divorce and personal-injury clients and thereby replace adversarial relationships with mediated solutions. Roger, a transplanted Brit with an empathetic face, applies his architectural skills to heal historic structures and put old forms to work in the present. Sarah interests her cool, laid-back biology students by bringing a lizard, or a lecturer who has traveled the world eating termites and other insects, into the classroom. Scores of other people—production-line workers, car mechanics, fire and building inspectors, financial planners, and nurses among them—are equally inspired in their work. Perhaps the presence of traditional arts and crafts in Collinsville helps us bring this spirit to mundane tasks, but the possibility of living and of seeing life as art exists everywhere. As with so many hidden wonders that sit in our midst—music, and buildings, and street-bound gardens, and the stories writ in tombstones—all that is usually lacking is an awareness of what surrounds us, and the courage to share our discoveries with others.

Government by People

*We do not say that a person who takes
no interest in politics is one who minds
his own business; we say that he has
no business here at all.*
—*Pericles*, Funeral Oration

Days of the Elect

You feel part of a community if you are part of a community. That is, you may reside anywhere and be counted in the census, but until you participate in some measure you do not truly live in that place. Like the revolution, community life will not be televised, cannot be read about in the newspaper, and is not visible from the bleachers. Your home may be set in an intriguing landscape of natural beauty, among handsome buildings where history runs deep and artists find inspiration, but it might as well be on a Hollywood back lot or in Mr. Rogers' Neighborhood unless you share in shaping its future. Explore a place and know it. Know a place well enough and it will grow in your affection, and seduce you to become involved.

Living within view of Town Hall, our household is gripped by more than the usual election-day anticipation. From the time polls open at six in the morning cars pull up on The Green and along Main Street. The village bustles with people rushing to vote, and from our porch we watch the clutch of candidates and their supporters in front of Eaton Hardware, doing their last-minute electioneering at the legally stipulated limit of seventy-five feet from the polls. Each car door slamming indicates another vote, and we approximate the turnout by how often vehicles park in front of our house. In particularly close elections we glance out the window and speculate on the outcome by an informal tally of Republicans and Democrats, elderly and young, and Collinsville and North Canton residents.

From the time they were chubby-cheeked babies being squeezed and kissed by first selectman, state senate, and school board candidates, the children have accompanied us on our way to the voting booth. Most kids love races and contests, and since they were old enough to play tag ours have been intrigued that the activity outside our house involves a competition. Elections have provoked dinner-table questions about winners and losers, personalities, and ideas. When Josh and Bekah became old enough to notice presidents and mayors on television, election day gained in gravity, and with the discovery of cliques in school they began to understand politics. Though the hip irony of adolescence now has Bekah in its grip, and tagging along with Mom and Dad is no longer cool, uncertainties about who to vote for and what the candidates will do still stirs endless questions. All the coming and going on the street remains a civic temptation, especially when there's a chance of being handed a pencil, pot holder, or chip clip bearing a candidate's name.

On election day we're sure to run into neighbors. We catch up on how the leaf-raking is going, the mischief the frost did in the garden, or the particulars of the kids' schoolwork. At his bike shop near Town Hall, Joe Carter sometimes ladles hot cider from a sidewalk table. Children run the gauntlet of candidates, circling skittishly on skateboards. With the election practically on our doorstep there has always been an element of holiday excitement in our house, palpable as Sarah and I go to work and the children attend school.

This is altogether fitting, since election day is by right a holiday. "Holiday" is a compounding of the words "holy" and "day," and what can be more holy in our national life than voting, the very symbol and basis of all democratic institutions? Not only should government offices and banks be closed, but so too should stores and restaurants, dry cleaners and gas stations, bottlers and electroplaters. The day should be celebrated with parades, patriotic speeches, picnics, and rituals urging people to the polls. Each year election officials fret for weeks over turnout and bemoan the declining number of ballots. We have only ourselves to blame. We set apart time to commemorate the first president's birth and Columbus's landfall on a Caribbean beach but treat the day we choose our leaders like any other. Wouldn't we do better to cheer that grand mechanism which embodies our traditions of self-governance and preserves us from the idolatry of strong personalities? Election day should be given its due as a celebration of a process rather than an event or a person, a fitting tribute to two and a quarter centuries of the peaceful transition of power. And unlike other holidays that merely honor the past, election day places faith in the future.

Most often Sarah and I vote at dinnertime when there is likely to be a long line extending down the hall toward the door. Even if I had the day off I would wait until this, the busiest hour, since the range of people I bump into at Town Hall is as interesting as who is on the ballot. The assembled voters move quickly into the auditorium with its scuffed hardwood floor and brick walls. The proscenium used by the Acts Factory Players is empty and still. Shuffling feet, low conversation, and the mechanical ring of voting-machine levers echo in the gymnasium-like room. Passing the sample ballot displayed on an easel, we arrive at the tables where poll workers sit, lists of voters organized by street in front of them. A familiar person crosses off our names as we ask the obligatory questions about the turnout and the quality of the coffee and donuts that fuel their efforts. I pull the big red lever that closes the curtain as I enter the voting booth and with a deep breath slide down the tabs under candidate names—a simple process for sometimes complex choices. The walk home brims with speculation on the outcome and is punctuated by periodic stops for brief bursts of conversation with neighbors.

Perhaps we don't value our franchise as much as we should because it doesn't come at a price. It's too cheap, requiring the nuisance of registration but no real cost. I often think that we should pay for the right to vote with a commitment to actually participate in our participatory democracy, to gain ownership by being involved. Many of our nation's founders believed that owning property was a prerequisite to responsible voting. Living in Collinsville has convinced me that they were mistaken merely in the character of the connection. It is not title to land that gives a people a stake in their community, but rather a willingness to volunteer time and effort for the common good.

Each local election day the names on the ballot—selectmen and finance and education board members—remind me of how essential our time and participation is to our way of life. Only those who are actively involved realize the extent to which their local government is influenced by ordinary citizens, and not a faceless bureaucracy of professional politicians and paid consultants. The people who make a community work are not just those sitting on the school board, zoning commission, or water pollution control authority. One need not be anointed at the ballot box, nor appointed by the selectmen: Chances to volunteer are everywhere.

I ran across enough opportunities to fill several lifetimes on a short bicycle ride around town last October . Coasting out of the driveway, I spotted Babe and her sisters planting mums on the north triangle of The Green, beautifying the village out of their own pockets as they have for many years. Denis, a genial man in his seventies who is hard-of-hearing from years in the Collins forge shop, was across the street sweeping the sidewalk in front of the Valley House. A couple of peddle spins down Main Street I waved to Dr. Carlton, standing on the historical museum balcony in his top hat. One of many docents who take visitors on tours through time in this vast attic of our past, his gentlemanly demeanor in and of itself recalls an age gone by.

Taking the bike trail east, Bridge Street on one side and the river on the other, I looked across the mill pond where a breeze whipped up the water, disturbing the placid surface that mirrored the clouds. This trail came about largely through the agitation, fund-raising, and planning of energetic citizens. The shore was litter-free, cleaned up by Farmington River Watershed

Association volunteers. Across the street a cannon from the Great War sits perched on a grassy little triangle that is beautifully maintained by the American Legion, whose members are the prime movers behind the Memorial Day parade. Bridge Street, lined with historic properties, is now a state scenic road due to the efforts of neighbors and the Collinsville Historic District Commission. I continued on, following the river, and passed the firehouse where the trucks, polished to perfection by the volunteer brigade, are visible through glass doors. Another group of civic-minded citizens, the Cawasa Grange, had recently purchased thermal-imaging devices for the firefighters to help them make their way through smoke-filled rooms. Along the river opposite the firehouse, in a park by the sewage treatment plant, the Lions Club holds an annual flea market to raise money for the blind, a children's fishing derby, and other charitable events. Beyond the park and river is the rugged slope of Sweetheart Mountain, preserved by land-trust volunteers.

Five minutes later I was in front of steep-roofed Trinity Church, where Bekah and Josh once attended a nursery school that parents help run. Getting off my bike, my legs somewhat rubbery from the ride, I dropped off a few canned goods for the food bank managed by Charlotte, a gentle older woman who has donated property to the land trust. I peddled another mile, following the Farmington upstream until I was beside a large field owned by the fire department that sits along the river. Several kids' soccer games were underway, sponsored by the members of the Canton Youth Soccer Association, who donate their time to coach, referee, and take care of the league's paperwork. Some of them go out of their way to buy trophies with money out of their own pockets, or give the players a pizza party at season's end to reward a job well done. I rested for a bit, prompted to move along only after a nine-year-old girl, kicking dead center above the goalie's head, got a hard-won score.

On my ride back toward the village I stopped at the new library, which was partially built and furnished with funds raised by the friends group that for many years was responsible for its operation. Across the street is the intermediate school, where the PTA's fund-raising has supported the field trips Bekah and her classmates take to museums and the ballet, as well as visiting musical performances and a week of nature education at a camp.

My impromptu survey of Collinsville's volunteer efforts continued on, due east past the home of Josh's first scout leader, around the parking lot at Mills Pond Park to the field where local folks patiently coached he and his fellow T-ballers, prompted solely by the love of the game. Just beyond is the wading pool that Sarah and her compatriots from Friends of Canton Park and Recreation built, having cobbled together grant applications and community donations. Far across the sloping lawn sits an abstract sculpture with images of fish and machine parts. Donated by the Creative Arts Council, it embodies the human and natural energies of the town. As I rode home I passed the houses of zoning and planning commissioners, selectmen, school board and inland wetland agency members, Girl Scout and church choir leaders. I'd cycled only four miles, but had mentally tallied tens of thousands of cumulative hours of volunteer effort—so much time given that had I pedaled the equivalent number of miles I'd have circled the world, and then some.

Though this brief ride might suggest we have volunteers aplenty, there is a great deal of work to keeping a community going, and volunteer organizations are chronically short of people and money. As Donald Connery observed in another small Connecticut town thirty years ago:

> Some people, of course, seem to do everything. They make up for those who do nothing. There are certain individuals, and even whole families, who can always be relied on to take minutes, bring flowers, recruit members, collect money, speak up at the PTA, boil hot dogs at a Community House fair, bake a casserole for the church supper, drive young people to a youth conference and call on the old lady who has not been seen in the village lately. The busier they are, the more they seem able to take on and the more they are asked to do. For all the complaining that people do about the way the welfare state is wiping out individual initiative and effort, there appears to be more demand than ever for volunteer services.

Perhaps that government governs best which fosters volunteerism most. Well-focused volunteerism not only makes communities better places to live, with more competitive schools and greener, cleaner public places—it saves vast sums of money in essential services, from fire fighting to overseeing sewage treatment plants. "No man is integral within himself," professed the first charter of Longmont, Colorado, in the late 1860s. "We are all parts of one grand community, and it behooves every man to know what his neighbor is about." Maybe these words, or something much like them, ought to be part of every constitution and town creed, set in the minds of the inhabitants and carved in stone on their public buildings. No one has any business just minding his or her own business. We learn more about our neighbors from how they spend their time than we do from how they spend their money, and the quality of a community can be measured by the degree to which volunteers are welcome.

In a small community perhaps the easiest way to volunteer is to attend the town meeting—if you can locate the finely printed notice or read a sign that can barely be scanned at the posted speed limit. Everyone has a voice here, and there is no long-term commitment: the meeting ends and you're done. These gatherings are often lyrically described as fountains of democracy, and just as frequently sharply condemned as anachronisms, where the minority opinion is squashed and decisions are skewed by the few noisy people who are either free or are able to break away from busy schedules. Both are true: Decision-making power is palpable, and a heated debate can forge or fragment a community. Though we frequently criticize politicians, when we make decisions ourselves we often realize, in sober terms, the delicate balancing of competing interests that they must master. There is something salutary in exposure to a wide range of vehemently conflicting opinions, and in the heartfelt airing of views we find ourselves akin to a family. As townspeople we agree on most things, so much so that votes are often unanimous, or very nearly. But disagreements can be bitter as a blood feud, and born of the same causes—money and appearances.

At a typical town meeting not long ago, the moderator gathered us to order. The town clerk read the call. A routine and reassuring parliamentary civility pervaded the hall as men in suits and flannel shirts and women in dresses and jeans gathered after a long day and a rushed dinner to discuss the budget. But the calm was deceptive, especially since taxes were the main topic for discussion.

The chairman of the finance board stood to summarize the numbers. A middle-aged man with a receding hairline, he thanked his colleagues for their long hours and described their battle to deal with inflation in utilities and teacher salaries, and how they trimmed the cost of a fire truck and deferred maintenance on the town garage. He explained these fiscal measures by pointing to pie charts with cost and revenue centers, occasionally gesturing toward the bar graph illustrating area mill rates.

Presentation done, the moderator asked if anybody had a question. A score of hands shot up among the hundred people seated in the high school auditorium, where a student production of *Fiddler on the Roof* had recently drawn many more people. Advising speakers to state their names and addresses, the moderator recognized a twentysomething man with a crew cut and diamond ear stud who wanted to know just what repairs were being deferred on town buildings. As a contractor, he pointed out, he knew that "putting off short-term fixes can cost big time in the future." The moderator asked the first selectman to respond. With words like "priorities," "weather tight," and "code violation" she elicited sympathetic nods from the questioner.

After a few inquiries about the number of catch basins and the price of textbooks, a big man with a florid face got up. The moderator soon interrupted the man's tightly wound speech about the cost of special education and the easy life of teachers to ask his name and address. The man looked dumbfounded. "Everyone knows me," he said belligerently. "I've lived here all my life." A titter of laughter rippled through the crowd. After a bit of verbal wrangling the man gave his name, "though it really doesn't make sense since they all know me better than you." He wanted to "get to the bottom of these outrageous school administrator salaries approaching six figures." After a long few minutes the moderator interrupted, asking if he wanted to pose a question to the school superintendent. "You don't expect him to say he's overpaid," the man snorted in disgust as he sat down. "We're the bosses," someone else shouted angrily from the crowd. "What kind of place is this where the employees make more than the bosses?" Thunderous applause. The moderator called for order.

An assortment of parents with kids in school stood up in defense of the school administrator: "experience," "years of graduate school," "long hours," "responsibility," "competitive salaries" was their mantra. Occasionally a chortle of disagreement erupted, but fierce looks from the moderator put a quick end to it.

Pleas were made to protect elderly people on fixed incomes. A firefighter questioned the sinking-fund cut that would delay the purchase of a new truck. "Young families won't be able to live here if taxes keep skyrocketing," a fiftysomething woman in a print dress loudly advised the crowd. "They sure won't come if we don't buy school computers," was the sharp retort from the seats. An undercurrent of agitated conversation rose from the audience. "I can't hear the speakers," a woman shouted. The moderator called for order. Respect for Robert's Rules goes only so deep, and the room was getting warm.

With both hands grasping the back of the chair in front of him, an elderly man with a thick European accent rose to ask about the steep liability insurance increases. On a nod from the moderator, the head of the insurance committee explained in a nasal tone that the figure was a high estimate because not all the bids were finalized. Before he'd finished his explanation he was forcefully interrupted by the old man, whose frail frame belied a powerful voice: "That's the way they used to do it under the communists. Never give you the facts!" Light applause greeted this pronouncement. The old man sat. A young woman beside me suggested he go back where he came from. People shifted uncomfortably in their seats. A former first selectman demanded to know where all the money was going. Before the finance board chairman could respond, someone in the back yelled, "You ought to know. You spent plenty in your day!" Laughter erupted, and some of the tension faded.

Most of the audience did not speak as the meeting wound on, but functioned rather like a Greek chorus, collectively murmuring hushed sounds of approval and disapproval. The explanations that the politicians offered for the complex problems at hand often fell on deaf ears—those who weren't swayed by the arguments and those who simply refused to listen at all. Many people grew frustrated with windy explanations that drifted far from the original question. It's hard not to take certain votes or statements personally, especially in such close quarters.

Round upon round of town meetings on routine subjects undercut their value, ignore government's complex realities, and test the limits of citizen commitment: Daily operating business clearly cannot be left to after-dinner legislators. But those subjects, however trivial, that define the character of a community—such as who should be responsible for clearing sidewalk snow, or whether a town should collect trash or maintain a transfer station, or if sewers should be expanded in the interest of development—deserve a face-to-face airing even if the ultimate decision is made by referendum. Public discussions and debate infuse a community with vigor, and prompt people to get to know their neighbors and grasp the diversity of viewpoints that complicate and enrich a democratic society. At a town meeting about leaf collection I was struck by the amazement of a woman who had never realized that those of us living on small village lots didn't have the option of raking our leaves into the woods. I was once similarly taken aback when I realized that while I was willing to be a good citizen and clear my sidewalk of snow, others might be less inclined to do so, *not* because they lacked public spirit but because there was no place to pile the stuff where they lived, or huge hardened mounds pushed up by plows sat where they had to shovel.

At their best, town meetings have the power to draw people in from the margin to active participation. Large cities might well take the lesson and so foster public debate on a few select issues, with simultaneous meetings at the precinct level to ensure manageable discussions. If town meetings don't draw well in this age of distractions, perhaps we ought market them and provide incentives, just as we do for everything else that vies for our attention. Better advertising; refreshments; a break on taxes for voting at a certain number of meetings; local businesses coupons—these and other possibilities might rekindle an interested in community involvement. Town meetings might not always arrive at the right decisions, but they do truly give us the government we deserve.

There is no magic to a sense of community. It's not an old-fashioned concept that has gone out of style, archaic as horsehair plaster, to be replaced with something more modern and efficient. It is timeless, and stems from the interactions of neighbors and citizens. In essence, communities belong to those who participate.

Voting does not just occur on the second Tuesday of November each year. We vote every day with our commitment of time, and our involvement does not have to be public or formal. There's no limit to what one person can do: design a neighborhood web site, or give a Halloween party for kids, or form a walking group, or organize a project like planting flowers in a park or cleaning up a vacant lot. Throw a pot luck dinner, or start a neighborhood association that sponsors street cleanups, plantings, car repair classes, tag sales, or home tours. Establish a book group. If you aren't that gregarious, you can hire local kids for odd jobs. Get out to a zoning commission meeting, help raise dollars for the PTA, check off names at the polls, vote at a town meeting. If you're not cut out to be a firefighter, help with the annual carnival, or take on a task for the Halloween parade, or teach Cub Scouts a skill.

Ours is the fault if we have no connection to our government, no relationship with our neighbors, nothing of interest nearby, and no place to walk. We get the communities we work for.

Notions of civic responsibility may sound sentimental or ponderous, and the concept of duty highfalutin or anachronistic, but when all is said and done there are practical reasons to be involved in the places we live. Sociologist Robert Putnam finds that "where civic engagement in community affairs in general is high, teachers report higher levels of parental support and lower levels of student misbehavior," principally because students are more engaged. Community connectedness also correlates with higher property values, and volunteerism more accurately predicts philanthropy than does wealth. In the final analysis, Putnam notes that "the more integrated we are with our community, the less likely we are to experience colds, heart attacks, strokes, cancer, depression, and premature death of all sorts." A point indeed to ponder, for if our own health is tied to that of our community, and volunteerism is the best prescription, we will be well by doing good.

For the Common Defense

*In the end Americans will get largely
the kind of physical space we demand;
if we don't really want more community,
we won't get it.*
—*Robert D. Putnam,* Bowling Alone

Rumors had leaked for weeks. At first I dismissed them, but their undercurrent had become so strong that by the time I walked into Eaton Hardware on a showery April afternoon, I knew that asking if they were true would confirm my worst fears. It was around closing time, and Richard, burly and bearded, was gathering in the wheelbarrows, ladders, and sacks of fertilizer displayed around the steps and on the sidewalk. Steeling my resolve, I posed the question, my voice low so a passing couple would not be privy to the exchange. He turned toward the shovels he was collecting, muttered something evasive, and told me to ask the owner, Rhett.

The wall of small wooden drawers with their treasures of bolts, washers, and fittings, the shelves of bright paint cans, and the racks of batteries and brushes had drawn me across the threshold of this temple of the practical for seventeen years. But now the familiar squeak of the worn hardwood

Eaton Hardware building, 1999. Tools, fasteners, paints, and chance encounters with neighbors. (Photograph by Walter Kendra)

floor seemed ominous and oppressive, and the small space piled high with useful goods felt claustrophobic. Rhett was at the register, cashing out the day's receipts as I approached him. "Yup, it's true," he answered. "I'm closing the store, first of July. Antique store is moving in."

"This is not as good a place to live as it was a year ago," my neighbor Eric later told me as we grubbed in our yards, hunched opposite each other across the property line. My friend Alan felt odd buying things marked down for clearance. "It's like picking at a corpse," he observed mournfully. Over the next couple of months I watched sadly as goods disappeared from the shelves at 15%, 25%, 50% off. The store slowly lost its sense of vitality, wasting gradually away like a cancer victim, and many of us felt its death struggle. Lost was the opportunity to walk down the street and buy the many last-minute and oddball necessities of life—light bulbs, mason jars, stove reflector dishes. Gone was a place where folks enjoyed chance encounters with neighbors.

The cannons of the Civil War had been silent but two years when people in the area first began stopping into this store for a pound of nails or pieces of stove-pipe. William McKinley was president when Rhett's great-great-grandfather stood behind the counter. The store was a constant through war and depression, and the fact that it lasted from the era of horse and buggy to the time of space stations was a source of pride and comfort to many. Whenever someone needed a paint brush or advice on fixing a crack in a foundation, the hardware was there. But the full weight of that history and the effort needed to sustain it, however glorious for the village, fell squarely on Rhett. No one could blame him for wanting to pursue other interests after decades of long hours spent in the retail trade.

Watching the storefront go from supplying us with practical neighbor-hood necessities to tempting tourists with antiques was hard. Still, it was part of a seemingly inevitable two-decade-long trend, the changes wrought as Collinsville increasingly traded on the past to survive in the present and attracted businesses aligned with artists and craftsmen.

Nevertheless, if Collinsville was diminished by the loss of its hardware store, the blame fell squarely on the residents. The polls may beckon but once a year and town-meeting ballots a few times more, but we cast a vote of confidence with our wallets every day. When we buy a pack of gum, a screwdriver, or a bottle of beer, we engage in a political act. By the goods and services we seek out, we make decisions about our community, and our local purchases are an investment in a way of life. Without Collinsville's small businesses the difference between the village and an ordinary suburb would be lamentably small indeed.

As all my treks through town have taught me, shopping is an opportunity for unplanned encounters, idle conversation, and the exchange of gossip, news, and opinions. Village businesses offer seniors who don't drive the chance to buy a gallon of milk, mail a package, or cash a check with a welcome measure of autonomy. They provide children a rite of passage, fostering that first sense of independence as they bike or walk to a familiar place to can spend their allowances on sweets or small toys. As we get to know our local merchants by name, they in turn come to know the products we prefer—be it a favorite flavor of ice cream, or whether we need black or brass screws for a certain job. This sort of easy recognition gives us a sense of belonging, and in this regard the big box cannot compete. "A small corner store," says the planner Andres Duany, "does more than a social club to build the bonds of community." In minding their shops, merchants give us something of themselves, and remind us that a village is a place where people both live and earn a living.

And earn a living they must. Just as birds and frogs are creatures of the natural landscape, businesses are fixtures of the built environment, with their own ecology and interdependencies. And like sunlight in nature, money must suffuse and flow through the system to sustain its varied niches, from the largest chains to the smallest and most vulnerable mom-and-pop stores. Perhaps if Eaton's balance sheet had been more robust, the hardware would have sold as a going business. If we want vibrant communities, and advocate to preserve historic buildings, and prefer the convenience of not having to drive miles for a loaf of bread, our course is clear. We are all partners in the nearby post office, bank, grocery, hardware, and restaurant, and investing in their future is as easy as mailing a package, buying a box of spaghetti or an apple, cashing a check, purchasing a can of paint, or ordering a hamburger.

Shopping at malls supports quite a different way of life. It's undeniable that they offer a wider range of goods and many items that are no longer available in the center of a small town or at the corner store. They have their place to be sure, but there are far too many of them, and too few alternatives. The high volume of large retail warehouses results in lower prices, though the savings are not as great if one adds in the cost of travel and of time spent. If prices are judged by the measure of value for the money, we must factor in the relative worth of our cordial relationships with shopkeepers and the chance of meeting our neighbors, commodities not so readily available at Home Depot or Wal-Mart. These are worth a premium: how much depends on a person's means and values. But even in more stringent times we can afford a few locally purchased items, although they may be the sorts of goods that are nationally priced and cost the same everywhere. Few among us can afford to buy everything we need at smaller local stores, but if we care about our community, the price of buying nothing there will be even more dear.

There are reminders of this everywhere. In the mid-nineteenth century one could walk down Collinsville's Main Street and satisfy any basic need, from groceries and clothing to medical care and shoe repair. By the time the Collins trip-hammers stopped in 1966, this was no longer possible. The pharmacy had moved to the highway strip, the dry goods stores had closed, and the professionals had fled to larger and newer offices. Collinsville became a backwater, an outdated and depressed village of decrepit storefronts.

As these changes rippled out and Collinsville slid toward becoming a slum of illegal apartments, vacant shops, and red-light zones, local boosters took up the cause of urban renewal. If businesses were leaving Collinsville for shopping centers, the thinking went, then a shopping center would have to be planned and built to attract and keep them. The narrow streets and two- and three-story commercial buildings with their decorative brackets and stone-accented brickwork would have to give way to lots of asphalt parking and low, flat-roofed buildings set with broad sheets of plate glass. There would be new businesses then—maybe a 7-Eleven, a Dunkin' Donuts, the latest outpost of a dry-cleaning chain, or even a small drug store. To some, such development may have been preferable to the decrepit remains of a century past, and boasted the added benefit of new tax revenues and increased property values, but it would have torn the heart out of Collinsville.

My neighbor Jim vividly recalled the bitter urban renewal debate. Neighbors were pitted against each other, and even families were divided. There were arguments on the steps of Eaton Hardware and at the town clerk's office. In hindsight it seems odd that the debate didn't focus on the preservation of the village, but in those days financial considerations and questions about the role of government were the more prominent concerns.

Some thought Collinsville was simply not worth the effort needed to preserve it. At a particularly acrimonious town meeting the advocates of urban renewal lost by the slimmest of margins. Jim admitted that it seemed a major failure to him at the time, a harbinger of decline and decay. There would be more empty stores, more broken glass. "I'd like to say my vote made the difference," he told me on a crisp morning as I stood in my yard leaning on a rake, "but I voted in favor." He watched a few bright yellow leaves fall from my big maple and drift lazily to the ground. "Worst vote I ever cast."

All of this was on my mind the day I learned Eaton was going out of business, and the cool drizzle seemed to match my mood as I stepped out of the store. I frowned at the handsome masonry and clapboard buildings that framed Main Street, knowing that except for Eaton and the bank each had seen a dozen or more businesses come and go over the years. Since before the Collins Company closed, downtown merchants had steadily shied away from meeting the mundane, practical needs of their neighbors. Clothing, auto parts, cosmetics, and now hardware were no longer a short walk away. The stores catered increasingly to out-of-town traffic, the visitors who came to fish or boat or bike along the river, to glimpse a bit of history and perhaps buy something from one of the antique shops to serve as a souvenir of their brief time in town.

Though Eaton's closure was the sure sign of a trend that had been building for half a century, I was not sanguine about the loss. Perhaps the urban planners of Jim's day were right in thinking that independent businesses would have to become more like shopping centers to compete with them. But instead of remaking downtown to resemble the malls, maybe what we needed to do was to take a lesson from the retail management and marketing strategies that make them successful—coordinated management, a strategic mix of businesses, retail continuity, and joint advertising their foremost techniques.

Some in town, lured by the extravagant promises of increased tax revenues, focused their attention on attracting big box retailers to Albany Turnpike with various zoning incentives. In doing so, they were setting existing businesses adrift. Rather than await what seemed inevitable, residents could assert themselves and institute measures to foster small businesses. After all, a group of neighbors had asserted themselves before, creating a historic district when the village's architecture was threatened. Why not do something similar to protect the fragile ecology of small downtown shops? As I started home, my rain jacket drawn up against the chilly mist, I realized that the failed push for urban renewal had left a unique cluster of buildings in which certain niche businesses could find a home. Moreover, the character of these buildings, and the atmosphere they created, could well draw an interesting group of entrepreneurs.

I remembered how crucial the architecture of the village had been in luring me to Collinsville almost two decades earlier, and I knew how much it had also factored in the home-buying decisions of my neighbors and in the location of many stores and offices. I crossed the street and passed the house

5 The Green as seen from Main Street. The Congregational church is to the left. Beauty is often found in the most mundane places. Note the air conditioners fitted into the siding in the building on the right. (Photograph by Walter Kendra)

opposite Eaton where gaping holes had been chainsawed into nineteenth-century walls to accommodate air conditioners in 1985, and glanced across the street at the Plexiglas vestibule that obscured the brick and brownstone entry arch of the bank. I paused momentarily, briefly refreshed by the fine mist on my face. These were the sorts of changes that had proved a call to arms and led to the creation of the historic district. No one wanted to ban air conditioning in offices, or stop the bank from putting up an entryway that would conserve energy and provide handicapped access, but there were cost-effective ways to meet these needs and still maintain a building's integrity.

Punctuated as they were by red-faced shouting from the opposing sides, and with angrily mumbled threats, accusations of creeping communism, and pleas to save the village, meetings regarding the feasibility of the district must have echoed the bitter urban renewal debate of the 1970s. And although more than three quarters of property owners voted for the plan, it remains controversial to this day. Despite the fact that it has approved a home satellite dish, the bank's automatic teller machine, a great many structural additions, and dozens of changes to roofs, chimneys, and windows, the Collinsville Historic District Commission is accused by some of treating the village like a museum diorama. In many ways the district is a sort of philosophical litmus test about the role of government. Some people understandably just want to be left alone, free from the need to seek approval when tinkering with their houses. After all, the appearance of one's home is a very personal matter. On the other hand, the district brings neighbors together to make key decisions affecting the community, something that is often equally personal. It recognizes that in a tightly packed neighborhood we live in relationship both to each other and the built environment.

When I finally got home from the hardware I found a note taped to the refrigerator: Sarah and the children had gone to visit a friend. Restless and distracted over the news about Eaton, and with nothing to hold me at home, I grabbed a wool felt fedora that I reserved for foul weather and ducked out of the house and down The Green toward Spring Street. I somehow sensed that I was on a mission, but its precise object eluded me. Perhaps a stroll around the village would offset the sinking feeling I'd been left with over this loss.

Three houses past the church Spring Street elbows to the left. I walked straight ahead and down to the factory, past a tiny spring house from which water still flows as described in Sam Collins's deed. Just beyond an iron cistern is a long and narrow wooden building that was once used to store steel; it is now the school bus garage. The buses have been there for decades, making good use of the almost two-hundred-foot-long structure. Now there was much talk of it closing up shop as well. Unlike Eaton, the bus company did not want to leave, and it was the neighbors who lived along the path of the daily run, tired of noise and diesel fumes, who were glad that it might go.

This rumored departure, however, was not due to the pressure of nearby residents but to plans for the redevelopment of the factory, about which many neighbors were ambivalent. A developer, Rusty Tilney, had contracted to buy and renovate the axe site for a project he called @COLLINSville. Over an eighteen-month period Tilney had pushed ahead, overseeing the creation of a new industrial heritage overlay zone for historically based mixed-use development, obtaining plan approval, getting the go-ahead for dividing the eighteen-acre property into twenty-one lots, performing a brownfield contamination investigation, and working to change the site's groundwater classification. But—according to Tilney—when it came time to consummate the deal the owner, Barbara Perry, had reneged and the closing was held with half the participants missing. Perry maintained that the developer lacked the ability to follow through with his plan as stipulated by contract, and that time had run out. The project was now stuck in limbo by litigation, and the future look and feel of Collinsville hung in the balance. As I stood beside the old rolling mill, a cavernous building of wood and corrugated metal stretching a few hundred feet along the river, I could tell by its sorry state—boarded windows, cracked siding, and a blue tarp that covered part of the roof—that the standoff couldn't go on too long before the legacy of neglect would answer all disputes with absolute finality.

The notion of redeveloping the axe factory had been a viable one from the day the company shut down. As the buildings aged and tenants came and went, there were occasional conversations—and napkin drawings—envisioning a rebirth with residences, manufacturing, and retail space mixed together in endless configurations. Barbara Perry's creative but unfulfilled ideas for developing the place herself fanned the flames. Redevelopment seemed inevitable in the early 1980s when the state identified the site as one of six top locations for a heritage park, but the idea came and went. Thus, when word got around early in 1999 that Barbara had an ironclad deal with a developer and it seemed Collinsville might get what it had asked for, anticipation was tempered with concern. Many residents had gotten accustomed to the gently run-down appearance of the quiet old factory buildings and enjoyed the bohemian influence and artistic reputation they lent the village.

Tilney's promise to transform the factory into "a village within a village" seemed both sensible and feasible. His stated vision assured that he would "preserve the architectural power of the existing buildings, favor the pedestrian over the automobile, and take maximum advantage of the views and recreation potential of the Farmington River . . . to create a sense of neighborhood and a feeling of community." It seemed too good to be true, this best of all possible outcomes. Factory buildings would be rehabilitated and preserved. New locally owned businesses would flourish. Housing would accommodate a range of ages and incomes. A vital new neighborhood in keeping with the character of Collinsville would be joined to the village.

Tilney preached his gospel to a range of interested parties: town officials hungry for tax revenue, local land-use commissions that fretted over design, and neighbors crowded into living rooms to voice their concerns about traffic and the threat to the small-town atmosphere. He spent long hours on the municipal circuit, brandishing maps, sample designs, and building elevations, and proudly brought out artists' renderings that showed people sipping drinks at outdoor cafes, and quaint shops with old fashioned signs, and restored buildings neatly accented with trees and shrubs.

Peppered with questions, he answered calmly and deliberately, like an old friend sharing a dream and not a developer out to sell a pitch. His responses were often noncommittal, reflecting, he said, the many uncertainties of a large project. The community's concerns were dizzying in their detail, and in the devotion to the village that they evidenced. With rents driven high by code improvements, what would happen to the artists and artisans? Would there be vehicular access through residential Spring Street? What about traffic and parking? How would historically correct restoration be assured? Would the development be phased? What were the uses? How would artists and artisans pay the market rents necessitated by code-compliant buildings? Would businesses or residences be the priority? Would there be loud bars? Did he anticipate the usual chain stores like Starbucks and Brookstone? What access would the public have to the site and to the river? Would this be a yuppie Disneyland, a mecca for tourists where residents would be strangers? All of these questions, and scores of others, helped shape the project as Tilney lobbied for acceptance.

Sitting on a couch in the home of my neighbors from across the street, or at a town hall table with selectmen, or on a metal folding chair in the audience at the zoning commission meetings, I listened intently as Tilney worked to gain our trust with direct answers and the balm of his smooth voice. He didn't want to disrupt the village way of life, but he couldn't guarantee how it would turn out. Some were suspicious of these vague pronouncements, while others took him at his word. After all, many reasoned, if nothing were done the place would fall prey to countless ills: Masonry needed repointing, sills needed replacement, roofs were not secure, and a canal wall threatened to collapse. Tilney was dubbed both a carpetbagger and the savior of Collinsville.

As I made my way deeper into the factory site, the gray shades of the three-story stone building blended perfectly with the gathering fog. Tilney initially said this might be turned into a small conference center, and went on to float various other ideas in rapid succession: a hotel, then offices, and finally housing. Over time his plans seemed to constantly change, and regardless of whether he was dissembling or merely refining them as he learned about the site, some people mistrusted him. What of his financial backers, some asked: wouldn't they make the decisions irrespective of what he told us? Still, the condition of the buildings spoke volumes.

I walked beneath the bike-trail bridge past the building where a saddle-repair company had done business for five years. It had recently moved, the uncertainty of redevelopment and of litigation hastening its departure. An increasing number of such vacancies invited vandalism, arson, and other mischief. Turning upstream, I slipped between a canal and a wood-frame building that had once been an inspection station, now home to a machine shop. Soon I was beside the boiler house near the huge brick smokestack. One of the paintings Tilney had carried from meeting to meeting referred this area as "Boiler House Square" and showed it blossoming with shops and restaurants. Later on someone heard him say the place might be demolished. Rumors were rampant.

The 1955 flood had already done its share of demolition, and a large area of broken concrete slabs marked the site where a number of buildings had once been crowded in near the boilers. The flood had also left a grass peninsula where a lower canal met the Farmington River. The developer had fended off those who argued fiercely that this should be a public park, and the whispered charges of his secret plans for a gated community were turning matters ugly.

I came to the polishing and packing shops. Clapboard and brick, with tall divided windows, an odd complement of doors, and varying rooflines, they appeared fragile despite their bulk. With a few changes they could look entirely different, and I played a bit with the mental image. Flush steel doors could replace those of made of planks; plate glass might stand in for twelve-over-twelve divided lights; a cupola could be removed; openings might be bricked up haphazardly. It wouldn't take much to remodel Collinsville out of what made it unique.

In time, and to the relief of many, Tilney and the Collinsville Historic District Commission hammered out an agreement to use the secretary of the interior's restoration guidelines and develop standards for new construction. After a short tug-of-war, the developer got a needed measure of flexibility and the community some of the means to protect its heritage. How well it will all work out depends on the vigilance of neighbors.

Rain began to fall steadily as I reached the stairs at the corner of the brick shipping building and made my way a flight up to street level beside Collinsville Antiques. I arrived at the gravel parking area across from the museum and was met by a downpour, the nearest shelter the eaves of the old freight station. I listened there to the deluge hammer the shingled roof and the parking lot beside LaSalle Market. The name of Gertrude and Alice's Coffee Bar remained in ghostly letters on the window, though the shop was dark and vacant. The former proprietor believed the coffee shop had been a victim of the Tilney-Perry dispute, left adrift when the parties could not agree to a long-term building lease needed to sell the business.

The point cannot be overstated: As the factory goes, so goes the village. In Collinsville, this has been the case for close to two centuries. The fate of the factory sets the character of the community, the range of businesses, and the value of property. Its appearance will determine both how we view ourselves and how others see us. If I had my druthers, I would leave the decrepit industrial site with its small businesses and artisan workshops alone. But our constant lesson is that the present cannot be sustained. The forces of entropy have the upper hand.

Rain cascaded off the roof and splashed my sneakers as it splattered on the coffee shop deck. On the far side of the parking lot across Main Street, partly obscured by trees, a low building of brick and bluestone built during the Eisenhower administration squats beside Town Hall. It had been the main post office, but with all operations save stamp sales and package mailing moved to a shopping center along Albany Turnpike, the letter-sorting and administrative staff were gone. Had it not been for a packed Saturday morning meeting presided over by a U.S. congresswoman, the first selectman, and reluctant postal officials, the post office would have joined Eaton Hardware as a sad example of the seemingly inexorable loss of community vitality. Instead, it stands now as a testament to the power of citizens to defend their vision of where they want to live.

The meeting had its origins in an April 2000 notice advising residents that the postal service was consolidating four zip codes, including Collinsville's 06022, to ensure more efficient operations. It seemed reasonable: who could object to a more efficient post office? But the five-paragraph letter was rather vague on the subject of the village name. I called the postmaster at his Albany Turnpike office and discovered that our street addresses would henceforth be subsumed in Canton, 06019. The name Collinsville would disappear. If mail is sorted by zip code, I asked, why was there any need to eliminate the village name from our address? He gave me some bureau-cratic mumbo-jumbo about the handling equipment in New Haven, and census tracts, and computerized sorting. At the end of twenty infuriating-ly polite minutes I knew less than when I had dialed the phone. "This is happening around the region," he advised me. "It's beyond my control and at this point it cannot be changed because the decision has been made." Mine was not the only call the postmaster received, and over the next cou-ple of months he sent out two more letters that purported to clarify the sit-uation, and demonstrated that he didn't understand what all the fuss was about. For those of us on the mail route, the postal service was not just con-solidating zip codes; it was stealing our identity.

Never in my years in the village had I seen so many people of all ages, backgrounds, and political persuasions united in a cause. It was a personal affront: we knew where we lived, even if the post office did not. Collinsville was a part of us, the watch-cry of our sense of belonging. A petition spon-taneously arose and quickly garnered a thousand signatures. Banners were hung on several houses, and a number of lawn signs sprouted along Maple Avenue and around downtown. The zip code was the subject of animated conversation at the museum, in the package store, on the street, and every-where else. There was a resurgent camaraderie among neighbors. Big Brother was picking on us.

A couple of months passed, and the first selectman, pestered by constant calls, tried to work out an arrangement guaranteeing the continued use of the village name. At length the post office gave in: we could use "Collins-ville" if we wanted, though we'd run the risk of late mail. Given that very few pressing things seem to come by post nowadays, the deal seemed sat-isfactory enough until we learned that we'd appear as Canton, 06019, to every database in the world. No one looking up an address or sending out a catalog order would find Collinsville—a regrettable state of affairs that stemmed from the fact that two place names could not be attached to the same zip, the miracles of modern technology notwithstanding.

Summer dragged on and many people despaired of ever recovering the village name. We felt we were at the mercy of inescapable and seemingly incomprehensible national trends. Then late in August the postmaster received a letter from the Federal Advisory Council on Historic Preservation. The letter, a response to an enquiry by the Collinsville Historic District Commission, questioned the impact of the address change on historic properties in the village and "the potential inhibition of heritage-based revitalization efforts in the Collinsville community that may result from the loss of their village-specific identity." If Collinsville's past was its economic future, we had argued, then its time-honored name was essential, identified as it was with our local heritage. Collinsville was as much a brand name as Goodyear or Xerox.

Shortly thereafter, the Collinsville postal battle came to the attention of Congresswoman Nancy Johnson, and notices announcing the epic meeting to discuss the issue plastered the village. Though it was held at 9:00 AM on a Saturday morning, so many people showed up that the crowd spilled out into the hall. We came well prepared with passionate and indignant speeches, but before the first of these could be delivered, the congresswoman called for quiet. The postal service had an announcement to make. A regional representative went on at some length about a computer program that would allow equal use of the Canton and Collinsville names in all listings, something that had never been done before. Cheers filled the room, and through our smiles we shared in the triumph of citizenship. We had beaten one of the biggest bureaucracies in the country and restored the village name.

Such occasions as this are a measure of a community where it seems as though we fight one battle after another. At times I have almost wished I lived in a sterile subdivision where neighbors are strangers and people are known only by the vehicle they drive. It would be less stressful. But Collinsville is a place that merits the struggle, and is worthy of our investment of the very stuff of life—time. These skirmish lines remind us that there is a synergy of places and people, and that a place can make life better for those who throw themselves into it. In a world of cookie-cutter conformity, we must ultimately stand for those places that cannot be mistaken for simply anywhere.

The damp finally defeated me and I walked away from the freight station, where comfort and company had only recently beckoned. I was confident that before long steaming mugs of java and homemade cookies would again be served here; this was the kind of place where people would demand it.

The rain let up a little as I made my way along Main Street, dodging under the awnings at LaSalle, Town Hall, Eaton, and the bike shop. Across the street was the old Collins office building, its roofline graced by a snow-and-ice guard sporting the company trademark, that familiar muscular arm rising out of a jeweled crown and grasping a hammer. It's a detail that lends a certain grandeur to the building, a sign of power and strength. After 1875 Collins blades were typically emblazoned with this symbol, the Latin *Legitimus*—right, just, proper, genuine—inscribed below. For the company the word was an acronym that encompassed its ideals: *Loyalty, Excellence, Genuineness, Integrity, Trustworthiness, Industry, Merit, Unity,* and *Success*. These remain the watchwords of the village the company created. They stand for the very quality that we seek in Collinsville, for something that cannot be found in a subdivision or strip development: authenticity. There is nothing like it, and its distinctive power is highly prized where it is lacking. The world's most successful consumer product is known around the globe as "The Real Thing." Billions of advertising dollars have been spent building Coke's image of authenticity. Collinsville needs no such hype.

However dull their day-to-day reality, the world needs places like Collinsville, those seemingly hidden enclaves with the power to rekindle the most deeply held of human ideals. They remind us that all places are more meaningful, engaging, and beautiful than we have commonly allowed ourselves to know. We can find inspiration not only in the picture-perfect worlds of films and novels, but also in real settings with peeling paint and cracked pavement, filled with people who argue and laugh and eventually die in their own unscripted ways. Such is the character and appeal of Collinsville.

People often dream of returning to a childhood home or summer hideaway. These tantalize and beckon like gracious fortune or a beautiful lover. The place I live holds that very magic, and it exists in the bright waking light of day. It is here for anyone willing to stay and find it, and savor the pleasures of that last undiscovered place.

A Note on Sources

The range of sources that served as midwife to this volume can be glimpsed in the epigraphs that precede each section and chapter. But the true wellspring of inspiration is Collinsville itself, the roiling synergy of natural features, architecture, and people—especially people, with their commitment and passion for their community. The works described below will provide a map to broader themes, but the gritty details of place are found only by mining obscure local sources. For this I owe the greatest debt to the dedicated volunteers, both past and present, of the Canton Historical Society, whose museum is at once a wondrous archive, attic, and time machine.

The one book I would strongly recommend to anyone wishing to explore their home ground is *Outside Lies Magic*, by John R. Stilgoe (Walker and Company, 1998). It offers both a methodology and a zest for discovering nearby wonders.

For communities and the politics of community building: *A Home in the Heart of a City*, by Kathleen Hirsch (North Point Press, 1998); *Bingo Night at the Fire Hall*, by Barbara Holland (Harcourt Brace and Company, 1997); *The Good City and the Good Life*, by Daniel Kemmis (Houghton Mifflin Company, 1995); *Reclaiming the Commons*, by Brian Donahue (Yale University Press, 1999); *One American Town*, by Donald S. Connery (Simon and Schuster, 1972); *In the Village*, by Anthony Bailey (Alfred A. Knopf, 1971).

For the relationship of individuals to their community and the natural world: *Staying Put*, by Scott Russell Sanders (Beacon Press, 1993); *Reading the Mountains of Home*, by John Elder (Harvard University Press, 1998); *Becoming Native to This Place*, by Wes Jackson (Counterpoint, 1996); *Sightlines*, by Terry Osborne (Middlebury College Press, 2001); *Biophilia*, by Edward O. Wilson (Harvard University Press, 1984); *The Primal Place*, by Robert Finch (W. W. Norton & Company, 1983).

For the broader relationship of people and landscapes over time: *Changes in the Land*, by William Cronon (Hill and Wang, 1983); *The Experience of Place*, by Tony Hiss (Vintage Books, 1991); *Reflections in Bullough's Pond*, by Diana Muir (University Press of New England, 2000); *Ceremonial Time*, by John Hanson Mitchell (Anchor Press, 1984); *Borderland*, by John R. Stilgoe (Yale University Press, 1988).

For the way people and communities are joined to the built environment: *How Buildings Learn*, by Stewart Brand (Penguin Books, 1995); *The Octagon House*, by Orson S. Fowler (Dover Publications, Inc., 1973, reprint of original 1853 edition); *Changing Places*, by Richard Moe and Carter Wilkie (Henry Holt and Company, 1997); *House*, by Tracy Kidder (Houghton Mifflin Company, 1985).

A glimpse into the spiritual relationship of individuals to a place can be found in: *Dakota*, by Kathleen Norris (Houghton Mifflin, 1993); *Pilgrim at Tinker Creek*, by Annie Dillard (Harper and Row, 1974); *Seeing through Places*, by Mary Gordon (Scribner, 2000).

Novels have always played a significant role in developing my sense of place. Some contemporary works that offered inspiration are: *Nobody's Fool*, by Richard Russo (Random House, 1993); *Spartina*, by John Casey (Alfred

A. Knopf, 1989); *Stranger in the Kingdom*, by Howard Frank Mosher (Doubleday, 1989); *Blue Moon*, by Luanne Rice (Viking, 1993); *In the Center of the Nation*, by Daniel O'Brien (Atlantic Monthly Press, 1991); *The Weight of Winter*, by Cathie Pelletier (Viking, 1991); *Edson*, by Bill Morrissey (Alfred A. Knopf, 1996).